Marx and the Western World. Nicholas Lobkowicz, ed.

Argentina's Foreign Policy, 1930–1962. Alberto Conil Paz and Gustavo Ferrari.

Italy after Fascism, A Political History, 1943–1965. Giuseppe Mammarella.

The Volunteer Army and Allied Intervention in South Russia, 1917–1921. George A. Brinkley.

Personalities and Policies: Studies in the Formulation of British Foreign Policy in the Twentieth Century. D. C. Watt.

Peru and the United States, 1900–1962. James C. Carey.

Empire by Treaty: Britain and the Middle East in the Twentieth Century. M. A. Fitzsimons.

The USSR and the UN's Economic and Social Activities. Harold Karan Jacobson.

Chile and the United States: 1880–1962. Fredrick B. Pike.

Death in the Forest: The Katyn Forest Massacre. J. K. Zawodny.

East Central Europe and the World: Developments in the Post-Stalin Era. Stephen D. Kertesz, ed.

Soviet Policy Toward International Control of Atomic Energy. Joseph L. Nogee.

Diplomacy in a Changing World. Stephen D. Kertesz and M. A. Fitzsimons, eds.

INTERNATIONAL STUDIES OF THE

COMMITTEE ON INTERNATIONAL RELATIONS

UNIVERSITY OF NOTRE DAME

Coexistence:

Communism and its

Practice in Bologna

1945-1965

Coexistence:

Communism and its

Practice in Bologna

1945-1965

ROBERT H. EVANS

 UNIVERSITY OF NOTRE DAME PRESS
NOTRE DAME — LONDON

Library of Congress Catalog Card Number: 67–22149
Manufactured in the United States of America

To
A. C.

PREFACE

Italy is a fascinating country to study, and the more one explores it, the more the complexities appear. Frustrating at times, I believe it is always rewarding in the end. My association with Bologna and Italy goes back to my student days at the Johns Hopkins Bologna Center of the School for Advanced International Studies, where later I returned to work. Those three years made me appreciate the beauty of the town and the charm of its inhabitants; thus, the Bolognese themselves as much as their local administrators are the subject of this book, the purpose of which is to examine the reactions of communism to a democratic environment.

Bologna was chosen above all because it possesses all the basic elements of a successful democracy: a long-established tradition of liberty, a people of independent mind, a balanced economy. Yet, in the Italian context it is a center of reference for the Italian Communist Party, which has administered the town since 1945. The questions to be answered revolved around this conquest and maintenance of power. Is there an inbred propensity of the population for extremist movements, or perhaps did not the dynamism of the PCI and the inertia of the opposition (or vice versa) become a leading factor in the take-over? Are not sociological evolution and weakness of the constituted groups more convincing arguments to explain the steady increase of popular support the Party receives than its own tremendous organization and the solutions it brings to local problems? Does the population see communism for what it pretends to be or for what it accomplishes? In brief, in the course of events how has communism reacted to the milieu that surrounds it?

Answering these questions would have been an impossible task had I not received help from many sources. Librarians went out of their way to assist me at the Mulino study group, at the *Centro Studi Amministrativi e Sociali*, at the Johns Hopkins Bologna Center, and at the Municipal Library; the archivist of the PCI also proved very cooperative. Bolognese political leaders were kind enough to give of their time, especially the federal secretary of the PCI and present mayor of Bologna, Guido Fanti; the assessor to public relations, Dott. Folco Ceechini; and the assessor to local finances, Avv. Umbro Lorenzini. All were most helpful in making available the resources of their departments. Nazario Sauro Onofri of the socialist *Squilla* opened up his personal archives. Dott. Giorgio Galli let me read his manuscript of a forthcoming study of communism and local administration in Italy. His Eminence Msgr. Giacomo Lercaro, cardinal-archbishop of Bologna, gave me many leads for this study, as did his collaborator Don. A. Toldo, head of the Center for Sociological Studies. Dott. G. Rubbi, Tesini, and Stupazzoni of the DC also helped me gather information. I cannot begin to name all the many businessmen and civil servants who opened their offices to me. Special mention must be made of those publishers who so kindly permitted me to employ extensive quotations from their publications (Einaudi and Il Mulino) and to reprint tables (Comunità). May they all be thanked profoundly.

This monograph would not have been possible without the cooperation of all those Bolognese who agreed to be interviewed. Most of them obliged gracefully, in keeping with the city's tradition of hospitality, while Dott. E. Brusatti and his collaborators of DOXA, who conducted the survey, were unsparing of their time in satisfying my requests. Finally, the guidance of Dr. Charles Micaud and the members of the faculty of the Graduate School of International Studies at the University of Denver, as well as a liberal grant from the Social Science Foundation of the same university, enabled me to perform the field work for this study. The Committee on International Relations of the University of Notre Dame covered the financial expenses of typing and editing, and my deepest gratitude goes to them.

I have attempted to be as impartial as possible, but the readers must be aware that many of my judgments coincide with those of a democratic lay-left, and not with the opinions of many who helped me in this research; it is unnecessary to point out that I take sole responsibility for the contents, as well as for the translations from the Italian.

TABLE OF CONTENTS

xiii

LIST OF TABLES

LIST OF ILLUSTRATIONS

LIST OF ABBREVIATIONS

Partito Comunista Italiano	PCI
Due Torri (PCI in local elections)	
Gigante (PCI controlled list in 1951 elections)	
Partito Socialista Italiano di Unità Proletaria (1963)	PSIUP
Partito d'Azione (dissolved 1947)	PdA
Partito Socialista Italiano (Nenni)	PSI
Unione Socialista	US
Partito Socialista Democratico Italiano (Sarragat)	PSDI
Partito Republicano Italiano	PRI
Democrazia Cristiana	DC
Uomo Qualunque (1946)	UQ
Partito Democratico di Unione Monarchica	PDIUM
Movimento Sociale Italiano	MSI

The word "Party" capitalized refers throughout the text to the PCI.

Part 1:
Background Factors

1: THE HISTORICAL AND POLITICAL ASPECTS
OF THE ASSUMPTION OF POWER

Under its guise as a calm and tranquil provincial town, Bologna is an example of the contradictions that riddle Italian politics. It was republican when it should have been monarchist, anticlerical when it was expected to be neoguelph, socialist when other cities were turning to the right—and now communist while its escutcheon reads "Libertas."

To a certain extent all these contradictions meet on the main square, Piazza Maggiore, which is one of the most beautiful examples of architectonic harmony and proportion to be found in Italy which ranks well with Piazza San Marco in Venice. To the north it is limited by the Palazzo del Podestà, erected by the twelfth-century republic which proclaimed liberty for serfs but held the young Enzo, son of Emperor Frederic II, a prisoner for twenty-three years. To the south King Enzo's palace is faced by the Basilica of San Petronio, originally intended to be larger than St. Peter's in Rome; only the strong will of Pope Pius IV could thwart this presumption of the Bolognese and effectively forestall any further extension of the church by constructing the Archiginnasio on the east to house the University. Finally, to the west the square is dominated by the tower and the buttresses of the Palazzo d'Accursio, which, after having served for centuries as the official residence of the cardinal legates who governed the town with an iron hand, today functions as the town hall for the communist administration.

Anticlericalism has always been a great factor in determining the political stance of Bologna and is the result of centuries of poor administration of the Papal States. Yet, the Bolognese are not against religion as such but rather are tremendously antagonized by the temporal powers of the Church. Violent during the last days of the papal administration, with occasional recurrences during the years that followed World War II, Bologna has apparently seen a *modus vivendi* reached between its cardinal and its population and administration. This accord has made anticlericalism more like pinpricks[1] than open hostility. Nevertheless, it remains a latent factor in the political situation. The Bolognese, from whatever political climate they may derive, are most affectionate toward their Madonna of San Luca, who every year is festively greeted on the main square; no miracles have been performed, but the Madonna has the great advantage of never having entered politics. Likewise, the population has never contemplated removing the image of the Madonna by Jacopo della Quercia that adorns the facade of the town hall, while the administration has always been most scrupulous about keeping a votive lamp burning at her feet. As Michelangelo learned, it is only where politics are concerned that the anger of the population can know no limits. His efforts and exhortations were futile when the wrath of the people decided that his bronze of Julius II was to be destroyed; later, nothing could prevent the removal of the statue of Gregory XIII from the center of the main square, yet this statue today blesses the communist administrators as they enter under the portal of the Palazzo d'Accursio. What can be done to antagonize the Church is done with delight and often with malice. Otherwise, how could one explain the administration's proposal that Victor Emmanuel's equestrian bronze have its hindquarters turned toward San Petronio, or why should the socialist administrators have made it a point of honor to build latrines along the flank of the cathedral against the cardinal's explicit desires? Or, more recently, why should the communist administrators adorn and illuminate the town hall on the feast of the Madonna of Lourdes if it was not to remind the Church that Togliatti had been an artisan of inclusion of the Lateran Pacts into the Italian Constitution.

If anticlericalism is an underlying factor in the political reactions of the town, republicanism is at least as strong. The first move of the administration after the popular vote that decided Italy would be a republic was to remove Victor Emmanuel's statue from the center of the main square and relegate it to the chic quarters of the Giardini Margherita. There the statue is more in keeping with the feelings of the rich bourgeois who can send their children and nurse to play hide-and-seek around its pedestal. By 1946 republicanism was present

---

[1] Arturo Carlo Jemolo, *Chiesa e Stato in Italia negli ultimi cento anni*, 2nd ed. (Torino: Einaudi, 1963) 438.

in Bologna for three quarters of a century; in 1870 when Italians rejoiced following Rome's inclusion in the kingdom, the Bolognese played hymns to Garibaldi and booed the Royal March, and the local administration voted that funds allotted for celebrating the king's birthday and for commemorating the anniversary of the Albertine Statute should be canceled.[2] Today the situation is no different, and only the few who suffer from nostalgia plus a more sizable group of protest-voters will cast their ballot in favor of the monarchist ticket.

The truth is that after the papal downfall Bologna, following the lead of the countryside which provided it with its wealth, was turning to socialism. Engineers arrived in the swamp-ridden areas surrounding the town to drain and reclaim the land, large shares of which still belonged to Roman pontifical patricians. The overexploited share-croppers and the equally miserable workers building the canals were prompt to ally, thus giving Bologna the example of a class-conscious group in open conflict with the contractor-tenant.[3] No large industry was required for socialism to penetrate this town which in a few years would break away from its anarchist and bakunian tendencies to practice modern socialism. By 1861 the Workers' Society (Società Operaia) was formed and soon established regular contacts with the first International; cooperative stores sprung up, and a newspaper entitled the Eco del Operaio, later renamed the Monitor del Proletariato,[4] was printed in Bologna. At the turn of the century the forty workers' societies and the Camera del Lavoro, which controlled 15,000 members and worked hand in hand with the Revolutionary Socialist party, could send two deputies to the Parliament in Rome, while the socialists entered the local administration in coalition with the Radical and Republican parties. This solidly grounded and dynamic socialist movement was in a position to score a triumph in the political elections of 1913 when quasi-universal suffrage became operative:[5] an absolute majority of votes sent five left-wing legislators to Rome, and the trend was confirmed by the local elections of

[2] L. Arbizzani, Sguardi sull'ultimo secolo. Bologna e la sua provincia (Bologna: Galileo, 1960) 34.

[3] P. Crocioni, "La Città di Bologna," La Squilla, October 23, 1964, vol. 63, no. 40, p. 10.

[4] L. Arbizzani, Sguardi 18–124.

[5] Males having reached 30 years of age, or those over 21 who could write and pay the census, could vote.

1914. With republicans refusing to enter a coalition with the radicals against the socialist assault, 46 per cent of the population preferred to stay at home, and by 1319 votes (3 per cent of the total popular vote) the "reds" won 48 out of the 60 seats in the Municipal Council.[6] Francesco Zanardi, the new mayor, was to become a mythical personage in Bologna, sincerely mourned by all at his death and more often considered a saintly man than a bolshevik. His radical plans, though greatly hindered by the outbreak of World War I, made it plain that Bologna was on the move: stables were transferred out of the city limits, latrines were built, wells were replaced by piped running-water systems, and above all prices during the War were held in line by a municipality that controlled twenty-eight stores and thus became a full-fledged entrepreneur (an example that would be closely followed by the communists).

By the end of the War Bologna seemed to be clearly dominated by socialist forces, which in less than four years were to be swept away by the fascist tide.[7] Bologna thus became one of Mussolini's strongholds and showcases. The reasons for this can undoubtedly be laid to certain stands taken by a Socialist party that was not as strong as it would make others believe; but the important fact is that the period from 1919 to 1922 accentuated a division of the town into two incompatible blocs, a division still partially obtaining today. The old town where the bourgeoisie were concentrated and the hills to the south to which they migrated and where they built luxurious villas were practically locked in a vise by the proletarian red belt of the suburbs. Prior to the War there was still a unified town; after 1919, it is not too much to say, Bologna was divided into two sides that cordially despised each other.

In November 1919 the populace sent seven socialist representatives to Parliament, and the municipal elections a year later clearly indicated that socialism was what the people wanted, 58 per cent of them voting for the extreme left. The immediate postwar period was

[6] Nazario Sauro Onofri, 28 Giugno 1914, i socialisti a palazzo d'Accursio (Bologna: Squilla, 1964) 10–22.

[7] The most complete study is L. Arbizzani's "L'Avvento del fascismo nel bolognese, 1920–1922," Movimento Operaio e Socialista 10, nos. 2, 3, 4 (April-December 1964). For a general view see F. Chabod, Italia contemporanea 1918–1948, (Torino: Einaudi, 1961), or Luigi Salvatorelli and Giovanni Mira, Storia d'Italia nel periodo fascista, 2nd ed. (Torino: Einaudi, 1964).

marked by disorders, strikes, and price increases that affected the proletariat above all. Throughout the summer of 1919 metallurgists, railway men, transport workers, and post office employees were on strike.[8] For the bourgeois, with the example of the Russian revolution in mind, bolshevism seemed at the doorstep. Simultaneously, the Socialist party did nothing to soften this impression, committed as it was to the doctrine that the State was the enemy. Its sixteenth congress held in Bologna (October 5–8, 1919) saw the *massimalisti* triumph, which "was equivalent to announcing the beginning of the revolution,"[9] and the local Bolognese congress reiterated that the general strike was the only weapon to obtain satisfaction. The slogan "The earth to those who work it" was winning favor.

This was to prove an ideal breeding ground for fascism. The bourgeoisie could no longer accept the red flags that floated over the city (September 1920), the factories occupied by workers, or the ever-growing rumors that a soviet would be established.[10] Thus, socialist violence became an excuse for fascist violence, and Mussolini's cohorts found it easy "to recruit large numbers of representatives of the lower, middle, and upper bourgeoisie: veterans, students, professional men, shopkeepers, houseowners, small and large landowners."[11] To the local Association for Social Defense, the aim of which was "to oppose a civil resistance to the disorders taking place in town,"[12] Bologna by the end of 1920 appeared as the only center where bolshevik socialism had maintained its strength and unity. The *mot d'ordre* was to become "Rid Bologna of the reds," and the swearing-in of the new administration loomed as the first opportunity to oppose this sizable entity, previous violence having been somewhat amateurish. On November 18 a leaflet was distributed throughout the town: "Let all women and those who love peace and tranquility stay home . . . Sunday, in the streets of Bologna, only fascists and bolsheviks must meet."[13] The main square became, in effect, a battleground: hand grenades were thrown from the town hall windows, a counselor

---

[8] L. Arbizzani, *Sguardi* 136.

[9] Salvatorelli, *Storia d'Italia* 103.

[10] *Il Resto del Carlino*, April 16, 1920.

[11] Salvatorelli, *Storia d'Italia* 168. For a view of Bolognese fascists, see C. Valente, *La Ribellione anti-socialista di Bologna* (Bologna: Cappelli, 1921).

[12] L. Arbizzani, *Sguardi* 85.

[13] Salvatorelli, *Storia d'Italia* 168.

of the minority was shot, and ten citizens were killed. Confronted by this massacre, the socialist administration resigned, while the Socialist party canceled a general protest strike. The left no longer felt protected by the law, and on December 1, 1920, the Bolognese fascist paper *Assault* could print

> Beware scoundrels! Do not touch us! Yesterday you were preaching civil war . . . and class tyranny . . . where you could have stuffed all your filthy lust of paranoiacs. . . . Well, we fascists are ready to defy you.[14]

During the first six months of 1921 the *Camera del Lavoro* was burned to the ground; one newspaper, six *Case del Popolo*, nine cooperatives, five peasant associations, and five socialist sections were destroyed. Despite the fact that the socialists maintained their majority in August (57.7 per cent), the left was ready to abdicate. The socialist *Squilla* could only write, "Workers, calm belongs to the strong, hatred to the wicked. Wait for better times."[15] Meanwhile, the newly created, pathetically small Communist Party had audaciously proposed opposing "strength to strength, weapons to weapons."[16] By the time of the fascist march on Rome (October 29, 1922), there was no resistance to fascism in Bologna, and normal political life disappeared until July 25, 1943.

Fascism crystallized the split between the two Bolognas, and the Resistance would provide only a first, timid step at bringing the antagonists together. For a majority of the citizens the fascist period was to become one of adaptation, increasing indifference, and passive conformism. For many, in particular the older generations, "the ethico-political education for modern life . . . stopped . . . and retrogressed to a new bourbonism."[17] As a leading young intellectual was to say,

> It would only be toward the end of the conflict, when . . . war materially uprooted men from their habits, obliged them to realize with their hands and their eyes the perils that menaced the foundations of each individual life, and persuaded them there was no possible safety in neutrality and isolation[18]

that Bologna would begin to move again.

[14] *Ibid.* 170.
[15] L. Arbizzani, *Sguardi* 274.
[16] *Ibid.* 261.
[17] Salvatorelli, *Storia d'Italia* 413.
[18] Giaime Pintor, *Il Sangue d'Europa* (Torino: Einaudi, 1965) 186.

For twenty years indifferentism would become the motto of a population that had renounced its freedom to think; the most striking example was at the University where, although it had always upheld the most glorious tradition of independence, only one professor preferred to resign rather than swear allegiance to fascism.[19] Socialism had practically gone into exile with its leaders, and the only group to remain active was the communist because "It had laid its plans for transformation at the very time it came, officially, into existence [1921], many years before the beginning of the exodus. . . . It only had to change from clandestinity to semi-clandestinity."[20] In its efforts its greatest ally was Mussolini's Special Tribunal, which fostered the impression that the only foe of the regime was the Communist Party. Seven hundred and three judgments were pronounced against Emilians, with sentences totaling over twenty-two centuries of imprisonment, wherein eleven men were to die. The names that were to recur are Dozza, Gnudi, Betti, Vignocchi, and Tibaldi, the leaders of the local Party after 1943.[21] On July 25, 1943, helped by its press[22] and a few sporadic strikes,[23] the Party would reap the harvest from the seeds it had sown. While Bologna was rejoicing and bells were pealing (July 25 in the town hall and July 26 in the church) and while the populace which was definitely committed to the left invaded the main square, the bourgeoisie had to make its choice. The communists had one, pre-eminent virtue: they alone had opposed fascism.

With the proclamation of the armistice the period of uncertainty came to an end, and Italy was torn asunder—Bologna following the trend. The bourgeois center, the "*sperzone*," was demilitarized, thanks

[19] Salvatorelli, *Storia d'Italia* 368–371.

[20] *Ibid.* 608. For a complete account of the underground period, see Giorgio Galli, *Storia del Partito Comunista Italiano* (Milano: Schwarz, 1958).

[21] L. Arbizzani, "Dal 1921 una lunga e gloriosa battaglia per la libertà di tutti," *La Lotta*, April 22, 1955, vol. 12, no. 16, p. 5.

[22] By 1930, 5000 copies of *Unità* were distributed in the province of Bologna. By 1933, a booklet was circulated on "How to Organize a Clandestine Printing Shop." L. Arbizzani, *La Stampa clandestina nella Resistenza bolognese* (Bologna: La Lotta, 1962) 11. For a more detailed account of the press see appendix one.

[23] 1926, strike at Molinella; 1929, outcries against salary reductions; May 1, 1930, celebration of the *Festa del lavoro*; March 1–8, 1944, general strike; manifestation by 1,000 women in front of the *prefettura*. L. Arbizzani, *Le Donne emiliane nella Resistenza* (Bologna: La Lotta, 1964) 24–25.

to the intervention of the cardinal; thus, even though some of the leaders of the Resistance lived in the shadow of the ancient towers, the mass of the troops would come from the suburbs, particularly from Corticella, where by the end of 1943 a workers' republic was established in which no military dared to set foot after dark.[24] On the outskirts of the town "The spirit of organization of the Emilian peasant . . . was reborn . . . intact. There, numerous, or relatively numerous, socialist and communist militants operated in a well-prepared terrain."[25] Hatred for the fascist militia and the prospect of being drafted by the Germans sent many men into the Resistance, but a PCI proclamation dated March 1943, inaugurating a systematic policy of recruiting, sums up the deep-seated motivation of many: "Only with a weapon in hand, confronted by the enemy, can we feel our dignity and humanity."[26] Bologna contributed 10,790 officially enrolled partisans divided into eighteen battalions: two socialist, one Christian democrat, two action-party, and thirteen communist.[27] Though the controversy is not ended, it seems reasonable to estimate the number of Catholics in the brigades at some 35–40 per cent,[28] while the social composition of the various groups was, for the most part, definitely working-class men and women[29] whose slogan was:

"The Germans, the fascists, and the boss
Are all one group to be thrown to the fire."[30]

[24] B. Pancaldi, Verso la libertà (Bologna: CVL, 1965) 52.

[25] R. Battaglia, Storia della Resistenza (Torino: Einaudi, 1964) 122.

[26] Ibid. 138.

[27] A. Meluschi, ed., Epopea partigiana (Bologna: ed. SPER, n.d. [1947?] 1. For a breakdown, see appendix one, p. 190.

[28] L. Arbizzani, La Lotta, April 22, 1955, gives the figure of 20 per cent Catholics. L. Bergonzoni, Clero e Resistenza (Bologna: Cantelli, 1965) advances that of 60 per cent. The truth probably lies somewhere in between.

[29] Percentage-wise, communist sources give the following (which is reflected in the success of the left in Bologna):

Workers and laborers	62.4	Craftsmen	7.1
Sharecroppers	15.4	Students	2.3
Employees, intellectuals, liberal professions	7.4	Housewives	5.4
			100.0

In Bonazzi, "Aspetti della Resistenza bolognese," Rinascita 9, no. 4 (1952). Quoted in Bologna è libera (Bologna: ANPI, 1965) 188. This division is also confirmed by the social composition of the 62nd Garibaldi. See G. Brini, La Brigata di Pampurio (Bologna: La Lotta, 1963) 1.

[30] Battaglia, Storia 393.

Militarily the strongest, the communists also held an advantage with respect to political organization, and as a consequence they alone were ready to take over the town when the German troops left and before the allied troops arrived. To a certain extent the repercussions of this are still being felt today. A year before the antifascist forces created the Committee of National Liberation (CLN) on a national level, the communists and socialists of Bologna had founded (in September 1942) the United Committee for Antifascist Action: republicans and Action party members joined in June 1943, while Christian democrats held back. Thus, what was to become the local CLN was composed exclusively of men of the left who knew how to use a well-organized press (between January 1943 and April 1945, 200 leaflets with a total circulation of 1.5 million copies[31] were distributed in town), while the same trend was to be found in the military organization or CUMER (*Comando Militare Unico Emilia Romagna*).[32]

By September 1944 Bologna was prepared to hope that the liberation of Florence would be the prelude to its own freedom. The town was "a volcano ready to vomit the white hot lava it had too long suppressed."[33] General Alexander's radio message of November 8 which put an end to the summer campaign had the effect of a bomb on the town: all the fighting that had transpired thus far in the hope of an early liberation now appeared almost useless, and moreover the PCI had revealed its strength among the general population. For the latter this was to be another winter of suffering and of persecution by the militia forces seeking to apprehend the GAP (Groups for Patriotic Action), the "terroristic groups of the Communist Party"[34] whose operations from the suburbs constantly kept the enemy on the alert. Nevertheless, for the bourgeoisie the red belt showed what it was capable of when 270 perfectly organized partisans held German tanks at bay for 15 hours, inflicting 216 and suffering only 14 casualties. This glorious episode of the battle of Porta Lame, the largest partisan battle to be waged in a town, witnessed not only the destruc-

---

[31] L. Arbizzani, La Stampa 45.

[32] Nazario Sauro Onofri, "I Socialisti e GL nella Resistenza," La Squilla, December 28, 1964, vol. 48, no. 47, p. 5.

[33] Battaglia, Storia 446.

[34] "Organisation der Italienischen Banden," p. v, appendix I of Epopea partigiana.

tion of an entire block that brought increased hardships to the population but also demonstrated the determination of the left when it was challenged. After this the situation became intensely dramatic in the town because there

> . . . the war was the longest and the most savagely fought, because the front was so close for so many months, because of the cruel, desperate, ferocious nazi-fascist oppression, more ferocious than elsewhere: here the nazi-fascists knew they were using their last resources before the inevitable disaster.[35]

When allied troops broke through the German lines April 17, 1945, eight partisan brigades were on hand in town.[36] One week earlier the PCI had called for rebellion, not "an explosion of popular rage, but an accelerated program of interruptions of work, of demonstrations, of strikes."[37] Ten thousand leaflets announcing the order were distributed in the city.[38] During the early hours of April 21 the town was occupied by the partisans, and at 6:30 A.M., the first Polish troops were greeted by the rejoicing population; because of the timely partisan action, little had been destroyed.

The CLN in 1944, had appointed Giuseppe Dozza mayor of Bologna "on the basis of tradition and the importance of the workers' movements."[39] The left controlled the town hall, the prefecture, and the police; a Christian democrat was appointed to the administration of the province.

> The CLN informed the allied command that the organs of local government were already in readiness, awaiting [allied] approval . . . [and that] only by the use of force would they be removed.[40]

The left clearly realized its strength and was ready to use it if allied forces should try to downgrade PCI authority in the town.

In reality, the fight for Bologna was more political than military—though this aspect has always been carefully disguised by the left, which has tried to play down the fact that it held total leadership

---

[35] Ilio Barontini, "Le Staffette," *Epopea partigiana* 18.

[36] A. Cucchi, "Liberi a Bologna," *Epopea partigiana* 107.

[37] R. Battaglia, *Storia* 531.

[38] L. Arbizzani, *La Stampa* 18.

[39] G. Dozza, "La Fine del fascismo a Bologna," *Epopea partigiana* 10–11.

[40] Nazario Sauro Onofri, "I Socialisti e la Resistenza," *La Squilla*, April 30, 1965, vol. 69, no. 17, p. 12.

in 1944. Instead, the left has boosted the Christian democrats, who as an organized group had actually joined the fight too late. For the communists the first objective was to be the liberation of Italy; but the second, and truly the more important objective, was to become one of the major components, if not *the* major one of the new Italian political life. These objectives dictated the communist attitude toward the Resistance. Military objectives thus took on political overtones. About the Garibaldi brigades Secchia wrote,

> If we have organizations of a military character which do not act, they will disintegrate and dissolve in a short period of time. On the other hand, action will harden them, experience will reinforce and strengthen them.[41]

But the ace in the communist hand was its appeal for unity among all antifascist parties addressed particularly to the socialists, but actually an appeal that none could refuse. In this the Party was very careful. As far as military units were concerned, it was made clear

> . . . that a military unit does not belong to the Party, is not a Party organ, does not and must not have the character of a Party. . . .[42]

This held true, even though it was evident that the principles held by Party leaders were sometimes at variance with actions of the rank and file and even though political commissars preaching the war for national liberation sometimes keyed their sermons to communist beliefs. As Gabriel Almond writes, "In brief . . . during the war the Party's objectives were to train cadres,"[43] to politicize the Youth Front and the Defense of Women groups and to help the freedom-fighters and the Defense of Peasants organizations.[44]

The immediate objective, nevertheless, was to enlist the aid of other political parties—Socialist[45] and Christian Democratic. The Resistance glossed over all contradictions, and the communists found it easy to offer guarantees of religious freedom, freedom of opinion,

---

[41] *Nostra Lotta* (November 1943), in Battaglia, *Storia* 169.
[42] Pietro Secchia, *Nostra Lotta* (May 1946), in *ibid.* 288.
[43] G. Almond, *The Appeals of Communism* (Princeton: Princeton University Press, 1954) 116.
[44] Pancaldi, *Verso* 24.
[45] *Nostra Lotta* (July 1944), in Battaglia, *Storia* 351.

and a democratic state.[46] The fight against fascism created an apparent unity which soon would be revealed for what it really was, a wishful myth. But it was too late; for the Christian democrats, backed as they were by the Church and a large popular vote, the break would come as a relief, while for the socialists, at the time such a break seemed impossible. Thus, in Bologna the PCI could count not only on votes stemming directly from its own military record but also on those that usually went to the Socialist party, its ally and, in fact, its vassal. By April 1945 the PCI held the necessary trumps to control Bologna—military strength and political support. It had fully comprehended the letter Togliatti sent to the Bolognese federation on March 2, 1945:

> The responsibility resting upon your shoulders, Bolognese comrades, is great because it is probable that your city will be the first of the large cities of the north to be liberated. To a great extent, the future developments of the entire Italian situation will depend on how wisely you operate in such a context.[47]

Confronted by this situation, the more traditional forces of the town were either passive or else hopeless that they could prevent the left from playing a predominant part in the local administration: the residential suburbs could only be silent and acquiesce if they wished to survive.

The occupation troops remained in Bologna for one hundred days. The new Italian regime was no longer an enemy, and the town appeared to be run by a united and capable administration; furthermore, it could take care of itself economically. The population saw no reason to be suspicious of the new administration; the myth of a united Italian Resistance was to be valid until the first elections. The tradition of liberty that had made Bologna famous was respected: after twenty years of suffering the inhabitants had had their share in bringing about fascism's downfall.

The only group which understood the perils of the Marxist teachings, the Catholic Church, was compromised by its ties to fascism[48] and thus had considered it expedient to remain silent and not disrupt

---

[46] Declaration of the PCI on the "Relations between Communists and Catholics," August 1944, in ibid. 360.

[47] P. Togliatti, quoted by L. Arbizzani in La Stampa 28.

[48] See Jemolo, Chiesa e Stato, in particular 465 and 438, 448, 482.

the newly won peace. Cardinal Nasalli Rocca, archbishop of Bologna, as well as a large number of his clergy, had been content in 1920 to be rid of the socialist mobs, and thus readily accepted fascism. In the fashionable parish of San Bartolomeo the faithful were able to contemplate a picture of the Virgin, "the Madonna of the fascists."[49] Consequently, official Church silence appeared necessary; moreover, the PCI did not seem anticlerical, and many Catholic intellectuals accepted the social dogmas of Marxism.

In sum, if we consider the leftist role in opposing fascism and the weakness of all the other parties, we need not be surprised that communism could take over the town so easily. It would do just that within two years. Bologna was faced with the total disintegration of a system that had governed it for twenty years; it was also confronted with only one properly organized party, a party, moreover, that rested upon a solid military organization which it had no hesitation in using. In various degrees the other parties appeared responsible for fascism; thus the choice was made simple,[50] particularly for young people "likely to call themselves communists precisely because they are young and have known only conditions conducive to extremism."[51] Catholicism, as it was traditionally practiced, offered no barrier.

Furthermore, communists and socialists were allied: if on a national scale their strength did not seem disproportionate, on the local scene it actually was. In military strength alone the communists were ten times as strong as the socialists. This alliance enabled the PCI to benefit from the whole tradition of Bolognese socialism and to make progress under its cover even when this meant reducing the socialist ally to little or nothing. Communism was helped in its task by the mentality of the population, which has always preferred extreme to moderate positions.[52] The generation of 1870–1895 was republican, that of 1895–1920 socialist, that of 1920–1945 communist. Thus, the

---

[49] *Ibid.* 447.

[50] Ideology does not appear to have played an important part. "An individual generally joins or votes for the Party because of the concrete experience he has had, and not simply because he has arrived at the logical truth." Hadley Cantril, *The Politics of Despair* (New York: Collier Books, 1962) 93.

[51] Elizabeth Wiskemann, "Socialism and Communism in Italy," *Foreign Affairs* 24 (April 1946) 484–493.

[52] See Murray Edelmann, "Causes of Fluctuations in Popular Support of the Italian Communist Party Since 1946," *Journal of Politics* 20 (August 1958) 544.

Party was profoundly convinced that the time for its own expansion had come. In this it would be greatly helped by the division of the town into two blocs, and it is now time to examine Bologna and its inhabitants.

2: BOLOGNA AND THE BOLOGNESE

The name of Bologna has traditionally lent itself to colorful adjectives. Most noteworthy among them *dotta* (the learned, referring to the city's University, which dates back to the eleventh century), *grassa* (the fat, alluding to its inhabitants' predilection for fine foods), and *rossa* (the red, underlining the ochre color of its buildings).

These terms today applied to the town of porticoes no longer accurately evoke the reality of a mere fifty years ago. More modern characteristics have emerged, and if the town is still well known for its University, its two towers, and the proverbial openness of its inhabitants, one prefers to think of it as the center of the homonymous province, as the most important town of Emilia and one of the most important of Italy, as the nerve center of the Italian rail and highway network, as a hospital center, as a nucleus for new industries—in short as an expanding, multifunctional, and politico-administrative industrial city with a population well on the way to a half million, enjoying a standard of living among the highest in Italy. Yet, the most noteworthy characteristic of Bologna remains that of *rossa*: *rossa* today, less for the color of its buildings than for its status as the largest city of the Western world to be administered by communists. In the Italian context Bologna stands as the point of reference for the nation's Communist Party.

Italian unity is generally traced to the 1860's. In a majority of cases it still remains to be achieved, since strong local particularisms make each Italian city totally different from its neighbors to the point where it is difficult to find one city representative of Italy as a whole. In this Bologna is but one piece of the mosaic-like Italy, and also a unique piece. The inhabitants tend to picture themselves in the role of a stereotype that has evolved over the ages but that today appears greatly altered by the twentieth century: by the inflow of immigrants which has doubled the total population and by the division of the town into two social groups. One can no longer talk of a red-black antagonism, but rather of a pink-grey cohabitation.

The sturdy men and opulent women of Bologna like to be considered uncompromising and outgoing people. To a degree this is true, for rare are the Italian cities that greet the foreigner—from abroad or from Italy—with so genuine an interest; few are the Italians who will go so far out of their way as the Bolognese simply to demonstrate the beauty and the uniqueness of the town to the occasional tourist, sympathizing with him and often striking up durable friendships. But the Bolognese also likes to be thought of as a man "all of one piece," who since the darkest ages has rallied to the defense of *libertas* against popes, dictators, and kings. "The extremist, the anticlerical Bologna" are frequently heard expressions, and yet, without denying their existence, one may well wonder how valid these concepts are today. Traditional anticlericalism has practically disappeared, with the possible exception of the local transport union, and what the Bolognese seem to resent above all is the Church's opulence and involvement in the earthly aspects of day-to-day life. In no way can this be considered as equivalent to atheism. The entire idea is that the Church should care only for spiritual questions and not meddle in politics; the Bolognese believe they are practical enough themselves to take care of the temporal aspects of their lives. "Areligious" would probably be a far better expression than "anticlerical."

The stereotype of extremist must also be modified. Barzini, writing of the Italians in general, declares they

> . . . are sceptical. They believe that all ideologies are equally right and wrong, that there is no abstract solution to their problems, that the world can somehow be made to function under whatever political institutions seem easier to accept at the moment, because all of them will always function defectively in Italy, where all have failed at one time or another, and will all fail sooner or later.[1]

This is undoubtedly true of the Bolognese industrialist or bourgeois who today survives and prospers under communism in the same way he did under fascism, possibly deriving less benefits but nevertheless remaining comfortable and respected by his peers. This is also true of many of the adopted Bolognese, the southern immigrants whose main concern is to work, who from experience know that they must,

---

[1] L. Barzini, *The Italians* (New York: Bantam, 1965) 235–236.

at least in appearance, honor the regime in power; it could also be true of many of the shrewd peasants who have been attracted by the economic possibilities of the town. Perhaps only the traditional Bolognese "proletarian" is an extremist; he is the one whose forefathers routed the popes and the Austrians and whose grandfathers were socialists before the party was even created—the one who more recently took to the hills to defeat fascism and resuscitate the traditions of the left. But today one may well ask how many of these still exist in an era of universal prosperity, of television and Fiat 500's! Is not the traditional Bolognese a race nearing extinction, or at least nearing integration into the general mass of Italians?

In no way does this exclude some remnants of provincialism, some characteristics peculiar to the town; yet, they too seem to be doomed. It is only with difficulty that one can uncover them, and it might not be too much to say they are condemned to survive in the films produced in Cinecittà. Traditionally, the Bolognese always sighs when speaking of his female companions, but how many really do believe in the uniqueness of the Bolognese woman? The widely known elegance of the inhabitants is also falling into a stereotyped Italian fashion vulgarized by two or three popular magazines, and if a majority of the women adopt purple one year rather than red, so do a majority of other Italian women in innumerable other towns. The local language, which according to popular belief can be traced back to Celtic, is also becoming a historical curiosity; it is spoken by the older generations but hardly understood by the younger ones. Not that its influence is negligible, for it does influence the general accent of the people; and its rabelaisian tones make the Bolognese manner of talk rather attractive and capable of more colorful expression than many other dialects. But this language, which prior to the twentieth century served as a link between the people and the proletariat of Bologna, no longer performs that function except for a very limited minority. Finally, the Bolognese is, and rightly so, proud of the culinary and gastronomic cult that has rendered his town famous. It is undeniable that this love for rich food is genuine and unique to a Bologna that harbors restaurants by the hundred. However, even this trait is disappearing: restaurants are no longer so numerous or active, their menus tend to resemble one another more and more, specialties are no longer created, and, horror of horrors, the local Communist Party has even set up a chain of self-service restaurants no different from those that cover the North American continent. While for the hurried tourist the uniqueness of Bologna and of the Bolognese may be still alive, in reality it is slowly dying. Since the end of the World War II and particularly since the beginning of the Italian "miracle," Bologna's populace has come to include more and more non-Bolognese who have brought with them their own traditions. Some of these they lose, others they adopt—all of which invariably modifies the customs of the original inhabitants. In this the local administration has played its part in relocating the newcomers, while the gap between the two towns, the rich and the poor, the bourgeois and the proletarian, seems to be narrowing.

Examining the social structures and the morphology of the town, one notes that changes have been rapid and that in less than a decade a complex system has grown up tending toward the distribution of functions in homogeneous zones.[2] The observer, when perusing statistics, is struck by the fact that the population doubled in less than forty years (1921–1958) and that it increased by one third between 1951 and 1964. It is no exaggeration to speak of a population explosion.[3] Coinciding with the Italian economic miracle, this explosion has manifested itself in a strong development of the secondary sector to the detriment of the others,[4] which furthermore has been totally attributable to immigration, despite a strong emigrant flow. Thus Bologna has been losing its "traditional" inhabitants (the natural increase of the population is practically nil), while receiving an overflow of immigrants either already oriented to the left prior to their arrival or soon oriented in that direction by the necessity of finding work. The first point is well made by Ardigò,[5] who notes that 70 per cent of the immigrants originate from the plains and mountains sur-

---

[2] See A. Ardigò, "Note sulle strutture delle città emiliano-romagnole," Civitàs 9, nos. 10, 11 (October 1958), and Paolo Giudicini, "Aspetti della morfologia sociale di Bologna," Elezioni e comportamento politico in Italia, A. Spreafico and J. Palombara, eds. (Milano: Comunità, 1963) 850–865.

[3] See appendix two, p. 191.

	1951(%)	1961(%)
[4] Primary	4.8	3.1
Secondary	41.2	44.8
Tertiary	54.	52.1

Compiled from: Comune di Bologna, Ripartizione Statistica, Annuario statistico 1963 (Bologna: STEB, 1964) 24–28.

[5] A. Ardigò, "Il Volto elettorale di Bologna," Elezioni 806–808

rounding the town,[6] regions which are traditionally oriented to the left. Hence, all new immigration toward Bologna has a bearing on the increase of the communist voting strength, and the author proves this empirically in considering the losses and gains in voting strength in the various localities from which the immigrants originate. The second point is also confirmed:

> . . . [the man from the countryside] feels alienated, inferior, humiliated. The sentiment of protest which ensues is translated into an always greater identification with the movements of the extreme left. . . .[7]

Moreover, this immigration is in the lower age bracket: 64 per cent of it is under age thirty-four, while only 48 per cent of the normal resident population is under that age.[8] Consequently, the quantity of labor offered by the immigrants is proportionally greater than that offered by the resident population and is accompanied by greater difficulties in finding work, or at least by more reliance upon the help of the municipal services. This strong immigration, the influence of the countryside (which until recently was the main factor in the expansion or contraction of the local economy), and finally the lack of large industrial developments and the predominance of small manufacturers allow further elaboration of the social structures of the town.

The Bolognese urban family of the middle and lower classes has remained one of the major channels of communication, having maintained strong links with both neighborhood and relatives very much along the line that can be found in a village. However, projecting upon our future findings, in many cases the urban family is integrated at the neighborhood level by social institutions that divide the town into rigidly separated blocs, cells, nuclei, sections of opposing parties, bars and recreative circles of different political hues as well as parochial and religious institutions. The consequences for the integration of the new immigrants are considerable, since they will be immediately snatched up by one or another opposing faction, the town hall tending to distribute them in zones where it already exerts strong control. In fact, this articulation of primary groups forms the basis of the structure of the political power of the town and gives the Com-

---

[6] See appendix two, p. 192.

[7] A. Spreafico, "Orientamento politico e identificazione partitica," Elezioni 724.

[8] Compiled from Annuario statistico 27–32.

munist Party a great advantage through its rigid and thorough organization. In some sectors of Bologna, such as in the Borgo Panigale or
Bolognina sections, the social-communist neighborhood has created
exclusive channels of communication between the base and the summit which can avert at least in part any activity that might be hostile to the Party. For instance, interviewers in these sections were
reported directly to the town hall as well as to the PCI federation
as soon as they had left.

It is interesting to note that if the dimension and nature of the
primary groups in Bologna extend to the large "capitalist" enterprises
(and they are few), they do not reach the social-communist cooperative organization. This organization, which grew out of a traditional
and special spirit of class solidarity, has since the war undergone great
strengthening, expansion, and concentration that have placed it on
the same level as the large-size enterprise. Thus there is a functional
diversity of associative structures, especially in the political and economic organizations controlled by the left. Primary groups will be
concerned with political propaganda, recreative life, public assistance,
and the creation of small groups of workers in the same enterprise,
while secondary groups will have the exclusive function of production.

We have already mentioned that the expansion of Bologna is a
recent phenomenon that can be traced to the turn of the century
when the medieval walls surrounding the town were torn down. More
recently, progress in building techniques has rendered suitable for
building the hills that formerly limited expansion to the south. To
some degree Bologna could be studied according to the divisions
implied by its historical and economic development, or the fifteen
administrative quarters might be used; or if one prefers more modern
techniques, it is possible to break up the town into twenty-two,[9] or
more simply six, homogeneous zones of residence.[10] The latter classification will be adopted. Nevertheless one must keep in mind that
the town is split geographically on an east-west axis by the Roman
via Emilia and by the Milan-Ancona railway, as well as socially on
a south-north axis between the traditional bourgeois and proletarian
quarters.

[9] P. Giudicini, Elezioni 850–865.
[10] A. Ardigò, Elezioni 801–819.

HOMOGENEOUS ZONES OF RESIDENCE

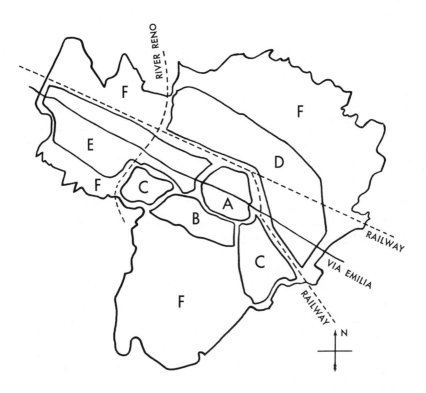

   Zone A, which corresponds to medieval and renaissance Bologna, is today bordered by the boulevards or *circonvallazione*. Originally a residential, administrative, and business zone, its residential role is gradually being abandoned as the population is relocating in more fashionable suburbs; and even with respect to administration and business the zone seems to be stationary, hindered as it is by the increased difficulties of finding adequate parking space in a medieval setting. Since the mid-fifties, the poverty stricken islands and the privately owned patrician palaces have been disappearing; the centers of poverty were eliminated while the palaces were sold to banks and other large organizations, the only ones able to afford the upkeep.

Yet this central sector is where Bologna continues to live, where things happen, where the piazza has not really lost its function of a noisy political debating center, and where discussions go on till the late hours of the night following appearances of the major political leaders. Long dominated by the bourgeoisie, this part of the town retains its traditional outlook, and in a normal electoral year[11] the DC can muster more votes than all the parties of the left put together (i.e., excluding 1956, when the voting was a plebiscitary type).[12] It is believed that this trend will continue: while the bourgeois tends to relocate in the suburbs (zones B and C), an even faster relocation of the proletariat and the smaller business enterprises in zones F, E, and D is also taking place. What is clear is that the steady decrease in population will give this part of the town less and less importance.

Zone B is the high-value residential area where considerable expansion took place following World War I, an expansion which continues today at the expense of zone F. The typical buildings of the first period, the large mansions or villas in which old Bolognese families dwelled, are outnumbered today by luxurious two- or three-story apartment houses surrounded by relatively large gardens. Since the cost of an apartment in this part of town is approximately 60,000 dollars, its conservative tinge is readily anticipated. Here it is that the PLI makes its best showing, though the PCI is not absent (red capitalism?), and here the DC polls twice as many votes as the parties of the left together.[13] It is worth noting that in these two zones the percentage of women, 55.25 and 55.38 respectively, is well above the local average of 53.1.[14] Since women, in general, are more conservative than men and since these zones also have the highest percentages of churchgoers, we may safely assume that a large share of the feminine vote goes to the Christian Democratic party.

Zone C is the "new" Bologna which exploded in a disorganized fashion in the fifties; while absorbing and burying the few islands of working people who lived there, it became a middle- and lower-middle-class residential suburb. It gives the impression of being a

---

[11] See chapter three.
[12] Appendix three, p. 193.
[13] *Ibid.* 194.
[14] Giudicini, *Elezioni* 864.

PROPORTION MALE/FEMALE IN A
SCHEMA OF THE HOMOGENEOUS ZONES
OF RESIDENCE

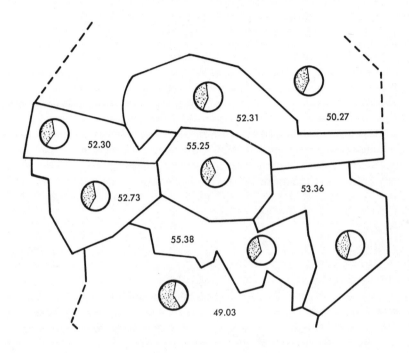

MALE

FEMALE (percentage of women
given in numbers)

Source: P. Giudicini, *Elezioni* 864.

typical, prosperous postwar Italian town, with large apartment buildings that have lost their once-bright colors; the observer is struck
by the total absence of gardens and by the proliferation of appeal-
ing service centers: groceries, bars, dry cleaners, rosticcerie, and so

forth. Undoubtedly, the area's rapid expansion, the predominance of younger people, and the rising standard of living of the working classes explain why the DC nearly equals the PCI and why the PSI and PSDI find here their most successful breeding grounds.[15]

Zone D, a popular residential suburb and service center, has traditionally been the appanage of the left, first socialist and then communist. Centered around the railway station, the gas works, and the meat and fruit markets, and comprised of rows and rows of *palazzoni*, only occasionally interrupted by surviving and decaying houses of the turn of the century, it is so uniform that the observer almost inevitably feels sad. Just recently this part of town has expanded to the north and to the east and has taken on a more attractive appearance. Though zone D is dominated by the left, perhaps because of its more recent expansion and the rise in workers' status, the PSI and PSDI are bettering their positions.[16] This phenomenon tends to confirm the hypothesis that a rise in the standard of living is more beneficial to the parties of the moderate left than to the extreme left or the center.

Zone E corresponds to the old industrial and artisan quarters of the town and centers around the two major Bolognese industries (today dominated by foreign capital), Sabiem and Ducati. The smallest zone, it is also the most homogeneous, inhabited almost exclusively by the proletariat. This is the zone where immigrants from the countryside tend to relocate, to so great an extent that part of it is known as "the village of the peasants." Here is the PCI's exclusive domain, where its own communication system is maintained and where no progress is possible for the DC.[17] PCI domination is so complete that it is doubtful that even a higher standard of living would attract workers to the PSI; instead, workers would probably seek relocation in more attractive parts of the town where they could actually make a choice without encountering hostility on the part of their immediate neighbors.

Zone F is the one-time agricultural belt of the town, now nearly nonexistent. It has become a popular residential suburb, particularly in the north, since efforts were inaugurated by public corporations

---

[15] Appendix three, p. 194.
[16] *Ibid.* 194.
[17] *Ibid.* 195.

such as the INA-CASA to implant new satellite nuclei. None of these is especially attractive, and as a result they have received a great many of the proletariat who originally lived in zone A. The rapid expansion and the combination of different types of population on the agricultural substratum have rendered the zone less amenable to the left than zone E.[18] Nevertheless, the proletarian origin of the inhabitants is clearly reflected by the fact that the left polls well over 70 per cent of the total popular vote.

This division of the town into homogeneous zones of residence supports the assertion that the gap which existed between the bourgeoisie and the proletariat in 1945 is progressively being bridged. Zones A and B are no longer hemmed in by the vise of the suburbs but have expanded to the east and the west, while zone C and the eastern part of zone D are being considered more and more as relatively high-value residential areas. This expansion does not mean that the proletariat has been pushed back but that it has transformed itself into the lower-middle and even middle class and has come to accept middle-class views in its ascent up the status scale. While the antagonism between the proletariat and the bourgeoisie has not been completely eliminated, it is worth noting that the traditional, derelict proletariat is becoming less and less numerous; and, likewise, the typical bourgeoisie with all its prejudices is also losing ground, no longer able to compete with the restricted group comprised of the upper upper-middle class. The reasons for this are not to be found in Bologna: the town hall has played no part in the expansion of these zones, though its over-all conciliatory attitude certainly has rendered communism, Bolognese-style, more palatable to the rich. The true explanation is to be found in the stabilization of the general Italian scene, and Italians should recognize the part Togliatti played in achieving this (his motivation is no longer important) and in the whole country's affirmation of the principles and validity of democracy as a system of government. In turn, these factors have made possible the continuous and tremendously rapid growth of prosperity that has benefited the workers, though we cannot close our eyes to the fact that capitalists certainly have reaped even greater material benefits.

At the present time there seems no reason for this trend to change, and the government is doing everything possible to maintain the

[18] *Ibid.* 195.

expansionist trend. In Bologna, as elsewhere, increased economic well-being is soon followed by a rise in social status, and then a change in political allegiances becomes noticeable, particularly toward the moderate left.[19] It is true that the democratic parties (PSI to PLI) are confronted with the PCI's closed channels of communication in zones E and parts of Zone D. But if the distribution of votes according to social status (manual workers and middle class) is examined, it can be maintained that as the size of the Bolognese middle class increases the votes of the extreme left will diminish. That a goodly percentage of Bolognese, particularly among the between-war generations, will continue to vote PCI is undeniable (15–20 in zone B where the upper-middle class predominates), but it does appear that economic progress, coupled with a dwindling immigration (1962–1965) and the creation of a new socialist party, could well disrupt the monoply on local government that the PCI has enjoyed for over twenty years.

While describing Bologna and the Bolognese, it seems pertinent to present a breakdown of the town according to the sample that was taken which serves as a guiding hypothesis for future chapters.

The collectivity or statistic universe that was examined is comprised of that portion of the adult population of the commune of Bologna which had reached the age of twenty-one, of both sexes and of all economic and social conditions. The size of this collectivity is approximately 350,000 people. To study it, a sample of 355 adults was selected by a method of random sampling. In a first phase, 63 electoral sections of the town were so extracted that they would be representative of the 633 sections which comprise the town. In brief, all zones and quarters of the town were to be represented in the sample. In each section a certain number of voters was chosen by lot, and these voters were interviewed in their homes during the months of December 1965 and January 1966 by five representatives of DOXA (Institute for Statistical Research and Analysis of Public Opinion).[20]

---

[19] This should not be interpreted as meaning that the PCI is going to lose votes in the near future on the national level. Italy has enough misery to keep the Party buoyant for many years to come.

[20] Originally 450 interviews were contemplated in the belief that at least 350 would be possible. Of the 95 that did not take place, 20 failed because the interviewee was absent; in 27 cases, the interviewee moved away; 3 potential interviewees died; 19 refused; and in the other 26 cases the interview was impossible because of lack of collaboration or for other reasons.

DISTRIBUTION OF VOTES BETWEEN PARTIES ACCORDING TO THE INCIDENCE OF MANUAL WORKERS ON THE ELECTORAL BODY IN 1956–1958

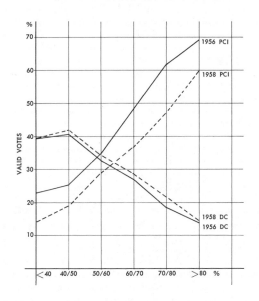

DISTRIBUTION OF VOTES BETWEEN PARTIES ACCORDING TO THE INCIDENCE OF THE MIDDLE CLASS ON THE ELECTORAL BODY IN 1956–1958

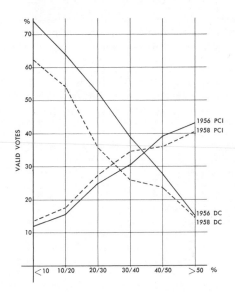

Table I

AGE OF PERSONS INTERVIEWED
(in per cent)

Age Group	Total	Males	Females
21 – 34	21	24	19
35 – 44	27	26	28
45 – 54	20	22	18
55 – 64	16	16	16
Over 64	16	12	19
	100	100	100

Elaborating the questionnaire,[21] which was established and codi-fied in collaboration with DOXA, was a far from easy task, and before it reached its final form it was revised three times. One of the first problems encountered was that an hour-long interview was the most that could be hoped for, and many relevant questions had to be sac-rificed. As a result, the number of open-ended questions was drasti-cally reduced and many accessory questions that might have rendered the interviews less political were eliminated. From the beginning, the dangers of an exclusively political questionnaire were considered, since Italians are notably reluctant to express their political opinions. Nevertheless, a questionnaire concerned principally with local politics was finally devised. An effort was made to keep the questions fair and balanced, and the people interviewed were asked about their political beliefs only at the end of the interviews. These political queries appeared acceptable to the authors of the questionnaire because it was sensed that the Bolognese are traditionally more open-minded and politically mature than the majority of their fellow countrymen. As a matter of fact their response was better than the national aver-age, though 63 per cent refused to name the party they had voted for in the last elections. A rather high percentage of "I do not know" answers to questions on local administration policies must be consid-ered less as refusals to answer than either a simple inability to answer or a lack of interest in the matter referred to.

Examining the representativeness of this sample provides a good

[21] Appendix four, pp. 197–202.

opportunity for exposing a more complete image of the Bolognese. The age groups of the interviewees, as outlined in Table I, practically correspond to those given by the town hall.[22]

The same parallel can be drawn with reference to sex (Table II) where a difference of one per cent appears.

Table II

SEX OF PERSONS INTERVIEWED
(in per cent)

Males	48
Females	52
	100

The economic and social status of the sample may also be considered representative, though well above the Italian average.[23]

Establishing the political tendency of the sample was possible through studying answers that indicated a political preference. The

Table III

ESTIMATED ECONOMIC AND SOCIAL STATUS OF THE FAMILIES
(in per cent)

	Bologna	National Average
Superior	11	8
Average	54	32
Under average	29	34
Inferior	6	31
	100	100

most probable political tendency of the people (Table V), calculated on the total sample (column 1) and specifically on those interviewees who clearly indicated a political leaning (column 2), is a reflection of the electoral returns of the 1964 local elections[24] if one excludes the PSI and the PSDI. The latter is considered the most

[22] See *Annuario statistico* 27, 28, 29.
[23] Mattei Dogan, "Stratificazione sociale dei suffragi," *Elezioni* 470.
[24] See p. 50.

Table IV

PROFESSION OF PERSONS INTERVIEWED
(in per cent)

Entrepreneurs, industrialists	1
Commerce	5
Artisans	5
High civil servants	1
Employees	16
Workers: specialized or not	19
Laborers	1
Unemployed	1
Housewives	36
Students	1
Retired on pension scheme	14
	100

democratic party by a majority of the population, and both parties fared better than previously in those local elections held in 1966 in other parts of Italy.

More generically, and with a smaller margin of error, it was possible to break down the sample into "certain or probable communist voters" (35 per cent), "certain or probable noncommunist voters" (48

Table V

MOST PROBABLE POLITICAL PARTIES OF THE PERSONS INTERVIEWED
(in per cent)

	Total (1)	(2)	Male (1)	Female (1)
PCI	29	43	31	28
PSIUP	–	–	–	–
PSI	7	10	8	5
PSDI	11	16	17	5
PRI	–	–	–	–
DC	14	20	9	18
PLI	7	10	7	6
PDIUM	–	–	–	1
MSI	–	1	1	1
Not deductible	32	–	27	36
	100	100	100	100

per cent) and undecided (17 per cent). This latter figure appears rather low in the Italian context and is an indication of the polarization of issues in Bologna. In view of the fact the PCI polls some 45 per cent of the vote in local elections, it can be assumed that perhaps 10 per cent of the undecided group will give the Party their vote.

Table VI

CLASSIFICATION OF SAMPLE BY POLITICAL TENDENCIES
(in per cent)

	Total	Male	Female
Certain communist voter	19	21	17
Probable communist voter	16	14	19
Probable noncommunist voter	12	12	12
Certain noncommunist voter	36	39	32
Could or could not vote communist	17	14	20
	100	100	100

The picture that obtains for Bologna is of a prosperous, dynamic, changing, and expanding town, even though deprived of any large industry. It is now appropriate to examine the communal system upon which the communist power rests, as well as the key issues that have confronted the Bolognese when called upon to vote.

3: VOTING IN BOLOGNA

Before examining the electoral returns and voting patterns, a few words must be said of the communal system and the problems of representation that are peculiar to Italy. In itself[1] the communal system is an ambiguous arrangement, a part of the heritage handed down by Napoleon and Cavour; it is supposed to perform as an organ of local government, and thus should be independent, but it also is designed to serve as an administrative unit of the central government which is rather contradictory.

The commune's basic organs are a common council (*consiglio comunale*), an executive committee (*giunta comunale*), and a mayor (*sindaco*). The common council is a deliberative (legislative) body, which in Bologna consists of sixty counselors elected by proportional representation; in case of a deadlock a commissioner appointed by the prefect can fulfill the council's duties. In turn, this council chooses its executive committee by majority vote (for the first two ballots) or by plurality on the third ballot. The mayor is elected according to the same conditions by the common council, but he serves two masters, being both the chief executive of the commune and an agent of the central government. In the latter capacity he has charge of registering births, deaths, marriages, and immigration; he is responsible for maintaining public order, safety, and health; he is authorized to issue building permits and to develop, administer, and regulate the various zones.[2] This latter function becomes of crucial importance in

---

[1] In English see: John Clarke Adams and Paolo Barile, *The Government of Republican Italy* (Boston: Houghton Mifflin Company, 1961) 109–123. Norman Kogan, *The Government of Italy* (New York: Thomas Y. Crowell, 1962) 153–155.

In Italian: Guido-Zanobini, *Corso di diritto amministrativo*, vol. 4, new ed. (Milano: Giuffrè, 1958–1959). Luigi Einaudi and Alessandro Repace, *Il Sistema tributario italiano*, 5th ed. (Torino: Einaudi, 1954) 373–425.

[2] See Giuseppe Dozza, "Il Reato di essere sindaco," *Rinascita* 8 (April 1951) 6–12.

a town where rapid expansion is the result of "red" immigration. Incidentally, it should be observed that the disorderly expansion of the building industry is as much attributable to the PCI as to capitalist circles, the local administration having relied upon the *piano regolatore* of 1889 ever since 1945; though the mayor proclaimed that a new plan was being followed, the "plan" appeared in fragmentary form only after 1956!

The central government controls the town by means of the prefect, a position which Clarke describes as "one of the nefarious legacies to Europe of its first modern tyrant, Napoleon Buonoparte."[3] To this phenomenon Luigi Einaudi devoted a now famous article, "Via il Prefetto" (Away with the Prefect), wherein he declared that "Democracy and the prefect are deeply repugnant to each other."[4] As already mentioned, the prefect is empowered to bypass the local administration when it cannot act (though sometimes intervention is solely for reasons of political expediency); the law which thus confers upon the prefect virtually unlimited veto power is based on the fiction that local government is a purely administrative function, that its acts and deliberations are administrative only. As a result, the prefect can base his veto of the acts of the common council on illegality, and furthermore he can reject the council's acts for lack of merit, of which he is sole judge. Thus, the prefect has a voice in all projects or disbursements that exceed three million lire. In Bologna this has led the leftist administration to divide projects unnecessarily and allot them to friendly cooperatives. In fact, however, the prefect's interventions have been quite reasonable, particularly when the budget was balanced. At least they have been more reasonable than the PCI pretends. In this context it must also be pointed out that when any important project is to commence, the *Prefettura* is often approached ahead of time, and whenever the town hall presses the affair further it is obviously seeking a political success and attempting to propagandize an issue that usually does not deserve it. This intervention on financial grounds is undoubtedly objectionable, but it can be understood when we consider the financial situation in which most Italian towns find themselves. What certainly is reprehensible is intervention on the basis of merit. Thus, in August 1965 the *Giunta*

---

[3] Adams, *The Government* 113.
[4] Luigi Einaudi, "Via il prefetto," *Il Buon governo* (Bari: Laterza, 1964) 52–59.

Provinciale Amministrativa and the prefect revoked all old-age pensions paid by the town hall to former state dependents who were already receiving too little from the state to survive.[5] In the sense that the local budget was unbalanced and that the state should be able to take care of its own employees, the arguments could be defended. But the fact is that the GPA had accepted these payments since 1949 without finding anything illegal about them; this action gave the PCI a golden opportunity to denounce, and rightly so, the arbitrariness of prefectoral controls.

What is evident is that

> Prefectoral controls are exercised in a partisan fashion, severely against the communes administered by Left-wing opposition parties. . . . The result is that the Left-wing communes are the best governed in Italy.[6]

This is what the Hon. Scelba (DC) expressed as, "If the prefect did not exist it would be necessary to create him. His function is essential: there is no replacement for him."[7] No doubt this centralizing and politicizing [8] of local government is nefarious for democracy as such. Yet one wonders whether in a country with so large a Communist Party the prefect has not been a safeguard for democracy at least during the early years of the republic.

More immediate and serious is the problem of local finances which truly undermines the effectiveness of local government. Deriving as they do from a tax base dating back to 1915 and 1931, balanced budgets from local taxes are impossible.[9]

There are five main sources of local tax revenue: a local property tax; a tax on items consumed in the commune; licenses on commerce, industry, trades, and professions; a tax on animals; and a family income tax.[10] Under these circumstances the equilibrium of the local

---

[5] *Resto del Carlino*, August 8, 1965.

[6] N. Kogan, *The Government of Italy* 155.

[7] *La Nazione*, September 25, 1960, p. 1.

[8] See Roy Pryce, *The Italian Election of 1956* (London: Chatto and Windus, 1957) 9–10, for a good description.

[9] In 1959, eleven communes out of 7,997 were solvent. Bologna balanced its budget until 1961. The laurels go to Messina, where all its income is insufficient to cover the salaries of its employees. For latest developments, see *The Times* (London), July 9, 1965, p. 11, which gives a good picture of local government in Italy.

[10] For a complete list see Einaudi and Repace, *Il Sistema* 373–445.

budget depends on state subsidies, which will be large or small depending upon the influence the local government can wield in Rome.[11] This explains the importance of a balanced budget for any communist town. In the measure that equilibrium can be maintained, as it was in Bologna until 1961, the central authorities have few means to bring pressure to bear upon the local government. Striving for this independence, Bologna managed to live on a shoe-string budget for years; for the communist administrators this meant greater freedom, while Bologna's status as one of the few Italian towns with a balanced budget provided excellent propaganda. Unfortunately, the consequences were that many necessary measures had to be neglected, sacrificed to the myth of equilibrium. Thus, it was only in 1965 that Bologna saw its last streetcar disappear, and rather than remove the useless tracks the administration saw fit to dispatch groups of workers with a handcart to cover them several times a year. In the long run this is certainly an expensive and antieconomic proposal. The point is, "That to make administrative progress local authorities must use political influence,"[12] and the Bolognese PCI certainly could not carry much weight with the government in Rome.

Also ". . . local elections reflect this situation: administrative and political problems are inextricably interwoven."[13] The result is that even a local election calls for a generalized political campaign in which national and local issues are liberally mixed, one that is organized from the national capital as much as from the local base. However, fundamentally, it can be said that in Bologna local issues tend to predominate in local elections, as was made clear in 1956. In general elections for the lower house, with the exception of 1953 (when the law would have required giving two thirds of the seats to the coalition that received 50 per cent plus 1 vote, a result that did not occur), the Italian system has employed a list system with proportional representation, the remainders being distributed on a national level and based on a natural quotient. In local elections, up to 1956, the voting was carried out with the list system but permitted pre-constituted alliances, and the *blocco* which obtained more than half of the popular votes would receive two thirds of the seats. The

---

[11] Since 1962, 25 per cent of the budget of Bologna is covered by Rome.
[12] Pryce, *The Italian Election* 10.
[13] *Ibid.*

remaining third was distributed proportionally. The system adopted in the 1956 elections, which reflected the changes that had taken place in the general political situation, called for separate party tickets, the seats being distributed according to proportional representation using the d'Hondt system.[14] In general and local elections the voter may indicate four names on his list as his preferences—the system's purpose is to prevent the central party organs from exerting too strong an influence upon the elector. In the case of the PCI, however, which controls a tremendous organization in Bologna, the measure is of illusory value, and *partitocrazia* seems to be the standard rule.[15]

The elections bear with them two problems which are peculiar to Italy: the high percentage of voter participation and the importance of the women's vote. To these can be added the importance of propaganda. The turnout for elections in Bologna is above the national average (92–94 per cent) as summarized below:

Political		Local	
1946	90.49	1946	84.83
1948	95.27	1951	93.60
1953	96.64	1956	95.41
1958	97.91	1960	95.52
1963	97.60	1964	95.69

In practice almost everybody votes, but it does not seem possible to consider this high participation as an index of political maturity. As the principal reasons for high electoral participation, many authors[16] suggest a reaction to twenty years of fascism, the grace with which the government accepted defeat in 1946 and 1953 (referendum and "fraud law"), and the polarization of the two major parties. These reasons are no doubt important, but more significant is the fact that voting is technically compulsory in the sense that a certificate of good conduct (required by nearly all employers) is issued, and upon this certificate electoral participation is recorded.

[14] Giovanni Scepis, "I Sistemi elettorali e loro classificazione," *Amministrazione Civile* 2 (March–April 1958) 59–69.

[15] See Luigi d'Amato, "Il Voto di preferenza," *Rassegna Italiana di Sociologia* 3, no. 2 (April–June 1962) 235.

[16] Adams and Barile, for instance, *The Government* 178.

It is difficult to assess the maturity of the town, but some ideas can be gained from studies made on a national level. Moreover, Bologna, like all northern Italian towns, must be recognized as possessing a somewhat higher than usual degree of political maturity because of the higher level of instruction that prevails.[17] Our sample indicates that the Bolognese level is two to five points above the general average, and also reflects the general rule that men receive more formal education than women.[18] (See Table VII.)

If we consider the frequency of political discussions (employing "often" and "occasionally" as measures) to be a means of clarifying one's ideas, Italy is on the same level as the United States, with approximately one third of the population using this means.[19] Comparing Bologna to other towns of the same size and considering frequent political conversation as an index of political maturity (or of political sensitivity, since 40 per cent vote communist), the town is some twelve points above the average. According to political tendencies, conversation as a clarifying means is often used: by PCI, 27 per cent; PSI, 18; DC, 10; PLI, 32.[20] Assuming 10 per cent for the extreme right, 15 for the PSDI, and using the electoral returns of

---

[17] On the importance of instruction see statistical results in Paolo Ammassari, "Opinione politica e scelta elettorale," *Elezioni e comportamento politica in Italia*, A. Spreafico and J. Palombara, eds. (Milano: Communità, 1963) 742–748, and Mattei Dogan, "Stratificazione sociale ed elezioni," *ibid.* 458.

[18] For the population of Bologna above six years of age in 1961 the following statistics were obtained:

Illiterates	7,751
Functional illiterates	35,748
Elementary school	261,225
High school	65,991
University degree	44,780
	415,495

Annuario statistico 1963 (Bologna: STEB, 1964) 119.

[19] Ammassari, *Elezioni* 760.

Frequency of Political Conversations in Towns Above 50,000

	In Family	With Colleagues	With Others
Often	10	11	4
Occasionally	28	19	10
Never	60	65	67
No Answer	2	5	19
Total	100	100	100

Bollettino DOXA (November 15, 1964) 177.

[20] *Ibid.* 176.

Table VII

LEVEL OF EDUCATION OF PERSONS INTERVIEWED
(in per cent)

	Total	Males	Females
Elementary or no schooling	65	56	74
Secondary school (*media inferiore*)	18	23	12
Lyceum (*media superiore*)	12	14	11
University	5	7	3
	100	100	100

1964 as a base for calculations, 71,114 Bolognese out of 356,611 of voting age—or 19.99 per cent—indulge in frequent political conversation, whereas the Italian average is 8. Evidently, because of the high proportion of communists, this can only be regarded as indicative of an *ordre de grandeur*.

As a further indication of political maturity, it is interesting to note the attitude of the young people, who, one might believe, would be attracted by the extremes. This is not, in fact, wholly true.

. . . . The movement toward the extreme left occurs *several years after* the first call to the polls. Thus a prolonged dissatisfaction about one's own economic conditions, a deeper mistrust for promises of economic and social betterment, and, in general, increasing negative expectations for the future are at the root of any electoral orientation toward political extremism.[21]

This holds true for Bologna also.[22]

The importance of the women's vote is summarized in the title of an article by Mattei Dogan: "The Italian Women Between Catholicism and Marxism."[23] Percentage-wise, in proportion to the total electorate of the parties, the situation was as follows in 1958:[24]

	PCI & PSI	DC	Others	Total
Men[25]	61	37	47	47.9
Women	39	63	53	52.1

[21] Joseph La Palombara, "Orientamento dei Giovani," *Elezioni* 514.
[22] A. Ardigò, *ibid.* 837.
[23] Mattei Dogan, *ibid.* 475–495.
[24] *Ibid.* 480.
[25] Proportion of male/female in Bologna 46.9–53.1 per cent.

The vote of women for the DC is plainly of paramount importance to that party, especially in a city like Bologna where one voter out of seven is communist. The relationship with the Church becomes clearer when it is noted that the majority of feminine votes comes from unmarried persons, or more precisely from widows and young girls, who are allied most closely to the Church.[26]

> As women are more religious, more attentive to the recommendations of the Church, more readily influenced by an intervention of the parish priest, it is natural and logical that they tend to vote more often than men for the DC party, or, to be more exact, against "atheistic communism and its allies."[27]

This general judgment should be modified in the case of Bologna. This is not to say that the Church does not influence the vote of practicing Catholics, but to assert that the Church has very little power over the areligious Bolognese in general.

Since the pontificate of Pius XII, this intervention has been clear and undisguised either through the Church or by means of Catholic Action groups. In 1952, in Bologna, Cardinal Lercaro used the *frati volanti*[28] (flying monks) to instruct people how to vote; in 1956 it was no secret that the hierarchy was inclined toward Dossetti, and the faithful were urged to vote in that way.[29] In 1963 the conference of bishops urged the faithful to vote DC, and to that end to sacrifice, if necessary, "personal opinions and particular interests."[30] As Jerkov observes, "In Italy, the lower degree of political maturity, the almost total absence of an Italian Catholic culture . . . have allowed the Church to maintain its temporal power, though the form has changed."[31] In a speech given in 1958 at the *Scuola Superiore di Formazione Sociale* of Bologna, Cardinal Lercaro explained:

> The Church gives autonomy to secular activities, but intervenes to judge *the morality of the act in itself* or to judge the *damage it could create* for the highest good of Faith or Grace, even if in itself the act, con-

---

[26] Mattei Dogan, *Elezioni* 484.
[27] *Ibid.* 488.
[28] Motorized priests who could easily go from one electoral meeting to another.
[29] On the intervention of the Cardinal see the *Avvenire d'Italia*, May 20, 1956.
[30] See Antonio Jerkov, "La Chiesa cattolica e le elezioni italiane," *Problemi del Socialismo* 6 (April 1963) 478.
[31] *Ibid.* 482.

sidered isolated, . . . could be moral. This is the basis of the "indirect power" . . . in political life [the basis of power] upon the voting power.[32]

This was expressed more clearly on the eve of the 1953 elections:

It is only in view of and considering your spiritual well-being that your bishops address you: if the actual electoral contest only concerned interests of the temporal, the bishops . . . would be happy to remain out of it. But today the highest spiritual interests are in contest: liberty and consequently the possibility of religious life in Italy.[33]

The communists point out:

If condemnation of a doctrine can represent a legitimate use of the potestas magisteri, then this use is quickly transformed into an abuse condemned by the law (art. 71 of the electoral law; art. 88 of the law on local elections) wherever spiritual weapons are used to violate the political liberty of the Catholic electors and thereby influence them for or against determined lists of candidates.[34]

However, the intervention has its limits. In fact:

The political power of the Church appears to be more effective negatively than positively. Its influence can apparently hold votes [women's] for the Christian Democratic Party, but it cannot gain votes for the party. It may block undesired policies but it cannot compel desired ones.[35]

Table VIII

DIVISION OF ELECTORAL BODY BY SEX
(in per cent)

	Total	Communist	Noncommunist	Undecided
Males	48	47	52	39
Females	52	53	48	61

Whatever the PCI may pretend, the essential point is that the Catholic Church cannot compel the votes it desires, and this is well reflected in our sample's distribution of communist and undecided votes. It appears that if we include probable communist voters

[32] Archidiocesi di Bologna, Il Cardinale Lercaro (Bologna: UTOA, 1964) 222.
[33] Bollettino diocesano (Bologna) June 1953, p. 76.
[34] "Il Clero e le elezioni," Rinascita 5, no. 3 (March 1948) 98.
[35] Kogan, The Government of Italy 75.

among all communist voters, women would make up 53 per cent of the PCI strength.

These figures tend to invalidate, for Bologna at least, the common assertion that in Italy men comprise two thirds of the communist strength unless we accept the unlikely alternative that a majority of the undecided men vote for the PCI. This clearly indicates the importance of the anticlerical or areligious tradition of the town where women are as dechristianized as men; it is our belief that the Church has totally lost contact with the vast majority of the population and can influence only that minority which regularly practices its religion.

The propaganda of the Church, though quite open, is as nothing when compared to that of the political parties, despite the fact that it directly influences party propaganda. Changes in national and international situations have materially influenced the Italian system of electoral propaganda: the crucial dividing point has come in the elections of 1956.[36] Up to that date the republican regime, while operating in an atmosphere of international tension that had come to a head in 1948, sought to strengthen itself and overcome fascist tendencies. Since 1956 the situation has been evolving toward normality; from campaigns based on emotion a more reasoned type of appeal has come about. The new approach demands more use of capillary propaganda and a greater personalization of political appeals, a trend that favors the larger and richer parties like the DC and the PCI.

The financing of the campaigns remains among the more obscure points of Italian elections. The amount of financial support given by the party or by individuals is impossible to determine with any preciseness. In any case it is an inordinately costly operation, particularly if one considers that in Bologna at least 68 per cent of the electors have made up their minds before the campaign. It is a fair estimate that an electoral campaign in Bologna, for general or local elections, must cost the major parties at least 200,000 dollars.

As long as the Church continues to give so much uncovenanted support to one party, it is unlikely that the other parties will agree to a general restriction which would handicap them unfairly in comparison.[37]

---

[36] See Luciano Visentini, "Osservazione sulla propaganda elettorale," *Elezioni* 277–299. For a good summary up to 1958 see Pietro Facchi, *La Propaganda politica in Italia* (Bologna: Il Mulino, 1960).

[37] Pryce, *The Italian Election* 27.

The most important point to consider in the Bolognese elections is the tense situation that exists between the left and the DC: in this it is impossible to dissociate the local situation form the broader Italian and international contexts, even though in Bologna local issues seem to predominate in local elections. The first postwar election could still be waged on the faltering basis of the unity of the parties of the Resistance, but above all it would be "red" against bourgeois, communist suburbs against inner-city and upper-class residential areas. As the communists were to say:

The enemies to be overcome are the camouflaged fascists, those who were friends of the fascists, those who left the people hungry for twenty years and made them suffer from war; the priests were the fascists' friends, the liberals were the fascists' friends, the bourgeois . . .; the socialists are our brotherly companions, and with them we will triumph . . . but to win we need organization. And who was ready to fight the Germans and the fascists? Who was always here, during twenty years, to give you hope in the darkest moments? Who helped you most in the past, and who has helped you most, from the standpoint of town hall leadership, during the past year? Who controls the partisans?[38]

Couched in such terms, old resentments could not die, and the "red" suburbs led the town to a communist victory. It was a victory for the party of Dozza and the socialist brotherhood headed by Francesco Zanardi, the man who had so distinguished himself as the first socialist mayor of Bologna in 1914; the more prudent bourgeois turned to the Christian democrats, thus indicating clearly the discredit into which the Liberal party had fallen. For Bologna, the question of institutions, as it was presented to the people, was a false problem, and no intervention by the Vatican could change the trend. The DC made the issue easier by not taking position on the referendum monarchy-republic, but insisting that democracy had to triumph over dictatorship. In the town 67.22 per cent of the population voted in favor of the republic.

The general election of June 1946, called to elect delegates to the constituent assembly, clearly showed where Bologna stood; though giving 7.81 per cent of its vote to the rightist Uomo Qualunque fad, Bologna delivered an overwhelming leftist majority, over-all.

---

[38] Gianluigi Degli Esposti, Bologna PCI (Bologna: Il Mulino, 1966) 29–30.

	Bologna	Italy
DC	21.75	35.1
PCI	33.73	18.9
PSI	28.09	20.7

The year 1948 provided a superlative occasion to set the two sections of town against each other. The very existence of democracy seemed to be in the balance; the choice appeared to be between a new *coup de Prague* and American imperialism, with these options being financially supported by the Cominform on the one hand, Washington and the Vatican on the other. On the Italian level the competition was between the government forces of the DC and the leftist bloc comprised of Nenni socialists and communists, the latter recently excluded from the government. In Bologna the issues stirred the electorate, and both antagonists were ready to use all possible means, legal and not so legal. From the very beginning the DC seemed certain to be defeated; they could scarcely count on support from the Sarragat socialists, who in Bologna looked more rightist than the Christian democrats themselves. On the other side of the fence, the PCI struggled to extract itself from the ambiguous situation of having participated in the government of the country. Thus, the PCI had to project itself as uncompromising, ready to expel the Americans, even though everybody knew that fear of being branded illegal would restrict the Party to its opportunistic policy for the present. On the other hand, while proclaiming its alliance with the Nenni socialists, the PCI did all that it could to diminish the Nenni influence, and it was clear that if the coalition were victorious, Bologna would be dominated by the PCI and not by an alliance between a dwarf and a giant. On April 18, the Bolognese proved they had understood:

	Bologna	Italy
DC	36.28	48.4
PCI - PSI	44.38	31.0

Contrary to all predictions, the DC polled 15 per cent more votes than in 1946, while the left lost 18 per cent, the PCI itself dropping at least 5 per cent of its support. The communist achievement was poles apart from the promise voiced in an editorial in the April 14 *Progresso:* "In four days we will overthrow this foreign dominated government." Nor would the pencils tickle St. Joseph's beard,[39] nor the proletariat dance in San Petronio, as had been promised. On April 22 all the *Progresso* could say was: "Only the Front was and is able to prevent clerical dictatorship."

Christian democrats, guided by a group of notables, never fully realized that they had practically defeated the left, and rather than take advantage of their momentum they preferred to fall back into the role of sterile opposition in the city council. There they automatically rejected all communist proposals and suggested nothing better than nineteenth-century solutions to twentieth-century problems. It was in this same spirit that they returned to the electors in 1951, and it spelled disaster for the DC. After the 1948 experience the PCI knew very well the danger with which it was confronted. Violence having failed, a new tactic had to be evolved, and this was helped along by the system of *apparentements* which was used for the first time. If the suburbs were not sufficient to guarantee success, the PCI would turn to the middle class of whom Togliatti spoke so highly. Bologna witnessed a flourishing of communist-controlled groups designed to protect small shopkeepers, little business men, and the like. Relying also upon the Bolognese sense of economy, efforts were made to present a balanced budget; and because it was apparent that the PSI was dominated by the PCI, a new electoral group was created. The *Gigante* group, which had as its symbol Gianbologna's nude of Neptune that adorns the Piazza of King Enzo, was led by top "bourgeois" communists who were members of the University. The group was formally headed by a gold medal winner of the Resistance who did not seem to suspect the role he was playing. The Sarragat socialists, who eventually polled over 14 per cent of the total vote, quickly denounced it in purely Bolognese terms: "Fa il Gigante la pipi nel vasino del PCI." The communist tactics paid off nevertheless: the PCI polled 40.40 per cent of the votes to the PSI's 7.37, while the DC (25.85) lost votes both to the liberals and the social democrats. With the help of the *Gigante* (1.02 per cent),

---

[39] The Front's symbol was Giuseppe Garibaldi, and his image is not too different from that of the traditional St. Joseph—thus the invitation to vote for St. Joseph!

the left entered the town hall controlling 40 of its 60 seats.
The 1953 campaign in Bologna was in a sense the campaign of a
dead man: Stalin. International tensions were diminishing even
though the DC refused to acknowledge it, and the government was
doing poorly with both its unworkable plan for land reform and its
antidemocratic *legge truffa*.[40] This was the PCI's leitmotiv. Stalin
had died some three months before election day, and Stalin was the
idol of the suburbs.

> He is what Mussolini never managed to be for anybody; Stalin is what
> the pope cannot be for his most obedient children: Stalin is everything
> the anticommunists, in their hatred, cannot find in the leaders of
> Christian democracy and the West.[41]

What greater tribute could the people pay to their hero than to vote
for his party? And so they did.

	DC	PCI
1948	36.28	25-30.0
1953	30.58	34.84

The 1956 campaign[42] was totally different from anything Bologna
had experienced until then, and for the first time the Christian democrats were on the offensive. They were somewhat hampered by the
fact that Dozza, with his record of moderation and achievement,
appeared as the conservative, while Dossetti, expressing hopes for the
future, appeared as the radical. Nevertheless, the DC hopes were
high, and the returns utterly dashed them:

	DC	PCI
1956	27.73	45.18
1951	25.85	40.40

The communist increase was far greater than the DC's, while the
PSI barely managed to hold its own, receiving some votes from the

---

[40] For the Chamber of Deputies the law allowed the alliance of two or more
parties and the attribution of a premium (65 per cent of the seats) to the group
polling more than 50 per cent of the total vote. This could only play in favor of
the government coalition.

[41] Degli Esposti, *Bologna PCI* 106.

[42] See pp. 54–63.

PSDI while losing as many to the PCI. The communists had shown their strength and the Christian democrats their determination, which for a few years would not waver. For the first time the DC made plain that it intended to seek votes in the red part of town and thus force a confrontation between the two antagonists. With the 1956 victory under its belt, the PCI could go to the polls two years later without too much concern. It is true that the Hungarian uprising shook the Party, but it also provided the PCI with a new wave of young theoreticians and administrators who would soon make headlines. However, Dozza and the Stalinists of the federation remained firmly in control. The intervention of the Church in state affairs (condemnation of the Bishop of Prato) provided Bologna with the type of ammunition it liked and at the same time undermined the DC. Socialist proposals for an "opening to the left," with which John XXIII seemed rather sympathetic, also hurt the DC. Never bothered by contradictions, the PCI delighted in criticizing Church intervention even while pointing out that Catholics could now vote for the left. The communists were fully aware that an extra vote for the PSI meant direct support for the PCI. Finally, immigrants were still pouring into town, and the local administration was taking great pains to insure their vote: the result was an increase in the communist strength.

	DC	PCI
1958	28.19	36.95
1953	30.58	34.84

The 1956 trend was to continue into 1960, and the DC this time had no recognized leader and reaped little benefit from its constructive opposition. The PCI hiked its share of the vote by .40 per cent and the DC regressed by .90. It seemed that the situation had stabilized, and it is in the general elections that one must look to discern a change in the Bolognese mood. The "opening to the left" preceded the 1963 elections by one year, and since it was still a faltering experiment, it did little to enhance the prestige of the DC with the Bolognese. Meanwhile, the PCI found it even easier to undermine what was left of the PSI electorate, in which the tendencies that were to lead to the creation of the PSIUP were already being felt.

LOCAL ELECTION RETURNS

	24-3-1946		27-5-1951		27-5-1956		6-11-60		22-11-1964	
	Votes	%	Votes	%	Votes	%	Votes	%	Votes	%
PCI (Due Torri)	71,369	38.28	93,043	40.40	121,404	45.18	138,256	45.58	149,433	44.79
PSI	49,031	26.30	16,982	7.37	19,957	7.42	25,992	8.57	25,265	7.57
PdA	1,200	0.64								
PSDI					23,253	8.65	26,384	8.70	27,715	8.31
US			32,438	14.09						
PSIUP									6,384	1.91
DC (Scudo Crociato)	56,543	30.33	59,532	25.85	74,501	27.73	81,383	26.83	73,643	22.07
PRI	5,343	2.87	4,409	1.91	3,487	1.30	3,312	1.09	1,671	0.50
PLI	2,940	1.58	13,837	6.01	12,496	4.65	14,992	4.95	36,786	11.02
MSI			7,716	3.35	13,622	5.07	12,976	4.28	11,200	3.36

Comune di Bologna, Ufficio Elettorale, "Elezioni politiche e amministrative," Bologna, 1965, mimeographed, n.p.

GENERAL ELECTION RETURNS

	2-6-1946†		18-4-1948		7-6-1953		25-5-1958		28-4-1963	
	Votes	%	Votes	%	Votes	%	Votes	%	Votes	%
PCI	67,876	33.73	99,946	44.38	85,856	34.84	107,772	36.95	135,829	40.40
PSI	56,533	28.09			23,922	9.70	37,432	12.84	40,036	11.90
US			9,984	13.31						
PSDI					24,038	9.79	27,650	9.48	31,598	9.50
PdA	3,076	1.53								
DC	43,770	21.75	81,723	36.28	75,357	30.58	82,204	28.19	71,289	21.20
UQ	15,716	7.81								
PRI	7,098	3.53	5,673	2.52	3,362	1.36	4,697	1.61	2,830	0.84
MSI			975	0.43	9,483	3.85	11,018	9.78	14,204	4.23
PLI					9,992	4.05	16,882	5.79	37,289	11.00

† Constituent Assembly.
Ibid.

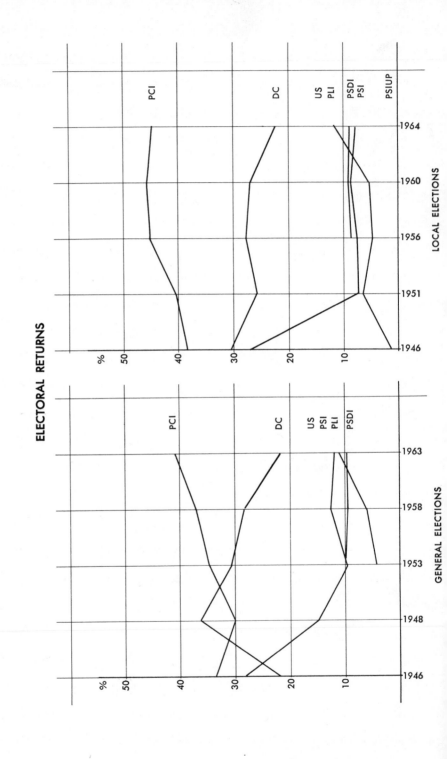

ELECTORAL RETURNS

LOCAL ELECTIONS

PCI

DC

US
PLI

PSDI
PSI

PSIUP

1964

1960

1956

1951

1946

% 50 40 30 20 10

GENERAL ELECTIONS

PCI

DC

US
PSI
PLI

PSDI

1963

1958

1953

1948

1946

% 50 40 30 20 10

	DC	PCI
1963	21.20	40.40
1958	28.19	36.95

In summarizing the electoral situation of Bologna, a constant increase of communist votes in local and national elections will be remarked. In local elections the total vote polled by the communists tends to stabilize around 45 per cent—which indicates a secure following—while in national elections the percentage of votes is increasing constantly and is approaching 40. This increase can be attributed to the heavy immigration Bologna has known since 1958, and it emphasizes the PCI's capacity for assimilation and encadrement.

The difference in returns on local, as compared to national, issues proves that a communist electorate exists which in administrative elections votes differently than it does in national elections. This difference does not even preclude a switch from DC and PLI when local issues are at stake. On the other hand, in local elections the DC shows a slow but constant decline, gaining nothing whatsoever from its opposition role. This is due neither to the effectiveness of the communist administration nor to a lack of constructive opposition, but more to a denial of support by the DC's central authorities in Rome, which consider Bologna as lost once and for all. Furthermore, the population has no great confidence in the Christian Democratic party. The DC's electoral efforts and, even more, its mistakes and scandals tend to help less clericalized groups, such as the PLI or the PSDI, which are not implicated in the Rome-Moscow controversy. But no benefit accrues to the PCI, which gets its recruits from the already "red" countryside.

In national elections the disappearance of international tensions (Moscow versus Washington, totalitarianism versus democracy)—the existence of which coincided with the DC's greatest electoral strength—the opening to the left, and economic difficulties have proved disastrous for the DC in Bologna. From the 1948 level of 35 per cent of the votes the DC now finds itself at its 1945 level of some 20 per cent. What has been said of local elections holds true for national ones.

In short, comparing the electoral curves of the PCI and DC in local and national elections in Bologna, the local election appears of lesser interest than the national one. In local contests the PCI's strength holds steady as DC power slowly dwindles; in national elections the PCI registers constant increases while the DC shows steady and sizable decreases.

The Christian democrat debacle and communist triumph in 1956 have already been mentioned. In retrospect, however, this election appears to have been totally different, both in form and consequence, from those which preceded and followed. The consequences, especially, demand a more extensive discussion which should focus on the general condition of the city's democratic life. In the differences that marked the 1956 campaign the reasons for the DC failure are readily apparent. The appearance and personality of the new DC leader, the development of the campaign itself, and the contradictions inherent in the new political formula proposed to the voters— all these factors played a role in the DC disaster.

Giuseppe Dossetti[43]—called the professorino (the little professor) because of his physical frailty—had won fame in Italy for the rapidity of his rise to eminence and for his progressive ideas. Born in Genoa in 1913 and a resident of Reggio Emilia, Dossetti was appointed a professor of ecclesiastical law in 1942. As a member of the Resistance, he became in 1945 the Christian democrat representative on the Committee for National Liberation even though he was not a member of the party. Despite this lack of party regularity, he served as vice-secretary of the Christian democrats from 1946 until he retired from Parliament in 1952—with the exception of the period 1947–1949. From the very beginning he was ranked with La Pira and Fanfani as a leader of the radical Christian democrats. This so-called doctrinal left was comprised of progressives who expressed their ideas in the Cronache Sociale, of which Dossetti became editor. In brief, Dossetti's personality and entire career weighed against him as a candidate in Bologna. The very progressivism for which he was noted tended to alienate from his cause a large segment of the local Christian democracy, oriented to the right and based upon the notables as it was. His mysticism, his profound Catholicism, and the cenobitic life he led after his return to Bologna in 1952 were completely foreign to the general population—traditionally carefree, open, gay, and anti-clerical. And, last but not least, to the chauvinistic Bolognese Dossetti was an alien, "parachuted in" from Reggio Emilia.

[43] La Stampa, March 17, 1956. Luigi Pedrazzi, "Il ritorno di Dossetti," Il Mulino 15, no. 54 (March 1956) 225–229.

It may appear strange that, confronted by such compelling reasons for rejecting a candidacy, a man as intelligent as Dossetti should instead accept it. Actually, Dossetti was forced upon the local DC, even as he himself was earlier "induced" to seek the candidacy by Cardinal Lercaro, on whose largesse the fate of Dossetti's Center of Theological Research was dependent.[44] Describing the relationship of the prelate and his candidate as a "battle" does not appear exaggerated if we consider that Dossetti had always made it clear, when in Parliament, that the Church should forego an active role in politics. Consequently, while Dossetti accepted in principle the proposal offered by the Cardinal, he made his formal acceptance only after all the DC supporters—who convened March 19, the feast of St. Joseph, his patron saint—had confirmed his candidacy. Moreover, he made it clear that he was not a member of the Christian Democratic party but was running as an independent. It can likewise be hypothesized that Dossetti agreed to be the Cardinal's candidate not only out of obedience but also on the grounds that while the Church should not intervene in national politics, local administration was another matter. Or, as it might be put negatively, he accepted the political intervention of the Church but hoped, once elected, to maintain a reasonable degree of administrative autonomy.[45] The natural consequence of this kind of thinking was that all secular parties and groups of the population, dismayed by the open intervention of the Church and the profoundly religious personality of its candidate, should harden in their opposition to Dossetti.

For Bologna the 1956 campaign was something different. The DC seemed to be filled with new energies and inspired by the personality of its leader. Its program was based on a break with the past, spelled out in full detail by a smoothly functioning brain-trust; the clear intent was to end the communist monopoly in Bologna.[46] Dossetti pitched his appeal directly to the voters rather than to the parties

[44] See *La Stampa*, November 13 1965; *L'Espresso*, November 12, 1955; Pryce, *The Italian Election* 80. It has been said that the Hon. Salizzoni, the local leader of the DC, exercised all his influence upon the Cardinal to have Dossetti run as the DC candidate.

[45] Lucio Magri, "Le Amministrative a Bologna," in *Dibattito Politico* 12 (April 9, 1956) 15–17, 22.

[46] Nicola Matteucci, "Dossetti a Bologna," *Il Mulino* 5, no. 57 (June 1956) 382–391.

and tried to shed new light upon the town's real problems. He struggled to keep his speeches from descending to mere anticommunist
rhetoric, and specifically from rhetoric involving the myth that
enshrined Dozza, his direct opponent. To sum up, while he was the
candidate chosen by a party that was moderate by definition, in Bolognese eyes Dossetti was the "bolshevik," the revolutionary. His
attack upon Dozza was accurate and was well documented by the
history of the town's earlier communist administrations: it was true
that Dozza was less the genial administrator than the cautious, fear-
ful mayor, less the revolutionary "red" than the bourgeois communist. But as always, truth is a two-edged weapon: by accusing the
local administration of conservatism and proposing a new program,
Dossetti was seen as an iconoclast by many small industrialists who
were moderately satisfied with the paternalism of the communist
mayor; by attacking the indolent and patronizing policy of the town
hall, Dossetti seemed bent on destroying the delicate equilibrium
that existed.

The Dossetti program, "formulated in the light of modern sociological techniques,"[47] stirred anxiety in the practical Bolognese. They
saw themselves confronted by the choice between communist immobilism "leading to a spiritual and economic decadence" (with which
they appeared satisfied) and an appeal to "unite and awaken Bolognese energies," to make the town "an active and propulsive center
for all national life" (for which they cared little). It was easy to
agree that "in the course of History the decadence of the Cities and
the States started when the creative impulse was replaced by the
politics of clientele," but in their secret hearts few saw the need for
renewing the "spiritual face" of Bologna even if this meant something "beautiful and generous . . . for the good of all." And still
fewer agreed when the new "spiritual face" was depicted as "a great
spirit of Christian fraternity and not of class hatred or egoism of
privileges." Furthermore, Dossetti's proposals to reform the town hall
by better coordination, to initiate a broad social inquiry to determine
the true necessities of the town, to undertake a policy of help to the
poor, the old, and the immigrants, to embark upon a policy of decen-

[47] The complete program is exposed in Democrazia Cristiana, *Libro bianco su
Bologna* (Bologna: Il Resto del Carlino, 1956) 10. More succinctly reference is
made in the text to DC, *Bologna a una svolta*, pamphlet put out for the elections.

tralization—all these modern and daring proposals the Bolognese equated with greater expenses and higher taxes, with destroying that balanced budget of which the communists—but also all Bolognese— were so proud.

In spite of this revolutionary program, however, Dossetti still entertained some hope of victory. On the one hand, Christian democracy—*volens o nolens*—devoted all its energies to winning the town hall, and in this effort it was actively supported by the Catholic Church, whose candidate Dossetti really was. On the other hand, the Communist Party was passing through a difficult national and international period, and for the first time the local Party seemed concerned and defensive.

Dossetti's candidacy was supported by all but four of the nearly 1,000 DC party members; with the mirage of the town hall before them, no energies were wasted, and the Church lent its active support as well.

> In fact all the clergy was mobilized. . . . The Demo-Christian activists have sounded the patriotic appeal, "Out with the agents of the Kremlin!" In Bologna the electoral campaign has been like a battlefield. Bloc against bloc: with Dozza or with Dossetti. The Cardinal has put his men on the move. . . .[48]

The attention of all Catholics was called to the fact that the electors must vote efficiently (no blank or split votes) and that it was a serious fault to vote communist or socialist. The Cardinal's message was published in the *Avvenire d'Italia* on May 5 and read at masses on May 20.

As has been pointed out, the communists were going through a particularly difficult moment, and the proposal of the Nenni socialists that the government might possibly find an opening to the left appeared to have isolated them; however large this "opening" might be, it was clear that it was not large enough for the Communist Party. Furthermore, the communists had suffered their first defeat in the shop stewards' elections at Fiat, an indication that their trade union policy had failed. Above all, the Twentieth Congress of the Communist Party of the Soviet Union was the source of great embarrassment; the condemnation of the personality cult was admitted by Togliatti on February 24, and Khrushchev's speech itself was pub-

[48] Bruno Biral, in *Il Ponte* 12, no. 6 (June 1956) 937.

lished on March 17. Blandly, the Party sought to carry on as if nothing had happened.[49] And this very line was most acceptable to the
DC, which was attempting to keep the campaign as dispassionate as
possible. Exciting fanaticism had been rewarding in 1948 but had not
paid off in 1953. Thus 1956 called for a more moderate line.[50]

If the DC had found a charismatic leader in Dossetti, the PCI had
a highly successful one in Giuseppe Dozza. Born the son of a baker
in 1900, Dozza interrupted his studies at an early age to become a
member (and later secretary) of the Emilian Socialist Youth. In
1924 he served as the national secretary of the Communist Youth
movement; in 1925 he was in France, in Paris and Toulouse, charged
with coordinating relations between the Italian Communist Party
and the International. Despite the fact that he had been condemned
to prison by the fascist regime, he went to Italy in 1930 to organize
the Fourth Party Congress, and in 1943 he returned to his homeland
for good, first to represent the PCI on the CLN in Milan, and then
in 1944 to become mayor of Bologna, an office he held when elected
to Parliament in 1946. Ever since, he has been regularly re-elected
mayor, with a large share of the preferential votes. Physically a stur-
dily built man with an open and jovial personality, he is in appearance the incarnation of the traditional Bolognese—more concerned
about his own well-being and the quality of the food on his table
than about politics[51] and cleverly disguising his ruthlessness under an
air of tranquil nonchalance.

The Party had carefully planned its campaign as far back as October 1955 when a series of articles pointed out the weaknesses and contradictions of the DC.[52] From that moment on, the accomplishments
of the Communist Party[53] and Dozza (whose photograph appeared
in all the issues of La Lotta from November 1955 to May 1956 with
the exception of February) were regularly pinpointed: the expansion

---

[49] Scarcely any mention is made of the new line in La Lotta, the organ of the
Bolognese communists, except as it referred to the different ways to socialism.

[50] On the campaign in general see: Alfonso Prandi, "La campagna elettorale
nella provincia emiliana," Il Mulino 5, no. 57 (June 1956) 403–411.

[51] See Time Magazine, November 20, 1964, pp. 38–39.

[52] La Lotta, October 18, 1955; November 4, 11, 1955.

[53] Renato Nicolai, "Realizzazione della amministrazione democratica della città
di Bologna," Rinascita (March 1956) 150–155.

of the building industry,[54] the equilibrium of the local budget,[55] the strength of the Party,[56] the importance of the University and the help given it by the local administration,[57] a higher standard of living in Bologna, and lower prices.[58] At the same time a series of eleven articles [59] pointed out how badly the DC administered the towns or villages around Bologna where it predominated, and the Lapirian Florence was held up as a special symbol of chaos.[60] Starting March 15, "the candidate of the DC," "the new man arising from his lethargy carrying the flag of anticommunism,"[61] the creature of the Cardinal was harshly taken to task, while the socialists who were presenting their own list were not mentioned.

The campaign in Bologna began two weeks ahead of the official April 8 date. On March 17, Dozza in a press conference[62] set the tone with a strong condemnation of Dossetti, consistently referring to him as "the Demo-Christian leader" foisted on Bologna by the Cardinal, who in the case of a leftist defeat would govern as did the "cardinal-legate" of tragic memory. Not content with touching off anticlerical passions, the mayor raised the specter of a prefectoral commissar who would rule in case there was no clear majority. On the other hand, Dossetti on March 19 declared himself confident in the campaign outcome,[63] but he also found it impossible to reject Dozza's accusations. In the socialist Avanti! the headline ran, "The Voice of the Cardinal. Dossetti, the Christian Democratic Candidate Has Not Presented 'His' Program, but That of the Church."[64]

On April 8 the campaign officially opened and the political charges began; the Communist Party was confronted with its responsibility

---

[54] La Lotta, October 1, 14, 21, 1955.
[55] Ibid., December 9, 1955.
[56] Ibid., December 30, 1955.
[57] Ibid., January 6, 1956; February 3, March 1, May 11, May 18, 1956.
[58] Ibid., April 4, 20, 27 and May 4, 11, 18, 24, 1956.
[59] Ibid., February 3 to April 27, 1956.
[60] Ibid., February 16, 1956.
[61] Ibid., March 22, 1956.
[62] Resto del Carlino, March 18, 1956; Unità, March 18, 1956. For the text see Renato Nicolai, Il Sindaco e la Città (Roma: Editori Riuniti, 1956) 123–145. A hastily put together answer to the DC white book.
[63] Resto del Carlino, March 20, 1956.
[64] Avanti! March 28, 1956.

as a political party[65] (the end of the Stalinist myth) and as a party of local administration (lack of initiatives), but this aspect was to diminish after May 21. The campaign, in fact, must be considered as the most important of the postwar era,[66] and the leading members of both parties appeared on the Bolognese scene, from Togliatti to President Gronchi.

With one exception, the local newspapers took sides. The communist Unità and the Lotta defended the list of the Two Towers, the Bolognese symbol adopted by the left, and wholeheartedly backed the positions taken by Dozza in his press conference. The socialist Avanti! stressed anticlericalism, while the Avvenire d'Italia proclaimed the hopes which rested on Dossetti's shoulders and all he would do if victorious. The most violent attacks against the Communist Party (on a national more than a local scale) were left to the Risveglio, the temporary organ of the DC. The Resto del Carlino, the most widely read of all Bolognese newspapers and indirectly influenced by the organized business pressure group Confindustria, assailed Dozza harshly with insinuations about the honesty of his administration and by pointing out the fallacy of a moderate Communist Party; but on the other hand, it was clear that the Carlino looked with jaundiced eye on the search for new "openings" or "adventures" projected by Dossetti.

Finally, one reason for Dossetti's defeat (PCI, 45.18 per cent; DC, 27.13) is to be found in his program, the way it was defended and the way it was understood by the other governmental parties in Bologna. It seems that in this campaign Dossetti saw the possibility of a new political formula. Apart from being a concrete civic goal, the program could also be developed on a national scale.[67] As interpreter of the necessities of the Bolognese situation, Dossetti addressed himself to all open-minded voters and examined with them the possibilities for an opening to the left; in such a way the DC would no longer appear isolated but the initiator of a new line. Instead, the Communist Party would be isolated in that its staticity and its lack of revolutionary impulse would be highlighted. For the communists, it would mean going over to the defensive. The move was undoubtedly

[65] Dossetti, "Togliatti, traditore dei lavoratori," Il Risveglio, May 21, 1956.
[66] Resto del Carlino, May 26, 27, 1956; La Stampa, March 17, 1956.
[67] See Matteucci, in Il Mulino 384.

proper, and four years later the DC would consider it orthodox, but in 1956 it was rejected by the parties (including the DC, on the national level). To the Bolognese moderate (center) parties Dossetti seemed too revolutionary, too involved with the Church. At the same time these parties saw him as an independent candidate who might steal their clientele. The responsibility for this reaction cannot be attributed to Dossetti but to the lack of dynamism in the parties themselves, incapable as they were of seeing beyond their limited horizons of selfish interest and unable to conceive that the ultimate benefit of the Bolognese and Italian society demanded their convergence. In fact, the dispersion of votes which took place in 1956[68] (PSDI, PLI, PRI, MSI) played in favor of the left.

Finally, Dossetti's defeat can be blamed on the way he presented and stated his program. In a Bologna particularly sensitive to ideological questions, in an election where the issue was pro or con communism, Dossetti insisted almost exclusively on citing concrete problems and refused to carry the discussion to ideology and politics; while his basic aim was to destroy the myth which had grown up around Dozza the administrator, he neglected Dozza the communist and thus failed in his attempt to capture the undecided or the protest-voters who for one reason or other saw communism as the panacea for their problems.

Last but not least, there is a "gastronomic" reason which must be taken into account to explain the DC defeat. Bologna and its inhabitants are rightly famous for the quality and richness of their cuisine, of which they have almost made a cult. Dossetti in his campaign mentioned that he could eat for 300 lire, and this was true for an ascetic who was satisfied with a large bowl of spaghetti—but it was not true for a typical Bolognese. Dozza seized upon the occasion and made a daily ironic comment to the effect that Dossetti, the foreigner, was ready to reduce the Bolognese to bread and water, while he, Dozza, had always been in favor of the rich *tagliatelle* or the expensive *tortellini*. Every day the mayor ate in a different restaurant, which thus became the center of attraction in his campaign, and every day he publicized the cost, always well above 300 lire. The Bolognese Christian democrats today admit that this trait made

[68] See page 50.

Dozza far more congenial to the population and probably gained many an undecided vote for him.

When the election returns revealed the communist triumph (+4.87 per cent) and the DC defeat (+1.88), the Bolognese situation looked catastrophic and the attitude of the Cardinal speaks clearly. Three days after the balloting, on the feast of Corpus Christi, May 30, he addressed the population assembled in the main square:

> O Lord, You have returned to this square which has greeted You in the past, and Your return recalls in our mind Your sagacious words to the apostle Philip: "Do you believe that when I return I will still find faith on the earth?" It is with bitterness that we recall Your words considering the apostasy of so many of our brothers who foolishly have allowed themselves to be de-baptized.[69]

However, one may well wonder if even the Communist Party had dreamed of so great a triumph. In all fields—international, national, and local—it had seemed to be on the defensive; its staticity and its lack of revolutionary spirit were patent, and its campaign, based on the slogan "Capacity-honesty" and promising nothing for the future, reflected this orientation. The great fear of a regression was clearly pointed out by the efforts made to import electors

> . . . who had the choice of voting in the commune where [they] were born, or where they had their business interests or their place of work.
> . . . . [In Bologna] the Communist Administration was said to have suggested to some 30,000 of its supporters living outside of town (but working in it) to change their electoral registration from their local village to the city.[70]

The communist victory, over-all, must not be attributed to political factors exclusively; as cited previously, the Bolognese voted for Dozza the cautious administrator (as much as for Dozza the communist) against Dossetti, his patron, the Cardinal, and "adventure."

Ten years later the communists' share of the votes in local elections has remained constant at 45 per cent, while the population of the city has sharply increased. This may be indicative of the fact

---

[69] Quoted by P. L. Contessi, "Bologna sbatezzata," *Il Mulino* 7, no. 58 (July 1956) 411.

[70] Pryce, *The Italian Election* 19. This move was legal and, in private, leading Catholics have admitted using the same tactics; the possibility of moving electors was abolished in 1965.

that the communists would in any case have obtained their majority, thanks to their cautious administration and their clever policy of capturing the votes of the new immigrants. It can also indicate that for the DC, no matter how hard it tries, Bologna is lost.

Today, however, it is plain that the results of the 1956 elections can no longer be considered negative and that Dossetti really fulfilled the task he had taken on of awakening the energies of the town and joining the two towns. Dossetti had expected defeat from the very beginning, as had the Cardinal, it is said;[71] however, his defeat impelled him and his successors[72] to establish a new and constructive minority that abandoned the sterile policy of obstructionism which up to that time had characterized the Christian Democratic party. Furthermore, the defeat saw the Bolognese Church withdraw from active politics.

At the same time, the Communist Party was forced to follow a more dynamic line and in the following years had made Dossetti's program its own. Starting in 1958, a study group turned its attention to the real necessities of the town, and an "Evaluation and Orientation for a Development Program of Bologna" that appeared in 1960[73] was nothing more than the social study called for by Dossetti in 1956. A policy of decentralization was put into effect by the municipality, and thus created the "quarters" called for in the DC White Book; at the same time, with an eye to the necessities of the town, the communists transformed the budget from an active to a passive factor, a measure that was implicit in Dossetti's proposals.

Finally, realizing that a campaign cannot be based on only one man and his achievements but that it needs to open up prospects for the future, the Communist Party began to play down the Dozza

[71] Interview with Don Toldo, director of the Center for Sociological Research and éminence grise of the Cardinal. The latter, in an interview, omitted answering questions related to the 1956 election.

[72] In 1958 he resigned his position as leader of the opposition in order to become a priest. In 1967 Dossetti was chosen by Cardinal Lercaro as his vicar-apostolic. Thus Dossetti, after having been the leader of the DC minority in the town hall, might well become the next archbishop of Bologna.

[73] Published in printed form but slightly modified in 1964. Valutazioni e orientamenti per un programma di sviluppo della città di Bologna e del comprensorio (Bologna: Zanichelli, 1964).

myth, thus again adopting one of Dossetti's principal aims.[74] The
accomplishments of the town hall are no longer those of Dozza but
those of the *Giunta*, which comprises minority as well as majority.
Unfortunately, while the DC quietly goes along with many proposals
which were originally its own, it prefers to emphasize the points of
disagreement rather than to shout loud and long that the new communist program is nothing more than what Dossetti proposed in
1956. The election results coincided with a general economic boom,
and over-all the life of the town has benefited remarkably.[75] At the
same time the results have made clear that, although it wields a
rather strong majority, the Communist Party has been obliged to
accept the basic rule of democracy in that its policies reflect the
desires of a sizable minority.

From this it can be concluded that in order to achieve its primary
goal of making a showcase of Bologna, the Communist Party has been
forced to adopt the very methods it condemns, to lose its impulse
when in power, to become, apparently, as conservative as many political parties which operate in the Western world it rejects.

[74] There were undoubtedly other reasons for this, such as the power Dozza
could have concentrated in his hands, the struggle of the young communist generations to come to power, the fact that Dozza's health was not as good as it
appeared to be; however, his conservatism seems to have been the main argument
used against him. It does not seem reasonable to cite "personality cult" as a reason for Dozza's loss of power; in fact, Togliatti was never really seriously "watered
down," and this is logical in a country where the CP is in the ranks of the opposition. However, Togliatti clearly minimized Dozza's role in the 1956 campaign. See
Togliatti, *Conclusion, Eighth Congress, Federazione Bolognese PCI*, November
18, 1956, reprinted in *Discorsi sull'Emilia* (Bologna: PCI, 1964) 39.

[75] At the same time the earlier cautious policy of the administration prevented
Bologna from suffering as much as other cities during the anticycle of 1963–1964.

4: COMMUNIST OPPONENTS, THE CHURCH AND THE DC

Opposition to the parties of the left can be found among all constituted groups in Bologna. However, since not all the bourgeoisie can be classed as totally unsympathetic to the local administration, groups such as the Liberal party, the University, and the Chamber of Commerce will be passed over in order to concentrate on the main opponents, those waging a total and no-holds-barred battle, namely, the Catholic Church and the Christian Democratic party. As will be seen, the differences between these two groups are less marked than each pretends, and, in many cases, what is said of one will apply to the other. This is particularly true in regard to those mundane aspects of the Church's activities which yet verge on the brink of politics.

When examining the role played by the Catholic Church in Bologna, three aspects are worthy of attention: the hierarchy and its problems as essentially related to the political sphere; the immense strength of the Church in Bologna; and its weaknesses, in particular those weaknesses stemming from significant local conditions.

In 1952 Cardinal Nasalli Rocca died. He had reigned over Bologna for some thirty years in an aristocratic manner, separated from the people and their problems. His successor, Archbishop Giacomo Lercaro, during the first years of his ministry in Bologna was to become not only the most discussed personality of the town but also one of the most discussed personalities in all of Italy.

Giacomo Lercaro[1] was born October 28, 1891, at Quinto al Mare (Genoa); he was the next to the youngest of nine children of a coxswain. The family was particularly devoted to the Church, and an elder brother and sister entered religious orders. Ordained to the priesthood July 25, 1914, the young Giacomo went to the Biblical

---

[1] Annuario diocesano 1963 (Bologna: UTOA, 1964) 61; Il Cardinale Lercaro (Bologna, UTOA, 1964) 11–51, passim.

Institute in Rome where he received the degree of Doctor of Theology. From 1918 to 1923 he was prefect of the seminary in Genoa, holding the chair of Holy Scriptures and Patrology while also serving as professor of philosophy and first chaplain of the newly created apostolate for sea-going people. The period 1927–1937 was devoted exclusively to teaching religion at the state school Cristoforo Colombo. From 1937 to 1947 Lercaro was a parish priest in Genoa (Santa Maria Immacolata parish), with the exception of the year 1943 when he went into hiding from German SS troops for having protected Jewish citizens. During this clandestine period the future bishop was to write his "Method of Mental Prayer." In 1945 he founded the *Didascaleion*, a higher institute of religious culture for laymen.

On January 31, 1947, Pope Pius XII appointed Lercaro archbishop of Ravenna, a traditionally anticlerical diocese which, "attached to old and worn-out prejudices of archaic bias, was not . . . the ideal terrain for the action of a bishop."[2] The war he waged there against communism and his attempts to modernize the ecclesiastical structures of his diocese soon won attention. On April 19, 1952, Archbishop Lercaro solemnly entered his new diocese of Bologna, and in January 1953 was raised to the rank of cardinal. It was ironically observed that the red cape was a necessity in such "red" surroundings.

As appears from this biographical sketch, Cardinal Lercaro's career and formation are characterized by their fullness: he fulfilled the roles of teacher, parish-priest, and bishop of a difficult diocese. Furthermore, it was not a "Roman" career spent amidst shrewd and cautious diplomats. The archbishop of Bologna became known for his energetic action against the Communist Party (as displayed in Ravenna) and for his ideas of renewing Catholic liturgy.

Physically, the impression given by the Cardinal is not one of great strength but of frailty compensated for by questing, penetrating blue eyes, a strong bass voice, and an attitude of modesty. In reality, the frail physical appearance is contradicted by an unbelievable capacity for work, combined with a superlative intelligence and a great sense of charity. The personage can be summed up in the two mottoes chosen at his ordination and at the fiftieth anniversary of his career. The first, *Maria mater mea*, is an expression of faith; the second, *Una*

[2] Marcello Morgante, "Il Buon seme della fiducia," *Il Cardinale Lercaro* 51.

manus sua faciebat opus et altera tenebat gladium, expresses a desire for innovation and creativity, on the one hand, and the impulsiveness of the warrior on the other. For both mottoes, examples abound. In 1947 Msgr. Lercaro became the first Italian bishop to institute an equalization of sacerdotal benefits; in 1953 he created the "flying monks," a kind of religious "truth squad," to fight the Bolognese communists; his views on liturgy have always been *avant-garde*. The impulsiveness of the Cardinal, particularly in matters relating to politics, has made him famous. His engagement in the 1956 campaign has already been discussed;[3] the opinions he expressed while in the United States regarding the inopportuneness of a meeting between Eisenhower and Khrushchev—"This meeting will contribute to perpetuate the communist myth pertaining to the possibility of coexistence between Catholic civilization and communism"[4]— created turmoil not only in the Italian Parliament but also in the Department of State. Many considered him a Curia conservative, while his mingling with the striking workers at Ducati led others to label him a dangerous progressive. In reality, most of his high-sounding acts were dictated by the political stance of Italy and Bologna prior to 1956 when violent anticommunism appeared to be the only answer to equally violent anticlericalism. Today it would seem more accurate to label Lercaro as progressive and possibly revolutionary in the ambit of the Church, while in the field of secular activities he appears to be at most an innovator, simply a modern prelate who has now ceased intervening openly in the realm of local politics. This position has been acknowledged by the PCI, which in November 1966 voted that honorary citizenship be conferred upon the Cardinal, the same man the Party had so violently denounced in the past. The goals, activities, and guidelines of so complex a person are innumerable and are probably best summarized by his communist opponents.

The roots of his philosophy that are never discussed are traditional Catholic spirituality and the social doctrines of the Church. These two cardinal points are to be found in all aspects of his activism.

There are three guiding rules for the activism underlying the crusade. The first is a new impulse for diffusion of religious science (ideological aspect), the second is a drive for an active and organized participation in the mass as adapted to the life of the Church (popular consensus), the

[3] See pp. 54–63.
[4] Quoted by Antonio Jerkov, *Il Punto*, August 29, 1959, p. 4.

third is an active and operative intervention in social questions (imposition of the authority of the ecclesiastical hierarchy on civil society).[5]

In the field of religious activities Lercaro is undoubtedly an innovator. Recognized as a pioneer and master of sacred liturgy, a member and president of the Concilium for Sacred Liturgy, a moderator during the Vatican Council, the Cardinal of Bologna is known worldwide, and his works are translated into several languages.[6]

In 1955 the first national congress of religious architecture and sacred music was held in Bologna. The problem of new churches for Bologna was and is one of his major preoccupations. In correspondence, the Cardinal launched his campaign by alluding to the fact that 58 out of the 79 churches in Bologna were in the center of town where less than one third of the population lives; he concluded by calling for 65 new churches, and on June 26, 1955, the Cardinal in one day blessed the grounds for 23 new church edifices to be built "with the help of God and of the Bolognese people." On the following Sunday, wherever possible, the Communist Party erected on nearby grounds a poster reading "Here will be built the new house of the people, center of democracy, peace, liberty and progress."[7] The problem of the parish is in fact critical for Bologna.

> In nearly every parish one finds an antiparish, almost always more fanatical in its faith, more severe in its discipline, more audacious and direct in its action. . . . For the first time the parish priest has become the pastor of only a portion of his flock; the "man of all" has been reduced to the "man of parts."[8]

To this it must be added that Bologna has only 199 priests for 69 parishes, that clerical ordinations are less numerous than clerical deaths, and that the general population is rapidly expanding.[9]

As can be seen from these figures, the fight against communism under these circumstances is on a less than even basis, and here the doughty Cardinal may be seen as the warrior, not only prepared

---

[5] Luigi Arbizzani, "Giacomo Lercaro, arcivescovo di Bologna," Rinascita 16, no. 11 (November 1959) 787.

[6] See E. Lodi, "Liturgo e pastore," Il Cardinale Lercaro 81–117.

[7] See L. Gherardi, "Rapporto Nuove Chiese," Il Cardinale Lercaro 117–136.

[8] Carlo Falconi, Le Organizzazione cattoliche in Italia, 1945–1955 (Torino: Einaudi, 1956) 345.

[9] For complete data see "Dati riassuntivi del censimento diocesano," Il Cardinale Lercaro 325.

to exploit momentary tactical situations but also possessed of a long-term strategic plan. The year 1956 was the turning point for the Church's activity in Bologna. As the Church's anticommunism became less violent and extremist, so the revolutionary impulses of communism, in turn, faded away. Until then, the anticommunism of the Church, which came to a climax in 1948 and 1949,

> ... like all phenomena characterized by the mixing of passions, emerged and consolidated itself in a clear-cut opposition of parts, with a simplistic dichotomy of history in movement. To communism, conceived of as a threatening and diabolic form and camouflaged as the enemy of violence, was opposed an equally camouflaged anticommunism, nourished by deprecations, condemnations, apocalyptical intimations, and dramatic alternatives and convinced that it was the depository for interpreting and rigorously guarding the "natural law."[10]

This outlook, which culminated in the episode of the "flying monks," had nearly disappeared ten years later, although in 1958 one could still find articles in the Avvenire d'Italia, dated "year XIII of the barbaric domination of Bologna."[11] Even in 1956 the electoral campaign supported by the Cardinal represented an attempt to hold a dialogue with the entire population of Bologna. Following the DC's failure, which the Cardinal interpreted as a defeat for his own policy and illustrative of the limitations on Church intervention, the goal became one of attaining a better understanding of communism by means of more efficient and less ostentatious tactics:[12] a Center for Religious Statistics was created,[13] as well as two Social Studies Institutes seeking to form priests and laymen for the fight against communism. With the same goal in mind, the social doctrine of Cardinal Lercaro has always been aimed at winning over the proletariat, "anticipating the Encyclical Mater et Magistra."[14] Indeed, Lercaro's abiding goal is well reflected in his Discorsi, the first volume of which is almost entirely devoted to the problems of the working class. Symbolically, the Cardinal discussed the encyclical Mater et Magistra

---

[10] Alfonso Prandi, "Il Pericolo del communismo e la coscienza cristiana," Il Mulino 13, no. 143 (September 1964) 957.

[11] Avvenire d'Italia, September 28, 1958.

[12] Interview with H. E. Giacomo Lercaro, August 31, 1965.

[13] Giacomo Lercaro, "Sociologia religiosa e azione pastorale," Discorsi del Cardinale Lercaro (Rome: Herder, 1964) 201–211.

[14] A. Toldo, "Il Magistero sociale," Il Cardinale Lercaro 195.

with a group of workers before officially presenting it to the diocese.[15]

As bishop of the Italian capital of communism, the initiatives taken by Lercaro are numerous. The Center for Religious Studies has carried out inquiries concerning the phenomenon "What the Bolognese Communists Think of the Church"[16] and has pioneered an "Inquiry Relating to the Church-going Bolognese" in eighty volumes. In 1961 the Bishop of Bologna held a conference for young Catholic graduates on the subject "Communism in the Judgment of the Church,"[17] later developed into "Pastoral Action and Communism."[18] In 1962 the last days of the diocesan synod were devoted to the problems of communism, examined under its local aspects and its methodology, in the light of the pastoral action required to oppose its expansion, particularly among young people and indifferentists.[19] The essence of this study can be summarized as follows:

> . . . convinced of the seriousness of the communist peril and of the impossibility of obtaining an immediate cure. . . . [Cardinal Lercaro is] initiating a broad pastoral program, evaluating all pre-existing structures and institutions and channeling people according to their talents, as the *sine qua non* for the fight against communism.[20]

Communism in Bologna can only be defeated by long-term action for which the Church is particularly well prepared, far better prepared than the weak and divided Christian Democratic party.

The strength of the Church appears immense but it is diffuse, and thus it is almost impossible to describe it with any degree of precision. However, nothing can dispel the impression that the Church's influence is felt at all political and economic levels; and moreover, a mere count of its numbers makes it a noteworthy factor in evaluating the DC's electoral record.

Religious capillarity is clearly obvious, but, judged in the short run, it does not appear to be the most efficient weapon. The some

---

[15] Lercaro, *Discorsi* 119.
[16] Unfortunately unpublished.
[17] Lercaro, *Discorsi* 280–307.
[18] *Ibid.* 308–339.
[19] Archidiocesi di Bologna, *Piccolo sinodo diocesano 1962* (Bologna: UTOA, 1963) 1–108. A copy of the *Sinodo* was given to all Catholic bishops by Pope Paul VI.
[20] A. Mazzioli, "Un piano pastorale aperto e lungi-mirante," *Il Cardinale Lercaro* 154.

two thousand members of the town's clergy and religious communities represent less than one per cent of the total voting population, but they do account for some three per cent of the total Christian Democratic party's electoral strength. Their influence probably stops there and, according to a sympathetic observer, "it seems that in relation to political orientations the parish does not cause appreciable variations."[21] As has already been demonstrated in the realm of politics, religious intervention does not gain votes, but at most only maintains established positions. Furthermore, the use of religious orders to fight communism (many of the communities were not truly familiar with the realities of the Bolognese situation) proved to be a disastrous experience. The violence of the "flying monks" and the extremism of their language had little influence outside the Church[22] unless it was to give weapons to its opponents. Bologna has pious institutions by the score, ranging from the Conferences of St. Vincent of Paul to the Committee for the Virgin of San Luca, and their number can be estimated at around 130 with some 2,000 members overall. These evidently are sure votes for the Christian Democratic party, but their influence is limited by a certain tendency to recruit among members of the local aristocracy and upper bourgeoisie. Furthermore, such votes can be considered already secure, since most members of the pious associations are already active in the rank and file of the Catholic Action groups. Such groups receive a good share of their younger cadres from the superior school of social sciences, founded by Lercaro in 1958 and directly attached to the local curia, the scope of which is "to prepare Catholics . . . for their responsibilities as citizens of a democratic state."[23] The school, which produces some thirty graduates a year after a triennial period of study, provides another example of the dual citizenships that are created; the graduates are not only militant in Catholic Action circles but also serve among the few qualified DC activists.

The strength deriving from these religious and lay institutions,

---

[21] [A. Ardigò], "Relazione sull'influenza territoriale dei centri religiosi (parrocchie) sull'orientamento politico (eseguite sui dati ricavati dalle elezioni amministrative del 1956)" (Bologna: CSAS, n.d. [1958]), n.p. [3], typescript.

[22] For good examples of this primitiveness: Lorenzo Bedeschi, Maleffatte della rossa Emilia (Bologna, ABES, 1953) 5–43; Tommaso Toschi, La Maschera e il volto, 2nd ed. (Bologna, ABES, 1953) 49–65.

[23] "Per l'attuazione del messaggio sociale," Il Cardinale Lercaro 225–229.

while diffuse, cannot be considered negligible particularly if one totals up the considerable assets they possess. Their strength is even more apparent in that they are part of what can be described as the mundane capillarity of the Church.

The Church's mundane capillarity arises from the fact that Catholicism is the religion of the State, and the Concordat is part of the Constitution (and at times in contradiction with it). For those citizens who associate the successes (and defeats) of the Church with those of the nation,[24] an emotional attachment is involved. The situation is epitomized in Bologna where anticlericalism, though on the downward trend, still appears strong in comparison to other regions of Italy. As an observer of the Italian scene put it,

> The policy of the Church . . . consisted in maintaining, once the limits and controls imposed by fascism had been eliminated, all the positions acquired during the fascist period, so as to render the Church always more secure against a return of laicism, to avert the communist peril, and, finally, to extend and enlarge the ecclesiastical influence to all the associated fields of life.
>
> A clash in this sector between the institutions of the State and those of the Church was obvious . . . but it was an unfair clash from the very moment that the defense of the State against the Church fell into the hands of a Catholic party which needed the Church to continue to govern the State.[25]

The Catholic jurist, Arturo Carlo Jemolo, says it more succinctly. Noting that Italy has become a confessional state, he writes, "The advance of confessional positions represents a verification of the physical law of a gas occupying an empty space."[26] One of the most striking aspects of this confessionalization of the state, noted by all observers, is the presence of religious authorities at all civil functions and ceremonies, and even more the scurrying of clergymen through the offices and corridors of all the bureaucratic offices—communist-dominated offices included—in search of favors, or at least the proper compensations for their parishioners or protégés.

The mundane capillarity of the Church can also be traced back to

---

[24] Jean Meynaud, "Chiesa cattolica in Italia e in Francia," Nord-Sud 9, no. 36, (October 1962) 22–42.

[25] Luigi Salvatorelli, "La Politica della Chiesa in Italia," in R. Petrazzoni, ed., Stato e Chiesa (Bari: Laterza, 1957) 30.

[26] Arturo Carlo Jemolo, Chiesa e Stato in Italia negli ultimi cento anni, 2nd ed. (Torino: Einaudi, 1963) 537.

tradition. Among the people, particularly among women, to vote according to the instructions of the parish priest has always been common.[27] But more concrete manifestations of this phenomenon are to be noted in Bologna, for example, the "clerical" banking institutes and the Catholic press, both of which were founded by Count Acquaderni in the early 1900's.

The Credito Romagnolo is the largest local bank, and its shareholders are approved by the Council of Administration only after they have been given the *nihil obstat* by the local parish priest. It is clear that in a medium-sized town like Bologna its influence, though almost impossible to assess, is strong. Apart from the official subsidy given to Catholic Action (two million lire per year), subscriptions to the Catholic press, free processing of statistical data for the Church and the DC, as well as contributions to the party coffers must be taken into account. Though there are no data to confirm this assertion, several businessmen and bank executives who were interviewed were privately convinced of this nonnegligible influence on behalf of the Church that the Credito Romagnolo can and does wield.

The Catholic press lists some eighteen publications in Bologna, seven of which are devoted exclusively to religious problems.[28] The most important is the *Avvenire d'Italia*, which publishes sixteen local editions. This newspaper is founded upon an ambiguity: while an organ of the Italian bishops, in Bologna it is also the newspaper of the Christian Democratic party, another indication of the interpenetration of the two. As is the case with all Italian newspapers, it is impossible to obtain exact circulation figures. These are either not publicized or else are grossly exaggerated for political reasons or publicity purposes. The "false" figure for the *Avvenire d'Italia's* circulation in the province of Bologna is 13,500, which would mean that circulation in

[27] See Mattei Dogan, "Le Donne italiane tra cattolicesimo e Marxismo," in *Elezioni e comportamento politico*, A. Spreafico and J. Palombara, eds. (Milano: Communità, 1963) 475–494.
[28] Catholic Press of Bologna, excluding religious periodicals: *Avvenire d'Italia* (daily); *Bollettino della Diocesi di Bologna* (bi-monthly); *Chiesa e Quartieri* (quarterly); *Il Regno* (monthly); *Agenda* (monthly of Catholic Action); *Amici del Cardinale* (monthly); *Bollettino Parrocchiale* (monthly) (113,265 copies in 1961); *Conquiste* (bi-monthly of ACLI); *Riparazione* (monthly); *Gioventu in Cammino* (bi-monthly); and *Riparazione all'amico Gesù* (bi-monthly).
From *Annuario diocesano* 1963 107.

the town would be around 6,800.[29] Actually under the most favorable circumstances the total figure for Bologna probably does not exceed 5,000 copies, 10 per cent of which go to religious institutions, parish priests, and favorably oriented institutes such as the Credito Romagnolo. To summarize, the newspaper reaches a limited number of people, at most 15,000, which is much less than the locally-run *Resto del Carlino* (circulation: 40,000), not unfavorable to the Church, and the communist *Unità* (10,000 daily and 30,000 on Sundays).

Finally, we must note the importance of the assistance and relief services performed by the Church (the Diocesan Committee for Assistance handles some one thousand cases a year),[30] as well as a phenomenon peculiar to Italy, *raccomandazione* (letters of recommendation), which is of considerable influence in the hiring of an employee. The communists (who use the same system) take great delight in discovering a letter of recommendation written by a priest invoking an employer's favors for one of the priest's protégés. Invariably they publish it as proof of the Church's interference in civic affairs.[31]

As mentioned previously, the distinction between political and religious capillarity in Church activities is artificial. In theory, the Church does not participate in such activities, and responsibility for activities of political capillarity is laid at the door of official Catholic Action groups and those groups which gravitate around them.[32] The Catholic Action movement is divided into the following branches:[33] Union of Men, Union of Women, Male Youth, Female Youth, FUCI (Federation of Italian Catholic University Students), Move-

[29] *Avvenire d'Italia*, Bozze di Stampa per la Società per la Publicità in Italia.
[30] "Caritas Christi urget nos," *Il Cardinale Lercaro* 190.
[31] See *La Lotta*, May 1, 1954 for a good example.
[32] Onarmo: National Institute for Religious and Moral Assistance to Workers, particularly known for the factory-chaplains in Bologna; ASCI: Italian Catholic Scouts Association; AGI: Italian Association of Girl-guides; ACLI: Christian Association of Italian Workers; FIDAE: Federation of Institutes of Dependents of the Ecclesiastical Authorities; UCID: Christian Union of Contractors and Managers; Catholic Union of Italian Artists; Catholic Union of Italian Pharmacists; Catholic Union of Italian Jurists; Catholic Association of Cinema Owners; Catholic Association of Italian Artisans; Italian Sports Center; and Center of Tourism for Youth.
Source: *Annuario diocesano 1963* 32–33.
[33] *Ibid.*

ment of Catholic Graduates, Movement of Catholic School Teachers. Theoretically, these groups are apolitical, being "the organization of the Catholic laity for special and direct collaboration with the hierarchy of the Church."[34] The fact that Catholic Action has always taken pains to distinguish between its actions as a constituted group and the actions of its individual members has seemed sufficient for it to proclaim both its nonengagement in politics and its independence from the Christian Democratic party.

This question of independence was the focal point of the dispute which preceded the return of Catholic Action groups to the political arena after 1945. In April 1945, Msgr. Montini wrote that "Catholic Action must contribute to the political education of the people";[35] in October 1951, Pope Pius XII spoke of the "necessary reciprocal compenetration of the religious apostolate and political action."[36] On the other hand, DC leftists led by Dossetti expressed the opinion that "social temporal action and social political action are not in the field of Catholic Action."[37] Usually—and Bologna is no exception— Catholic Action groups seem to function as wholly political instruments of the hierarchy.

> The Catholic lay militant has been pressed into service as a twofold intermediary between the Papacy and the modern state: as a member of Catholic Action he responds to the hierarchy . . ., but as a Christian Democrat he assumes direct political responsibilities that the hierarchy must shun.[38]

It is quite symbolic that Catholic Action headquarters in Bologna also houses DC headquarters, both groups sharing one building attached to the bishop's palace.

The strength of Catholic Action groups can be found in the influence they wield as schools for DC cadres and in the role which has been assigned them by the Cardinal; their weaknesses, however, arise from their small number and from the social composition of the various groups.

---

[34] Annuario diocesano 1963 159.
[35] Falconi, Le Organizzazione 369.
[36] Ibid. 388–389.
[37] "Cronache Sociali" (November 1948), in ibid. 378.
[38] Richard A. Webster, The Cross and the Fasces (Stanford: Stanford University Press, 1960) 185.

According to the latest available data,[39] members of Catholic Action groups number 12,172 (Bologna's total Catholic population is 437,672, but only 104,677 practice their faith regularly) and are divided as follows:

Male Youth	4166	in 59 parishes
Female Youth	3429	in 59 parishes
Men	1422	in 64 parishes
Women	3155	in 78 parishes
	12,172	

Not only is the number small, but even more worrisome are the movement's evolutionary history and social composition. Considering only those Catholics who practice their faith regularly (104,677), we discover the following:

Enrolled in Catholic Associations	M	%	F	%	MF	%
Never	19,753	51.50	35,743	55.60	55,496	54.06
In the past	9058	23.61	15,578	24.23	24,636	24.00
In the present	7668	20.00	10,373	16.13	18,041	17.58
No answer	1878	4.90	2596	4.04	4474	4.36

Furthermore, 76.47 per cent of the enrollees are among the nonactive population (young people, housewives, students, retired) while only 17.16 are among the gainfully employed.

Among the reasons for the high withdrawal rate from Catholic groups (60 per cent of these taking place upon reaching the age of 25) must be noted

the impression . . . that the associations are not a center of life and warmth . . . but a closed and monotonous milieu, principally concerned with questions relating to their own prestige.[40]

It is true that these figures must be considered from more than a statistical standpoint; many who abandon formal Catholic Action can

---

[39] "Censimento diocesano 1961," Il Cardinale Lercaro 324–325.

[40] D.F., "Practica religiosa e atteggiamento politico a Bologna," Questitalia 5 (November–December 1962) 662.

be found in other groups such as the FUCI or the Catholic Masters' Association. Furthermore, since the aim of the association is formative, leaving it is not the same as renouncing its principles. In short, a large majority of those no longer enrolled can still be relied upon when it comes to the question of voting DC. Thus the Bolognese DC members of Parliament and the municipal counselors have been formed and trained by the various groups, and many still remain active in their organizations. Another source of strength for these groups derives from the role assigned them by the Cardinal; they are not only to be formative but also representative of militant Catholicism. The least that can be said is that Cardinal Lercaro, who believes in the importance of mass demonstrations, employs these groups most liberally; it is also true that these mass-rallies are comprised more of young teenagers and the old than active workers. Nevertheless, the showings are always impressive (Carnevale Dei Bambini, Feast of the Madonna of San Luca, Ferragosto at Villa Reverdin).

The most avidly political sections of Catholic Action groups, the Civic Committees, still remain to be studied. The Civic Committees were created before the 1948 elections when the Church realized both the immense potential of the Catholic laity[41] and the possibility of a communist electoral success. Immediate opposition to the plan was voiced by the left wing of the Christian Democratic party grouped around Dossetti-Fanfani-La Pira, who feared that the DC might be taken over by such Catholic Action groups. While Cardinal Lercaro, then bishop of Ravenna, envisioned them as a means of retaining "contacts with all the organizations and individuals acting on the same level, parties, parliament, municipal and provincial councils,"[42] they were "a level of encounter of the Catholic forces to act on the civil front."[43] In practice this means:

> The person in charge of elections takes care of the organization of the electoral campaign and its related services. In particular, he must take a census of the existing electoral districts in the parish and on this basis distribute the list of the voters "to be controlled," so as to see that all are enrolled on the electoral lists: . . . he must establish a list of those

[41] At the end of 1947, 120,000 young people convened in Bologna when only 50,000 were expected. Falconi, Le Organizzazione 377.

[42] Meynaud, in Nord-Sud 40.

[43] Director of Civic Committee in A. Settembrini, "La Chiesa in Italia," L'Astrolabio 1 (June 25, 1963) 36.

voters who are ill or invalid, so that they can be taken to the polling place; he must select those to be nominated as candidates and as election commissioners and forward the list to the DC; he takes care of all the technical means of propaganda . . .; compiles the list of friends who have cars to be used on election day. . . .

The person in charge of activists in one or two "evenings" prepares the local committee for the task of . . . "activating the base." . . . In particular he gives the themes of local propaganda and counterpropaganda . . . to orientate the electors toward the DC.[44]

In short, through the Civic Committees Catholic Action is placed in charge of a large portion of the DC's electoral campaign, and it seems no exaggeration to say that the Committees were created for purely electoral purposes.

However, their efficiency in Bologna must be weighed in terms of the people's anticlerical attitude. It is true that in 1948 the DC increased its vote by some 15 per cent, but this was apparently due more to the tensions of the international situation than to the activity of the Civic Committees. In 1956, when Civic Committees were most used, the DC increased its vote by only 1.88 per cent, and the Civic Committees' forecasts proved completely wrong (103 per cent of DC votes but 44.75 of communist and socialist votes).[45] If nothing else, the result proved that the Committees' knowledge of their opponents' strength was extremely limited. Since 1956, use of the Civic Committees has been practically eliminated, or at least such use is no longer as evident as it was in the past. This policy coincides with Fanfani's attempts to create a base for the DC without having to rely on the hierarchy. However, in terms of opening up new administrative units in Bologna since 1963, and with respect to the possibility of a dialogue with the left, the Civic Committees have been dusted off again, but their activity has been restricted solely to the interests of the laity in the local administration.

As pointed out previously, it is next to impossible to evaluate precisely the strength of the Church in town. That it penetrates all spheres of public life and can exert its influence, when necessary, on

---

[44] Vicariato di Roma, *Bollettino d'Informazione* (March–April 1956) 88.
[45] [A. Ardigò], "Dalla previsione ai risultati delle elezioni amministrative del 1956 nel comune di Bologna. Indagine campionaria" (Bologna: CSAS, n.d., n.p. [1957, p. 29] 24, typescript.

most levels of Bolognese society—not only in religious but also in political and economic matters—must be admitted.

At this point, in view of the limitations imposed on Catholic Action groups by the areligious atmosphere of Bologna, and considering the prestige and activism of the Cardinal, it can be seen that the latter is not only a key figure in, but enjoys an exclusive representation of, the political strength of the Church. His towering personality and his immense prestige make him the leader and guide of the Bolognese laity.

The weaknesses of the Church—unlike its strength, which is widely diffused—are easier to describe and can be attributed to organizational and purely religious problems, as well as to facets peculiar to the Bolognese mentality. The major organizational problem is that of the overabundance of Catholic organizations, some different in purpose but many so similar in their goals that their only distinctive characteristic is their name. In fact,

> During the period since the war, the Catholic world has multiplied its organizational efforts and given life to a series of organisms, the intent being to get nearer to the most diverse milieus; thus, for the majority of committed and organized Catholics a series of *multiple citizenships* has been created, which necessarily has reduced the feelings of obligation toward individual associations, has contributed to the confusion of ends and means, and has generated among the members fatigue and a great amount of skepticism.[46]

Bologna has attempted to alleviate this situation, and since 1958 a *Consulta* has been created to coordinate the activities of the different organizations, "operating on the level of parish and diocese in cooperation with the regular and secular clergy."[47] Seen some seven years later, it can be said without exaggeration that this *Consulta* has failed miserably. This is due less to the multiplicity of organizations to be coordinated than to the egotism of the different associations jealous of one another and of their independence, eager to absorb others but not to be absorbed. More serious than the organizational problem—which could be solved if more energy was employed—is the Bolognese practice of religion, which provides a true measure of the

---

[46] Luigi Pedrazzi, "Cattolici non-democristiani," *Il Mulino* 10, no. 108 (September 1961) 640.

[47] Msgr. L. Bettazzi, "I Laici, parte viva della Chiesa," *Il Cardinale Lercaro* 80.

Church's influence among the population. Bologna is no exception to a situation that holds good throughout Western Europe, and the conclusions reached for Paris by Gabriel Le Bras are valid here in "Catholic" Italy. Religious practice is proportional to economic well-being: the percentage of workers who go to church is very small; women are twice as numerous as men in church; and the largest group of churchgoers is made up of people still at school and women past the age of fifty.[48]

It is no exaggeration to describe "Catholic" Italy as a myth, although 99 per cent of Italians are baptized. Figures are misleading, and instead of considering non-Catholics it is more interesting to study outright opponents or indifferentists who, after baptism, remain Catholics in form only.[49] In many cases these people are members of the Communist Party. The religious statistics for Bologna, probably the most complete in Italy, speak clearly.[50]

Catholicism in Bologna (1961)

Under seven years of age	28,141
Active	13,529
Go to church on Sundays	104,677
Indifferent	272,343
Hostile	18,982
Total	437,672

If going to church on Sundays can be considered a sufficient criterion for separating the "good" from the "bad," 24.13 per cent of Bolognese Catholics follow this ecclesiastical precept (37.3 men, 62.7 women). Compared with all of Italy (53 per cent go to church on

[48] Quoted in Falconi, Le Organizzazione 33.
[49] Regarding figures on people having no religious faith, the first statistic to be found is for 1911. Out of 874,532 Italians who declared no religious belief, 258,288 were in Emilia. In 1941, for the diocese of Bologna, 2,750 were considered non-Catholics, and in 1961 in Bologna the figure was reduced to 963. In the first case each citizen declared his faith; in the other two, the statistics only considered nonbaptized people. See Falconi, ibid. 23–26, and "Censimento diocesano 1961," Il Cardinale Lercaro 325.
[50] For all that follows see "Inchiesta sulla messa nel commune di Bologna," Il Cardinale Lercaro 322–324, and D. F., "Pratica religiosa e atteggiamento politico a Bologna," Questitalia 651–660.

Sundays, 45.0 men and 61.0 women), the figure is significant.[51] Bologna is, in fact, the town with the lowest proportion of religious practice in the entire country. In general, statistical studies show Bologna with below-average percentages of religious practice at all ages as compared to the whole country: there is a sharp decrease among males over fifteen years of age and among females over twenty, while a very slow increase among males over fifty-five years of age and a somewhat stronger increase for females around forty are also registered.

The situation waxes most critical when church attendance in the different parts of town is compared to the political returns. The discrepancy shown in all zones (except for the center where the proliferation of churches attracts those who do not want to be known as practicing Catholics) between the number of practicing Catholics and DC voting strength demonstrates on the one hand the weakness of the Church, whose voting directives are ignored by a large percentage of Catholics, and on the other the existence of a traditional following made up mostly of women who will regularly vote for the clerical party. Briefly, there appears to be a clear relationship between economic conditions and social status and practicing Catholics, just as there is between social status and DC votes (Zones A and B). The weakness of the Church is more evident if one considers that only 28.66 per cent of the regular churchgoers are from the active generations, which is equivalent to 15.16 of the total active population. The Church in Bologna has lost contact with the workers (Zones D, E, and F), only 4.77 of whom practice their faith regularly, and is going through the same process with respect to the prewar and postwar generations (Zone C).

Unfortunately, no data are available concerning the situation of the intellectuals and the Church, though the general consensus is that the rigidity of the Italian Church leaves little room for active research. It is certain, however, that the Center for Religious Documentation founded by Dossetti has no influence upon the town, while the Center for Social and Administrative Studies headed by Achille Ardigò apparently functions as a research group for the local DC leadership. The situation of the leading review and study group in Bologna, Il Mulino, is different. Formally independent, Il Mulino

---

[51] "Lei è stato in chiesa," Bollettino DOXA 3–4 (February 26, 1962) 49–54.

STRATIFIED REPRESENTATION OF SUNDAY CHURCHGOERS

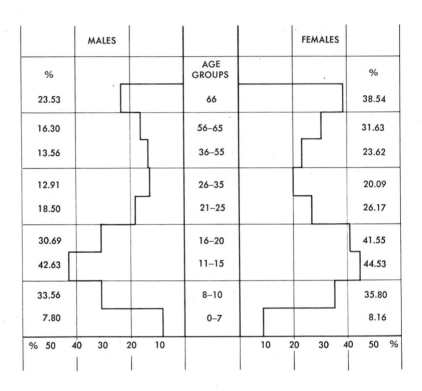

MALES				FEMALES	
%		AGE GROUPS			%
23.53		66			38.54
16.30		56–65			31.63
13.56		36–55			23.62
12.91		26–35			20.09
18.50		21–25			26.17
30.69		16–20			41.55
42.63		11–15			44.53
33.56		8–10			35.80
7.80		0–7			8.16
% 50 40 30 20 10				10 20 30 40 50 %	

has undoubtedly attracted many Catholic intellectuals frequently associated with the left wing of the DC, and, when it is not being accused of being an instrument of Confindustria,[52] it is often charged with being linked to the DC. All in all, one can say that this group is inspired by modern Catholic principles and has a definite impact on the intellectuals of Bologna; its debates are often focused on the ambiguities of the local administration but also reflect those of the Church and of the DC.

A broader explanation of the Church's weakness (and in turn, the

[52] Joseph La Palombara, *Interest Groups in Italian Politics* (Princeton, Princeton University Press, 1964) 185–190.

DC's) comes to light when we consider the mentality of the Bolognese and some apparent compromises made by the Church. The confusion between Church and State and the creation of a confessional Italian state after the war have already been pointed out. The matter would be relatively unimportant if the milieu were indifferent. The problem takes on a new aspect in the case of a Bologna divided, as it is, between "reds" and "blacks"—where communists appear far less extremist than their Catholic foes. Furthermore a majority of Italians (and Bologna is no exception in this respect) have clearly indicated that the Church should abstain from politics.[53]

To the question "In your opinion does the clergy of Bologna participate too much in politics," the following answers were received:

	True	False	Do not know	Total
General sample	35	19	46	100
Males	39	18	43	100
Females	31	19	50	100
Communist electorate	57	2	41	100
Noncommunist electorate	29	36	35	100

By its unwise actions—particularly in 1956—the Church has antagonized the anticlerical segment of the population, and this in turn has diminished its moral influence among the people. Percentages are all the more significant in that the Church abandoned its active participation in politics after 1956.

Another explanation of the weakening of the Church's influence is to be found in the progressivism that many attribute to it. Though Cardinal Lercaro should be considered a modern reformist, he has been, and is, judged a revolutionary (the "Cardinal of the masses") and a progressive by a majority of "nonengagés" and by those leading groups of the DC which clearly belong to the center and right wing of the party. While the majority of the initiatives taken by the Cardinal, especially since 1956, are in the fields of liturgy and social doctrine, their translation into the field of politics is easy. And the communists, who sometimes accuse the Archbishop of being a "reac-

---

[53] "Diritti e Doveri del Clero," *Bollettino DOXA* 17 (1958).

tionary," do nothing to diminish this image of progressivism. In practice

> Progressivism accepts history, denounces the collusion between Christianity and established interests, questions the so-called missionary spirit and the misleading hopes underlying the obvious subordination of earthly interests to religious values, discusses and derives the methods, the short and long-term objectives of another interpretation, confounds the assumption that the ethico-social doctrine of Christianity— . . . — is the cure for each and every injustice, the foundation of stability. Furthermore, it puts to the test the historical process of Christianity, . . .
>
> From this stems the social vocation of progressivism, which reaches its full development in a revolutionary outlook and in faith in the validity of the concept and practice of revolution. Thus one may grasp the foundation of the Marxist theory of history and the place man occupies in that theory.[54]

This marginal encounter between Catholicism and communism, taking place, as it has, in the ambiguous atmosphere of "the opening to the left"—where a dialogue between Marxists and non-Marxists appeared possible—and at a moment when the Catholic hierarchy was confronted by rebellion,[55] can only work to the advantage of the communists, particularly in Bologna.

Finally, the July 1, 1949, decree of the Sant'Uffizio, which the Communist Party cleverly exploited in Bologna's leftist atmosphere, also aided the communist cause. Many parish priests in town felt that this condemnation of communism was more harmful than helpful to their ministry. Communist attacks have always omitted any mention of the incompatibility of Catholicism and Marxism. For reasons of strategy,[56] the PCI has found it useful to try to live with the Church[57] and has apparently played the game honestly. The Church's condemnation of the Marxist heresy—a completely orthodox move from the religious standpoint (though after the 1948 elections it bore

---

[54] Alfonso Prandi, "Il Pericolo del comunismo e la coscienza cristiana," Il Mulino 13, no. 143 (September 1954) 959.

[55] "Monito del papa ai fedeli contro l'indisciplina sistematica," Il Corriere della Sera, July 15, 1965.

[56] P. Togliatti, speech of July 9, 1944, in Rome, Politica comunista (Rome: Edizione PCI, 1945) 83–84.

[57] P. Togliatti, "Sui rapporti tra Chiesa e Stato," speech in Parliament, March 25, 1947, La via italiana al socialismo (Rome: Editori Riuniti, 1965) 91–109.

clear political connotations)—was used by the Party as an example of the Church's extremism and authoritarianism. This argument proved especially effective in a country where liberty had just been restored after twenty years of dictatorship. Moreover, communists could point to their condemnation by the Church to emphasize the alliance between the Church and its Christian Democratic party.

The communist version of the decree claimed, first, that all those who had voted communist were *ipso facto* excommunicated (the communists used this "fact" to retain the votes of those who had in the past voted the red slate) and, second, that any Italian who had voted for the Party would be denied the sacraments. This was a potent weapon, especially as applied to the sacrament of matrimony, since a church-blessed marriage constitutes the most important moment in the life of an Italian. In this communist version the decree was warped almost beyond recognition. In point of fact, the decree[58] clearly distinguished between active supporters of the Marxist heresy and those *gregari* who merely gave their votes to the Party; the decree regarding marriage was released on August 11, 1949.[59] The same distinction held true here, and in *all* cases communists were allowed to contract matrimony in the presence of a priest, with more or less solemnity. This distinction was never made clear and explicit in the press, of whatever party or persuasion. In the mind of the Bolognese communists, who had believed themselves excommunicated and who now suddenly realized they could be married in church with a priest as witness, it appeared that Rome was compromising and had not in reality totally rejected Marxist ideas. The cartoon carried for several months by *La Lotta*—a candle as a symbol of excommunication, becoming smaller with every new issue, until it was reduced to a stub—probably reflected the views of more than one communist supporter: compromise could be achieved.

The clear consequence was (and is) that a decisive majority of Bolognese communists who receive the major sacraments of baptism and matrimony see no contradiction whatsoever between Catholicism and Marxism. On national and local levels, the answer to the ques-

[58] Suprema Sacra Congregatio, "Decretum, I Julii, 1949," *Piccolo sinodo* 1962, 123–125.
[59] "Declaratio de communistarum matrimonii celebratione," *ibid.* 126.

tion "Can one be a good communist and a good Catholic?" is as
follows (in per cent).[60]

	Sympathizers			
	National		Local	
	PCI	DC	PCI	DC
Yes	71	16	71	23
No	20	73	8	61
I don't know	9	11	21	16
	100	100	100	100

As one can see, in Bologna the number of wavering Christian
democrats is higher than the Italian average. While one might interpret the total figures as an indication of the strong influence the
Church still wields in Italy, inasmuch as the masses either ignore or
have not understood Marx, it may also be interpreted as showing that
the Church is at least presently unable to convince the masses.

To sum up, in surveying the strength and weakness of the Church in
Bologna, it seems that its strength is due more to tradition and habit
than to its organization and its penetration of the social milieu.
Conversely, its weakness seems to stem from an anticlericalism that
is rooted in history and from an inability to convince the masses that
it offers a valid alternative to Marxism. Bologna should be considered
as "terre de mission."

The most important political ally of the Catholic Church in its
fight against communism is the Christian Democratic party. Created
in 1943, the party is the heir of Don Luigi Sturzo's short-lived Popular party, abolished by Mussolini in 1926.

Formally, the Partito Popolare[61] sought not to be considered a
Catholic party, although its aims were "to support the political and
moral program of the Christian people . . . the liberty and independence of the Church in the full accomplishment of its spiritual teachings."[62] In supporting the Church, the party in turn received aid,
especially from the Church's parochial organizations. It is no surprise

[60] "Religione e politica," Bollettino DOXA 4–5 (March 23, 1963) 38.
[61] Gabriele La Rosa, Storia del Partito Popolare (Bari: Laterza, 1958).
[62] Luigi Salvatorelli, Storia d'Italia nel periodo fascista, 2nd ed. (Torino:
Einaudi, 1964) 31–32.

that some saw the picture as that of "two armies, marching divided, to fight united."[63] Unlike its principal opponent, the socialists, this Popular party had no broad program of its own, nor did it even have a flag or a slogan—all serious faults in a party seeking a mass following. Even at the party's first congress in Bologna in June 1919, these weaknesses were evident. While moderate and Catholic, it was able to sweep to a nationwide victory in 1919 on the strength of the Church's influence and the War's ending; but its long-term chances were slim in Bologna, which was known for the extremism of its population, its anticlericalism, and its deeply rooted socialist tradition. Furthermore, a lack of parliamentary experience led the party to adopt a neutral stance during fascism's early growth. Indirectly, this neutralism (for example, refusing to agree to Giolitti's return in February 1922 and its criticism of the democratic state in December 1922) abetted fascism's upsurge. Finally, it, too, succumbed to Mussolini in 1926. In Bologna, the neutralist policy of "no collaboration, no opposition," which Don Sturzo called for during the 1924 election campaign, could not possibly satisfy the general population. A majority of the Bolognese had witnessed the red fiasco of 1921–1922 and were now prepared to support this new form of extremism that preached the greatness and supremacy of Italians.

For some twenty years the Christian democratic ideal fell into oblivion. In Bologna, where parties of the left spearheaded the resistance to fascism, the ideal was almost totally forgotten. Moreover, the Church did little to rekindle the embers of the Christian democratic ideal; the hierarchy was hesitant to support those of its members engaged in the Resistance and even, at times, hindered their action. Because of this, while in 1946 the Christian democrats were victors nationally (DC, 35.1 per cent; PCI, 18.9), in Bologna they were weak (DC, 21.75 per cent; PCI, 33.73; PSI, 28.09). In some cases DC votes came from former fascists, but the majority was cast by Catholics and moderates who saw in Christian democracy "the only mass party not committed either to an immediate revolutionary transformation of Italy or to an alliance with the Soviet Union."[64] The cement holding the group together was the same mixture of Catholic

---

[63] Ibid. 33.
[64] Webster, The Cross 172.

doctrine and Church influence that had worked for the Popular party in 1919.

A coalition of young and old, of recent converts from clerico-fascism and ancient foes of the regime, of theocrats longing for the days of Innocent III and Boniface VIII and admirers of French and American Church-State separatism . . . brought together by a common faith, common enemies . . . and by a common aim of social reconstruction and defense of Catholic principles, the Christian Democrats of 1943–1945 were less self-reliant than the Popular Party militants . . . but . . . by training and mentality far closer to the hierarchy and the Holy See.[65]

The formal organization of the DC in Bologna is rather schematic.[66] A provincial committee with several specialized sections (youth, press, organization, local administration, study) has been established, and in practice it is frequently confused with the municipal committee on which the twenty-two sections located throughout the town depend.

National Committee

Provincial Committee Sections $\left\{ \begin{array}{l} \text{Organization} \\ \text{Youth} \\ \text{Press} \\ \text{Local administration} \\ \text{Study groups} \end{array} \right.$

Municipal Committee

Sections

This vertical form of organization implies that the base can make its influence felt on the municipal, provincial, and, eventually, national committees. In fact, however, this does not happen; the party is a party of men and cross-currents of opinion, and these alternately make their influence felt in the national committee. Thus, it is possible that the grass-roots views of the provinces and sections will be in complete contradiction with those of the summit. Actually, at the very most the influence of the base extends to the level of the provincial and municipal committees. Committee members are theoretically elected by the general membership but in reality are appointed

[65] Ibid. 118.
[66] Based on interviews with G. Rubbi, provincial secretary of the DC, and G. Tesini, secretary of the DC in Bologna.

by the committees themselves. In Bologna, the secretary of sections acts for the municipal committee, while the section on local administration is controlled by outside experts who can be summarily removed by Rome.

This rigidity and consequent lack of dynamism combine with great material poverty to explain the weakness of the local DC. Except for election times, the DC could scarcely be said to exist in Bologna. Among the numerous ailments of the Bolognese DC, its complete lack of dynamic and well-known personalities must be cited. Our sample shows that the local members of Parliament, the local leaders (Felicori, Tesini, and Rubbi), and the major theoretician (Ardigò) are virtually unknown to the people of Bologna. The sole exception, the Hon. Salizzoni (undersecretary to the Presidenza del Consiglio), is more interested in national than local politics. And the single outstanding candidate the DC has had, Giuseppe Dossetti, hailed from Reggio Emilia—a fact bitterly resented by the chauvinistic Bolognese.

Materially, the local DC is poverty-stricken. Blame for this can be attributed both to its own scanty political activity and to the meager financial support supplied by the national committee in Rome, with all the consequences that this implies. Paid and full-time party functionaries in Bologna numbered one in 1961[67] and two in 1965, with six or seven others working in public offices (*Delta Padano*) or in journalism (*Avvenire d'Italia*). Such tasks leave little time and energy to devote to the party but still provide grounds for accusations of *sottogoverno* and clerical intervention. The twenty-two sections are apparently active only on paper; at the most, seven sections might meet the "active" requirement. The youth circles (two to our knowledge) have a small following and devote their activities to academic problems, where they are competing with the FUCI and with Catholic Action groups in general. The local DC press (*via Emilia*) died from lack of support in 1959, and to make its opinions known the party is forced to rely on the Catholic *Avvenire d'Italia*. In short, so far as formal organization is concerned, the Bolognese DC seems moribund, which makes one marvel all the more at its survival. The reason for this survival is the direct and indirect

[67] Luigi Pedrazzi, "Cattolici non democristiani," *Il Mulino* 10, no. 108 (September 1961) 639.

help the party receives from the Catholic Church. Though the Church employs no cells or similar organizations, the interchange of personnel between DC and Catholic Action makes the success of one the success of the other. In sum, the influence of the Church on the DC is paramount and is the only way the DC's electoral successes can be accounted for. The DC's political activity, such as it is, demonstrates the weakness of the party itself. But it also demonstrates the strength of the left and that of the Church as well.

Exact figures on the number of Bolognese DC party members are impossible to obtain, and figures cited by such "official" sources as the local secretary seem wildly exaggerated. For example, the "official" DC figures for 1965 claim 12,000 members in the Bolognese federation or province and 3,000 in the town of Bologna, compared to 1,000 in 1953 and 1956. The discrepancy in the town-province ratio (one to four), while not reflecting the two areas' population difference (one to two), is normal, since the DC has always been stronger in the country. The figure of 3,000 for town membership is questioned by most observers, even in the DC, and it probably should be reduced by at least 50 per cent; furthermore, it must be realized that many party members also belong to Catholic Action groups in which they have an important part to play: this "dual citizenship" obviously reduces their efficiency. The tiny entity that ultimately comprises the DC becomes all the more tragic to behold when it is compared to the Communist Party and its some 50,000 members. The explanation of the local secretary that the party seeks votes, not members, fails to convince when considered in the light of the poverty of the Bolognese DC. Not only is it obvious that the local DC could use more funds, but in other parts of Italy one of the party's goals is to have as many card-holders as possible. The party's weakness is also revealed by its inability to mobilize large groups of people for political or even cultural purposes. Both the PCI and the Church can do this, and the DC must often rely upon meetings called by the Church, which are frequently presided over by some of the DC's "dual citizen" members.

How, then, can we account for the fact that the DC still manages to poll some 25 per cent of the votes in Bologna (about seventy-five votes for each party member)? It is our opinion that this comparative success stems partly from the fear of communism among the relatively well-to-do and partly from the masses' willingness to follow the Church's injunction to vote for the Christian party.[68] Finally, the DC emphasizes that it is a middle-class party, comprising some 20 per cent women, the majority of whom are not politically active. Because of the lack of statistics, this is impossible to prove. However, Bologna's DC leaders themselves openly admit that they have little success with the proletariat, and they confirm that the votes they gain in that area are usually feminine; actually, the votes the DC normally wins come from employees and middle-class groups. Furthermore, among the DC's local clientele the proletariat is almost non-existent yet its PCI rivals manage to attract sections of the middle class. In can safely be said that political participation in the DC is negligible, and that which does exist is confined to the middle and upper-middle class.

It has already been mentioned that the local DC group has to rely upon Rome for its financing, whether in unimportant matters (buying stationery) or in important ones (elections). This makes the party all the more sensitive to the struggle among the various groups in the capital; and to this could be added the petty jealousies among local DC leaders, many of whom believe their own election to Parliament would solve all problems. Until 1954 (the Naples Congress) the Bolognese DC followed the rightist current and was governed by the *notabili*. When the national situation was such that the PCI's violent or pacific intentions toward taking over the government were undetermined, this line was normal; moreover, it could be explained by a lack of personnel which forced the DC to employ old figureheads who were conservatively oriented. But this policy, plus political inexperience, led to that sterile kind of opposition which was kindled by an illusory hope of victory in 1951 even if it meant alliance with the fascist MSI. At any rate the final result was certainly not to the town's benefit.

The Congress of Naples in 1954 accented the problems of local administration and the necessity of local autonomy, and it coincided with the arrival of new and younger personnel who are still in power today. The outstanding characteristic of these new men is their knowledge of local problems and, even more, their leftist orientation along the line Fanfani-La Pira-Dossetti. This orientation has led to a more constructive opposition, but it has also had the disadvantage

[68] See appendix five, p. 207.

of contrasting the progressive DC with the conservative PCI; thus the DC appears *plus royaliste que le Roi*. As a result, its leftist reputation—particularly since 1956—has rendered the Bolognese DC both hostile to Rome and at the same time suspect to many Bolognese. Under such conditions, the DC knows it is fighting for a lost cause but refuses to admit it; it couches its hopes for final victory in long-range terms, thereby adopting the same pattern as the Church. The only hope for change resides in a genuine center-left coalition in local government, one that may possibly include the unions. With the reunification of the socialist parties, this might be possible after the local elections in 1969. However, it may well be doubted that the DC will reap many benefits from the coalition, since the leading wing is comprised of the socialists, and even if they are not the most numerous, they will appear as the most dynamic element while the DC will be seen merely as a brake. In reality, as the DC now stands— and its local policies must take into account the positions held by the Roman central organs—it seems to be little suited to a Bolognese mentality that leans heavily to the left, a left which for the last twenty years has been dominated almost exclusively by the PCI. It is the latter we must now examine.

Part 2:
The Bolognese Communist Party and Local Administration

5: LOCAL ORGANIZATION OF THE PCI

The local Communist Party has acquired enormous power from some twenty years of continuous and competent administration. And not the least effect of this long tenure is that in the mind of a large segment of the population the Communist Party, though actually a monolithic bloc, and the local administration, in which the minority plays a role, have become identified. Obviously, this confusion helps the Party in that it can exploit, as if its own, initiatives which have been proposed by the opposition and accepted by the municipal administration; by the same token, the very presence of the mayor at the inauguration of a new project sometimes gives the impression that he and his Party are the instigators of initiatives which, in reality, have been the work of the Christian Democratic party. For example, the idea of creating permanent buildings for the annual fair was the DC's (Dossetti); the DC originated a society for achieving this purpose (Felicori) and built the necessary pavilions; the proper location was discovered by the DC and contracted for by the town hall, but it was not paid for. The impression remains, however, that the local administration and the PCI created the fair; actually, they were only the artisans of a somewhat dishonest transaction.

Furthermore, when studying the Bolognese Communist Party, it must be remembered that it is only a part of a major complex, the Italian Communist Party. Undoubtedly, by virtue of its own strength the Bolognese federation wields power nationally and can thus take rather daring initiatives on its own; but in the final analysis it must submit to Rome. The case of the Bolognese *rinnovatori* (modernizers) is a perfect example which will be described in detail. The fact that this allegiance to the national Party is not always visible can at least partially explain the popularity of the local communists among population groups which either do not understand or actually totally reject Marxism.

Finally, we must recall that until 1956 the Italian Communist

95

Party existed solely and exclusively as a satellite of the USSR, and though it developed a few individual characteristics, it remained very close to Stalin, the protector of its leaders. It is true that the development of polycentrism and the insistence upon the Italian way to socialism have rendered the Party less defensive and more congenial, but the observation of an acute student of communism remains valid:

> Born Leninist and developed Stalinist, in a few years of life in the Italian milieu the Party has taken on most of the characteristics of the old social democratic movements, integrated with those peculiarities of its own formation, namely, bureaucratic monolithism, an atmosphere of Inquisition, the congenital use of lies and slander as an arm of the political struggle. . . .[1]

When one thinks of the name Bologna, one usually means not only the town but also the homonymous province and, to a certain extent, all Emilia, of which it is the largest town and capital as well; and since "Emilia holds a key position in the Italian economic and political situation,"[2] all the more importance attaches to Bologna's role.

In the province of Bologna, the Party can rely upon 126,000 members, distributed over 5,000 cells, 306 sections, and 15,000 cadres: it can employ 246,000 members of the leftist trade-union CGIL: it hands out 15,000 copies of the daily Unità, and it controls some 590 cooperatives.[3] This gives one an idea of the strength of the Bolognese Communist Party.

In 1963, of some 1,614,886 Italian communists, Emilia could count 411,563 among its population of 3,600,000[4] (or one out of nine), while Bologna alone had 50,000 in a population of 475,000. At the same time, it is estimated that one third of all the cadres in the whole Italian PCI originated in Emilia.[5]

Bologna has become the stronghold of communism in Italy, and this prominence is reflected in the attention the Party's leaders devote to it, considering it, as they do, a decisive testing ground.

---

[1] Giorgio Galli, Storia del PCI (Milano: Schwarz, 1958) 319.

[2] Togliatti, "Intervention at the Provincial Conference of the PCI," Bologna, March 8, 1964, in Discorsi sull'Emilia (Bologna: PCI, 1964) 90.

[3] Piccolo sinodo diocesano, 1962 (Bologna: UTOA, 1962) 3–4.

[4] Unità, May 1, 1964.

[5] At the height of its strength, 19,798 cadres out of 58,634 came from Emilia. "Forza e attività del partito. Dati statistici," confidential, VII Congresso Nazionale del PCI (Rome: PCI, n.d. [1950]).

An entire booklet of Togliatti's speeches on Emilia has been published;[6] Togliatti reserved for Bologna his comments on the importance of the middle class (ceto medio)[7] and the necessity of an alliance with all nonmonopolistic producers against the large monopolies; it was in Bologna that Amendola developed his somewhat heretical views on local communism in 1958.

The concept of a political party in Italy may be compared with membership in an American church,[8] and this is all the more true for the PCI where the commitment has the totality of religion and demands an unbreakable allegiance. Today the PCI in Bologna has some 48,000 card-holders who presumably contribute regularly to the Party finances. From a splinter group in the early 1920's the Communist Party has become the giant which dominates the local scene.[9] At its birth in 1921 it probably represented less than 0.6 per cent of the total population, and while fascism helped enhance its prestige, it did little to increase communist membership; according to Party sources, at the period of Mussolini's downfall the total membership did not exceed 300, or less than 0.1 per cent of the total population. This ridiculously low figure was well compensated for by the Resistance activities of its members, by sympathy for the Party enlisted in the suburbs where many were communists without being officially enrolled, and also by a good deal of opportunism. In less than two months the PCI had increased threefold, and when Bologna was liberated in April 1945, membership had risen to 3,600. At the Party congress in November the Bolognese federation could boast 16,800 members in the town alone, while by the following June the total had reached 30,000. Certainly, the validity of these figures may be doubted, but it is felt that they do contain a high degree of truth: the PCI enjoyed a considerable following among the people; it headed the local administration and thus became the purveyor of jobs, food, and shelter, and finally it was never reluctant to impress members at the point of a gun. In those days, in fact, Bologna became known as one of the summits of "the triangle of death."

Since the end of World War II, the Party has gone through dif-

---

[6] Discorsi sull'Emilia (Bologna: PCI, 1964).

[7] Ibid., 1946, pp. 7–36; 1964, pp. 61–68.

[8] John Clarke Adams and Paolo Barile, The Government of Republican Italy (Boston: Houghton Mifflin Company, 1961) 157.

[9] See appendix three, pp. 193–195.

ferent periods coinciding with the general economic and political situation of Italy. From 1945 to 1952, when dissatisfaction with prevailing economic conditions was at its highest and when many still believed in the possibility of violent revolution, membership increased by approximately two thousand a year. Between 1953 and 1961 the increase continued at a regular though considerably diminished pace of about one thousand per year. Since 1961–1962, when the economic boom hit Bologna, the PCI has decreased and stagnated at approximately 47,500 members. When confronted with the increase in population, the figures became all the more relevant: until 1951 the PCI represented between 10 and 11 per cent of the population; from 1952 to 1961, between 11 and 12; in 1962 it was equivalent to 10.75. In 1965 it represented only 9.62 per cent of the population, which is equivalent to its strength at the end of 1947. The figure remains impressive, but we must be careful to note that maintaining it has only been possible by a carefully planned policy of immigration and even more by transfers from the Communist Federation of Italian Youth (FGCI).

The FGCI was established in 1949 to attract young people between the ages of fourteen and twenty-one (extended to twenty-five in 1957) and thus to give them a political formation which would make them secure allies of the Party. By the end of 1949 the FGCI had 25,514 members in the province of Bologna, equal to 6 per cent of the total number of young Italian communists, while the province's total number of young people represented only 0.2 per cent of the national population under twenty-one.[10] In Bologna, the proportion of young workers in the FGCI is predominant (40 per cent in 1956; 67.5 in 1958),[11] followed by students (8.0), with the remainder being distributed among self-employed girls, employees, and seamstresses. The most common age bracket is seventeen to twenty-one. In absolute figures the following is offered:[12]

1951	1952	1953	1954	1955	1956	1957	1958
5614	5975	5991	6351	6470	6081	5380	5412

[10] VII Congresso Provinciale del PCI, "Documenti statistici" (Bologna: PCI, 1950) [n.p.].
[11] Federazione Bolognese PCI, "Federazione Giovanile," n.d. [1960], n.p. [2], mimeographed.
[12] Ibid.

Today the figure can be estimated at 4,500, and each year some 15 per cent of the membership reaches the age of eighteen and enters the Party. For the period 1953–1957 this transfer was to a great extent responsible for the Party's increase in numbers.

	1953	1954	1955	1956	1957
Transfers from FGCI	900	950	975	910	775
Increase of Party	20	850	1452	1844	770

It cannot be doubted that the FGCI is a secure reservoir for the Party.

On the other hand, the efficiency of the Pioneers' Organization (age seven to fourteen) is doubtful, since the figures may well have been faked.[13] Until 1956 all the cards sold by the center (though not necessarily distributed) were counted, and it is known that only "forty groups have a continuous activity"[14] out of a total of 160. It nevertheless remains true that perhaps some 25 per cent of the Pioneers will join the Communist Youth Movement.

Another source of worry for the PCI is the suspicion that the Party is unable to attract enough young people to take the place of the older generations, as 61.5 per cent of the members were over forty years of age in 1965 and only 13 per cent under thirty.[15]

There is no doubt that the predominance of the prewar generation is total and can be satisfactorily explained by the fact that these were the age groups that witnessed the transformation of the PCI into a mass party. It cannot be denied that the powerful Party machine has been unable to recruit as many young people as desirable. And this is especially so since economic affluence has become a characteristic of northern Italian society; this means that the Party is inevitably going to witness a decrease in membership.

---

[13] Ibid.

1953	1954	1955	1956	1957	1958	1959
11,000	15,000	18,000	16,500	11,500	8,000	6,200

[14] Ibid.

[15] Federazione Bolognese del PCI, "Campagna di tesseramento e proselitismo, 1966." (Bologna: PCI, 1965), mimeographed.

Age Group	%	No.	Age Group	%	No.
18–25	5.4	2,574	41–50	25.3	12,064
26–30	7.6	3,624	51–60	20.5	9,775
31–40	25.6	12,207	61–	15.7	7,486

Adversaries of the PCI rejoice over this, and they rejoice over other figures that likewise indicate a drop in PCI membership. Yet such an outlook does not consider the problem in its entirety: the other parties are even less successful among the young people; their own effectives are not increasing; and the PCI, all percentages considered, remains the giant among Bolognese parties. Furthermore, it has in its possession certain trump cards that give its enemies no cause for rejoicing. First, the percentage of women card-holders is tremendously high, some 10 per cent above the Italian average, running around 40 per cent.[16]

1951	1955	1958	1965
37.6	39.7	43.2	42.2

Second, when studying membership figures and the percentage of communists compared to the total population, it must be remembered that membership in the Party begins at age eighteen. Consequently, when we say that the communist population is 10–11 per cent of the total population, electorally speaking, we are saying that this communist strength may be put at 20 per cent. Comparing membership figures to electoral returns, we observe that in municipal elections each member of the Party influences between 2.3 and 3.1 more votes.

1946	1951	1956	1960	1964
2.3	2.3	3	2.6	3.1

Third, the social composition of the PCI electoral body shows it has been capable of gaining votes among relatively privileged sectors of the population, both among males and females. (See Tables IX and X.)

It is true that the Party does not cross class lines to any great extent, but no Italian party actually does, and it cannot be called a genuine weakness that the PCI recruits among the lower income bracket and less educated people. If we consider the economic and social status of the PCI electors and the undecided, it can be seen that dissatis-

---

[16] Conferenza Regionale del PCI, "Tavole statistiche, Documenti per delegati" (Bologna: PCI, 1959) 35; PCI "Campagna di Tesseramento" (1965).

Table IX

PROFESSION OF PERSONS INTERVIEWED BY SEX (MALES)
(in per cent)

	Total	Probable PCI Voters
Entrepreneurs, industrialists	2	2
Commerce	8	2
Artisans	6	8
High civil servants	2	–
Employees	26	8
Workers, specialized or not	34	54
Laborers	1	2
Unemployed	2	3
Students	1	–
Retired on pension scheme	18	21
	100	100

Table X

PROFESSION OF PERSONS INTERVIEWED BY SEX (FEMALES)
(in per cent)

	Total	Probable PCI Voters
Commerce	2	–
Artisans	3	3
Employees	7	3
Workers	6	10
Housewives	69	72
Students	2	–
Retired	11	12
	100	100

faction is not the sole reason why people in Bologna vote for the PCI; and while it remains true that most PCI voters are among the less educated, a change in the level of education is not something that can be brought about in a few years. In any case there will always be sufficient grounds for dissatisfaction to allow the Party to be the mouthpiece for the discontented.

Table XI

ESTIMATED ECONOMIC AND SOCIAL STATUS OF THE FAMILIES
CLASSIFIED BY POLITICAL BELONGING
(in per cent)

	A*	B*	C*
Superior	1	8	—
Above average	3	9	7
Average	47	60	49
Under average	40	20	32
Inferior	9	3	12
	100	100	100

* A represents certain and probable communist voters; B, noncommunist; C, undecided.

Table XII

LEVEL OF EDUCATION ACCORDING TO POLITICAL BELONGING
(in per cent)

	Total	A	B	C	Total A Males	Total A Females	
Elementary or no schooling	65	86	48	73	56	88	74	84
Secondary school (*media inferiore*)	18	10	23	19	23	7	12	14
Lyceum (*media superiore*)	12	2	20	8	14	3	11	1
University	5	2	9	—	7	2	3	1
	100	100	100	100	100	100	100	100

To sum up, while we do find reasons to believe that membership in the PCI will diminish as the years go by, this will not necessarily be translated into an increase in membership among the other parties. The PCI is losing its older members and recruiting fewer younger people, but it remains the largest party and compensates for its weakness by its tremendous organization and electoral machine.

The strength of the Party is maintained by what, without exaggeration, can be called an army of cadres. The figures obtainable indicate that the Bolognese federation had at its disposal 21,665 minor cadres in 1950 (17.22 per cent of the total enrollment in the Party) and 18,928 in 1956 (14.40 of the total enrollment).[17] Today the figure

[17] "Studi sull'organizzazione del PCI in Emilia-Romagna" (Bologna: CSAS, 1958) 20, mimeographed.

should be put around 15,000. While these minor cadres are not entirely dependent upon the Party, many derive their income from front organizations, such as cooperatives or municipal enterprises, and are consequently dedicated to the Party.

For the town of Bologna alone, the Party in 1956 appointed 42 civil servants (funzionari), 34 secretaries of sections, 107 party members in the trade union, and 53 political cadres in the cooperative movement, all of whom depended entirely upon the Party.[18] In 1964 the figure for section secretaries was 74. However, a subjective approach gives a better impression of the organizational strength of the Party. Via Barberia is known today as the central headquarters of the Bolognese federation of the PCI. In the palace that shelters it the main offices on the first floor are reached by a monumental staircase, surmounted by the hammer and sickle symbol covering an old patrician escutcheon. This and painted ceilings are all that is left of the past. From that point on, we see a modern organization with several scores of civil servants, secretaries, and typists, all of whom seem tremendously more efficient and courteous than their counterparts in other administrations. While the central headquarters of the DC appear empty, the PCI swarms like a beehive.

The members of the Party are organized on the classical line of cells and sections, the latter divided into zones and coordinated by a municipal committee (Comitato Cittadino), which has jurisdiction over the 14 zones of the town corresponding to the different quarters and the 74 sections including some 1,300 cells.[19] These cover the town as follows:

Sections		Sections		Sections	
Centro	12	Mazzini	4	Barca	3
Corticella	5	S. Stefano	6	Borgo	
Bolognina	10	Stadio	3	Panigale	7
S. Donato	6	Colli	4	Saffi	3
S. Vitale	4	S. Viola	3	Lame	4

The high concentration in the center is explainable by the presence of the federation, while the Bolognina (10 sections), Borgo Panigale

---

[18] Via Emilia, October 16, 1957, p. 7. It is interesting to note that at the period the DC disposed of no more than five cadres, of which only one was full-time.

[19] X Congresso Provinciale PCI, "Documenti per delegati" (Bologna: PCI, 1962) 8, 9, mimeographed.

(7 sections), and Corticella (5 sections) are traditionally the reddest districts in town. It is impossible to say how many cells are attached to each section, the number being variable. To give some idea, in 1958 the smallest section had 13 cells and the largest, 71.[20] The variation between 46 sections in 1958[21] and 74 in 1962—while total membership in the Party remained almost constant—reflects both the Party's attempts to achieve better and more thorough organization and also its efforts to secure greater participation by means of a fairer distribution of responsibilities. It is impressive to observe that the PCI owns approximately two thirds of the seats of the Bolognese sections, which are directed by a committee of nine, eleven, or thirteen members elected during the Congress of each section and presided over by a secretary. The latter directs a secretariat of three or four of the faithful and is actually all powerful. In fact, the secretary can veto a majority decision of the section and appeal to the higher levels of the Party. General meetings are irregular but are usually held two or three times a month.

The section secretary is charged with the political direction of the cells—divided since 1947 into male and female cells, plus factory cells. Each has 30 to 35 members, guided by a cell committee of 5 members and coordinated by the chief collectors (capo gruppo collettore) in the ratio of 1 for every 8 or 10 members. The latter is one of the key figures in the entire organization, not only collecting the dues but also visiting the families regularly; thus they keep informed regarding the members' orthodoxy and their most pressing desires. Chosen because of his outgoingness, cordiality, and reliability, the chief collector has taken the first step up the stairs in the Party hierarchy. General meetings take place two or three times a month, while, in the case of the sections, the specialized study groups may convene more often (e.g., press and propaganda). Among factory cells (some 10 per cent of the total) coordination of activities is assigned to a Party factory committee composed of the cell secretaries, the most influential members of the factory's internal commission, and the trade union delegate.

This strength in peripheral organs rests upon the somewhat doubtful principle of democratic centralism which conceals the seat of

[20] CSAS, "Studi sul" 16.
[21] Ibid.

power, while allowing for an appearance of democracy at the lower levels. This is well illustrated in the mechanics of elections and decision-making in the Party. According to their status, the members of the cells convened in a Congress of Sections elect the section's directing committee, and this group in turn chooses its secretary.[22] Actually, the leaders of the cells are chosen by the secretary of the section, and the secretary is in turn controlled by the organization and the cadres' commission of the local federation.

The section secretaries, the secretary of the *Camera del Lavoro*, the secretary in charge of coordinating the cooperatives, and the mayor elect the municipal committee, the secretary of which is chosen from among members of the local federation. The section delegates who are controlled—or more accurately, chosen—by the cadres' commission of the local federation constitute the Federal Congress which elects the federal committees, the federation secretariat, and the secretary. This latter functionary has, of course, received the approval of the Central Directorate in Rome. Finally, the delegates of the Federal Congress make up the Provincial Congress, which chooses the secretariat and secretary of the provincial federation (the names for which are proposed by Rome), while the executive committee formed by the directors of commissions of the local federations of the province (chosen by the secretary who is controlled by Rome) shapes the political line of the various local secretariats.

On the surface there is a democratic structure of cell, section, municipal committee, local federation, and provincial federation wherein the base elects the summit; as a matter of fact, all elections are controlled on two levels, either by the central committee in Rome for the local federation or by the local federation for the municipal committee and the sections; in turn, the sections, but even more the local federation, control the cells (see diagram, p. 106).

In the case of Bologna, it is clear that the most important organ is the provincial federation (practically absorbing the municipal committees), which exerts its influence by means of a certain number of commissions subdivided into various sections and which is itself controlled by the all-powerful local secretary chosen by Rome. The federation has nine commissions at its disposal, commissions which

---

[22] What follows is derived from CSAS, "Studi sul" 6–15, and personal observations.

ELECTION AND CONTROL SYSTEM IN THE PCI

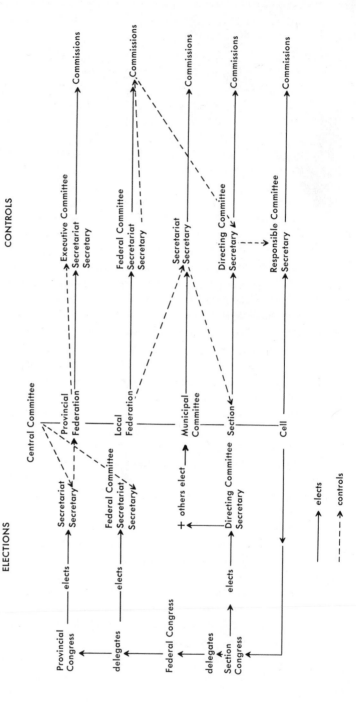

ELECTIONS

CONTROLS

→ elects

--→ controls

theoretically should also be represented on the municipal committee. In turn the sections and cells direct the activities of four commissions (administration, press, organization, and mass), to which are added specialized study groups when necessary.

It is interesting to consider the commissions of the local federation controlled by the local secretary and the powers of control they have at their disposal which extend to all levels of the Party (see p. 108). The organization commission is the most important and has among its members the directors of the following commissions: mass, cadres, *enti locali*, press and propaganda, and feminine. The principal purpose here is to give political and organizational instructions to all sections of the local federation in the province of Bologna; as a consequence, it coordinates all the political activities of the municipal committees and of the secretariats of the different sections and thus handles the relations between federation and sections and between sections and cells. To perform this task, it is divided into five working committees: city (Bologna), plain, mountain, statistics, and armed forces, the latter committee being in charge of all activities in the barracks and among retired military men.

The commission *enti locali* (local administration) directs the activities of the League of Democratic Communes and insures that the communes' policy is in harmony with Party objectives. The leader of the majority in the town hall is directly responsible to the commission.

The cadres' commission has a threefold mission, reflected in the division of the working committees. The vigilance committee (in charge of "negative" cadres) directly controls all PCI cadres which have had divergences with the Party; when necessary, it isolates the most influential of the dissenting militants; it also has the exclusive right to handle all contacts with members of the municipal and national police forces. The ideological committee is in charge of the cadres' political formation, assigns instructors to the sections, and in particular controls the provincial and national party schools. The committee for positive cadres is in charge of all promotions within the Party. Each month the group leaders present a report to the federal secretary concerning the political and moral attitudes of the cadres they control, and having the ear of the federal secretary is often equivalent to being the *deus ex machina*.

The feminine section is divided into two parts: one committee is in charge of the political work in the cells and sections; the other is

CONTROL SYSTEM VESTED IN COMMISSIONS UNDER
GUIDANCE OF FEDERAL SECRETARY

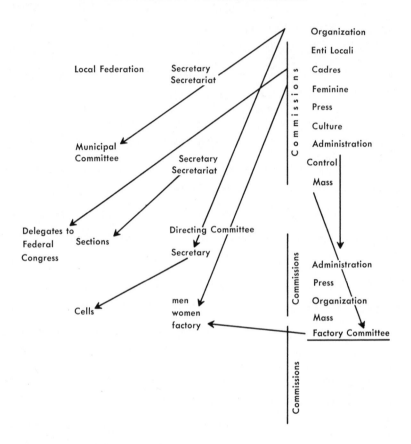

responsible for directing the activities of the various feminine mass organizations, such as Union of Italian Women, Pioneers, Association of Mothers of Deceased Partisans, Association of Cooperative Members, and others.

The press and propaganda commission supervises the local communist press, as well as the town hall publications and those of the union and the cooperatives controlled by the Party. It also supervises the press commissions of the different sections and handles the distribution of books, reviews, and newspapers which must be relevant to the milieu wherein the section is most influential. The propaganda branch is responsible for political demonstrations and for assignment of speakers to the different sections. In Bologna this commission has at its disposal four regular cadres.

The cultural commission supervises teachers and university students and directs the Cultural Circle Antonio Gramsci (1,500 members), the Circle of Friends of the Cinema, and the Association for Friendship Italy—USSR. The administration commission has charge of the Party's income, handling both ordinary revenue (Party cards, monthly and support stamps, subscriptions, and the month of the communist press) and extraordinary revenue (administration of the patrimony of the Party, kickbacks from cooperatives, and financial operations abroad). Each month the ordinary revenue group, through the administrative commissions of the sections, checks the financial activities of the cells.

The control commission collaborates with the federal committee and the secretariat in controlling the administration of the Party's rules, as well as the ordinary functioning of the Party; also, together with the cadres' commission, it directs the activities of the Party schools; it investigates the morality of accused Party members and judges all questions relevant to the internal discipline of the Party.

The mass commission is charged with dictating the political line of the four principal sectors: trade unions, cooperatives, small associations (commerce, small houseowners, small builders, cinema owners, etc.), and agriculture. In every case it can make its influence felt by means of the communist cadres which permeate those associations.

In an organization such as this, which is characterized by a multiplicity of organs and controls, the result is that no aspect of life, public or private, can escape the eye of the Party or that of the secretary of the local federation. It is also evident that this complex system of controls creates a certain rigidity within the Party, but happily from the standpoint of communist leaders it also prevents all possible discussions—except those that take place at the level of the federation, which are then controlled by Rome. In fact

If the direction remains compact, the opposition can crystallize itself in single cells or sections where, led by a militant, nuclei offering an alternative can be formed. In fact, however, they remain isolated, with no horizontal link between themselves, unable to exert a vertical influence, because the functionary, the cadres' commission, has full control of the situation on the federal level, and carries on its task until it receives clear and precise instructions from the center. Furthermore, at the beginning opponents tend to legalize their attitude, thus acknowledging a legality in the Party which kills them.[23]

Acceptance of Party legality means recognizing the validity of democratic centralism, a notion which rejects the very concept of opposition. The modernizers and the rare Sinophiles have had occasion to realize this quite concretely.

The costs of maintaining so complex a machine are immense. Yet it remains practically impossible to obtain reliable figures on the financing of the Party in Bologna. At the most, only estimates of the strength and influence of the communists can be given. We have already alluded to the fact that Bologna subsidizes the central organs of the Party in Rome. The amount of this subsidy is unknown and probably depends upon necessities which vary from year to year, particularly where elections are concerned. Local experts maintain that two thirds of the ordinary income and one third of the extraordinary income go to Rome.[24] On the other hand, the past federal secretary, Guido Fanti, mayor of Bologna since April 1966, completely rejects their view, saying that 20 per cent goes to Rome, 20 per cent to the local sections, and that there is no such thing as extraordinary income. This is doubtful; otherwise, it cannot be explained how the Party lives on the footing it does today in Bologna. Thus it is believed that the extraordinary income which the Party has at its disposal in Bologna must be considerable.

The ordinary income handled by the local federation of the Party is distributed as follows[25] (in millions of lire):

	1961	31-X 1962	1963 (forecast)
Monthly contributions	72	65	74
Party cards	22	22	
Support stamps	16	19	
Press campaign	80	80	
Total	190	186	74

[23] Giorgio Galli, Storia del Partito Comunista Italiano (Milano: Schwarz, 1958) 349.
[24] CSAS, "Studi sul" 14.
[25] PCI, Federazione Bolognese, X Congresso Provinciale, "Documenti" 14.

Bringing the figures for 1962 up through December, and using the figures of 1962 to project 1963, the following would result:

	1961	1962	1963
Total	190	199	195
in dollars	306,500	321,000	314,500

with an average in lire, per party member, of

1961	1962	1963
3,800	3,980	3,900

Thus in 1962 the Bolognese federation would have been in a position to use between 65 and 119 million lire. The minimum salaries (lire 1,200,000) for fifty functionaries (and it is more probable that it employs over a hundred) would be 60 million; and this does not take into consideration all other expenses of the secretariat, electoral campaigns, and so on. Therefore, it is likely that ordinary income barely covers the current expenses of running the Party machine; this also gives a hint of what the extraordinary income of the federation must be. The federation certainly appears flourishing and prosperous, a fact that seems all the more remarkable if the estimate that the federation can actually use only two thirds of this income is correct.

It is impossible to estimate the extraordinary income; however, it should be noted that the Party controls eighty-three Case del Popolo in the province and fifty-six Party headquarters, which sometimes pay rent to the Party and which, in nearly every case, were either built by the workers at their own expense or by Party-controlled cooperatives, at cost, if not free. The Party also receives a considerable commission on transactions where it serves as an intermediary, plus kickbacks from all the cooperatives it controls. For Emilia these cooperatives have a budget running around 70 billion lire[26] (113 million dollars). It is also well known that the Party receives contributions from the commercial agencies attached to Italcoop, which handles trade arrangements with Eastern Europe; moreover, funds destined

---

[26] Vinicio Araldi, Emilia rossa (Roma: Vito Bianco, 1964) 41. If Bologna received 1 per cent of this, it would have some 700 million lire at its disposal, or seven to ten times more than its ordinary income.

for travel in Eastern Europe are said to remain with *Italtourist,* represented in Bologna by CAMST.

In conclusion, there is no doubt that the organizational capacity and the financial wealth of the PCI outweigh all those factors of weakness that have previously been cited. An illustration of this can be found in the problems connected with recruitment, formation, and dissociation from the Party.

There is little doubt that a majority of the PCI members come from a politically uncultured group which understands agitational goals but which is in no way conversant with Marxism. In Bologna three waves of recruitees can be distinguished. First, those who joined between 1922 and 1943 constitute the true believers, those opponents of fascism who had nothing to gain and everything to lose; they were bound together either by secrecy or by ties of common immigration. They make up the old guard, the very incarnation of which is Dozza, mayor of Bologna from 1945 to 1966. The second wave arrived during the period of armed resistance, or immediately following, from 1943 to 1947, and the greater part of these recruits had known no other politics than dictatorship; the Resistance and its ideals formed the basis for their faith, a foundation that was cleverly exploited by existing communist political cadres who were still able to make revolution seem possible. In Bologna these men, led by Lorenzini and Soldati, constitute the new wave which came to power in 1959. In the third wave, since 1947, the recruits were largely "protest" members *par excellence,* dissatisfied with economic conditions, impressed by the power of the local Party, and convinced that the communists could do better—or certainly, no worse—than the other parties. Since 1959, when the Italy of the economic miracle emerged, dissatisfaction has not been as rife. As a result, Party effectives are not increasing, and to a considerable degree they remain at the current level only because of immigration and the transfer of young communists to the Party ranks.

Recruitment, during all periods except the first, has always gone through three stages, which are admirably summed up by Gabriel Almond. First, there is the commitment or joining, which rarely involves a clear perception of the esoteric party. Second, the new member is "activated," which means he is kept under pressure so that he has little time to judge his new experiences; and this in turn means that possibly five out of seven evenings each week are devoted to the Party. Third, the member is "sloganized," or indoctrinated. To progress beyond this point is to break through, or to break away. The formation of the Communist Party member takes place at all times and at all levels, during discussions and upon mere contacts, while the atmosphere of suspicion within the Party requires that certain patterns of reasoning be adopted. Gradually these patterns become second nature.

In its task the Party is helped by the schools it has created, where

> . . . the individual loses, little by little, the faculty of judging facts and situations objectively, and begins to reason not by virtue of his own intelligence but . . . using from time to time those very reasonings with which he has been indoctrinated, and which for him have now assumed the value of an axiom.[27]

In Bologna this is the role of the Marabini school, better known as the Marxist University (its only equivalent is in Rome), which has several modern, well-planned buildings on the outskirts of town. Exactly how many frequent the school is not certain, but it is generally agreed that one thousand party members take a course every year. A fair guess would be that at least one third are Bolognese. This is confirmed by the only statistics (for 1945–1950)[28] that are available.

		Male	Fe-male	Co-ed M.	F.	Total
1945	2 provincial courses (2 months)			43	9	52
1946	2 provincial courses (2 months)			29	7	36
1947	4 provincial courses (2 months)			57	22	79
1948	75 section courses (8 lessons)			850	250	1100
	3 provincial courses (2 months)			76	18	94
1949	132 section courses (8 lessons)			1700	300	2000
	3 provincial courses (3 months)	36		68	11	115
	History of the C.P.			934	128	1062
1950	2 provincial courses (3 months)	80				80
	1 provincial course for youth	39				39
	Stalin courses (3 lessons)			2200	800	3000
	2 courses for local administrators	74				74

---

[27] Gabriel Almond, The Appeals of Communism (Princeton: Princeton University Press, 1954) 115.

[28] Federazione Bolognese del PCI, VII Congresso Provinciale, "Documenti per delegati" (Bologna: PCI, 1950) 45.

In the words of Lenin, "We must train people who shall devote to the revolution not only their spare evenings but the whole of their lives":[29] this means total engagement for the good of the Party.[30] In the case of Bologna, this was true—as far as can be judged—during the first postwar years when all members believed in the imminence of revolution and devoted their entire energies to this purpose. And it is significant that figures extending beyond 1950 for the activities of the Marabini School are not to be found. Today the political commitment of many communists is doubtful. The cadres have to overcome bourgeois tendencies that in some cases are marked by conspicuous bank accounts; for the greater portion of new members, joining the Party represented a protest against economic conditions, and these conditions are now no longer so bad.

The cadres' entire life depends upon the Party (psychologically and often materially), and they continue their life as activists either from habit or in quest of greater responsibilities in the Party. This explains the difficulty encountered in breaking away from the organization and the reason why exclusion is such a tragedy for the militant.[31] Finding in the Party a way of life, the militant lives among a closed group of initiés with whom he shares the same mentality and problems. The militant does not easily switch to the weaker parties of the left; and once excluded, he feels lost, his knowledge of life limited to but one trade, that of a professional agitator.[32] And this vocation is no longer useful.

The political groups within the Bolognese Communist Party can be classified by age and by the place they occupy in national political groupings. The distinction between "old guard" and "new wave" has already been made; the first, predominantly of proletarian origin, came to power as a result of migratory movements, was under the pro-

[29] V. I. Lenin, Urgent Tasks of Our Movement, Collected Works, vol. IV, book 1, p. 57, quoted in Almond, The Appeals 52.

[30] See Almond, ibid.: on Party and friendship, p. 123; personal relations, p. 160; and family, p. 157.

[31] The most notorious cases of exclusion (Cucchi, 1951 and Soldati, 1963) will be examined under the weaknesses of the Party in chapter six.

[32] Almond, The Appeals 339, points out that 58 per cent of Italian defectors go through serious difficulties or at least a difficult period, while only 22 per cent have no problems at all. In Bologna, this proportion would be higher, due to the economic dependence of a large share of the base on the Party.

tection of Stalin (Dozza would have been Molotov's Italian pro-
tégé), and made the Party what it is. The second, created by the
Resistance, govern the town today; they oppose the centralizing tendencies still upheld by the old-guard Roman leaders; they appear to be
from the lower middle class, have often had university training, and
at times appear clearly heretical. The other point to note is that those
members of the Communist Party who represent it in Parliament
come predominantly from the middle class. In local politics, however,
leadership is more proletarian, as illustrated by these statistics for
Bologna: 43 per cent proletarian origin, 17.5 per cent rural lower
middle class, 29.6 per cent urban lower middle class.[33]

The militants and the base carry out the central office's orders pertaining to agitation or propaganda. Agitation was the focal aim during the first years (1945–1950) when revolution was possible and
when it was clear that "Mass movements can rise and spread without
belief in a God, but never without belief in a devil"[34] (American
Imperialism, NATO, the Government). As hopes for a revolution
dissipated, agitation characterized by violence was replaced by propaganda. This is a more constant weapon, and, in employing it, attacks
on the government become not only a defense of the Party but even
more a kind of proselytism which reaches its height at election times.
In this form of activity the militant has only one role to play—that
of catalyst for the masses—and he has no decisions to make.

The problem of the base's political activity is probably one of the
most important and most pressing confronting the Bolognese Communist Party, where appearances differ greatly from reality. The Party
is capable of organizing the largest demonstrations in town for the very
simple reason that it is the only true mass party that exists. Furthermore, its centralized structure enables it to make its influence felt
upon the base whose dissatisfactions it interprets. Examples of this
abound, particularly during election campaigns when big names of
the Party speak to more than 15,000 people packed into the main
square. However, the more usual kind of demonstration is the Festival dell'Unità, which demonstrates that politics alone are not enough

---

[33] [Giorgio Galli], "Il PCI e la DC nelle amministrazioni locali," Bologna,
1965 manuscript, p. 231. Noteworthy is the case of the DC, the local and national administrators of which are almost exclusively from the upper middle class.

[34] Eric Hoffer, The True Believer (New York: Mentor, 1963) 86.

to attract the Bolognese population. The festival is held each September (the month of the communist press), and its aim is to collect money for the press while propagandizing the slogans currently being employed.

In 1965 the slogans were "Against the Center-Left," "Against American Imperialism," and "United in the Spirit of the Resistance." The base had been motivated by careful propaganda within the sections ("All at the Festival"), and many of these sections set up stands at their own expense. Slogans exploiting the communist version of current events were abundant: "The Center-Left Does Nothing to Alleviate the Crisis," "In Vietnam the SS Nazis Are the American Marines." However, over the four days of the Festival neither the lighted panels bearing these slogans nor the two political demonstrations (Sunday afternoon and Monday evening) attracted as many of the 100,000 attending as did the daily variety shows featuring the more popular Italian singers, the dancing (beat music of course), or above all the gastronomic festival. As a matter of fact, the Party is tending more and more to organize a county-fair type of gathering, with tortellini, sausage, and polenta on the menu, than a political meeting for the masses. It is able to achieve the latter only when elections or violent rallies are in prospect.

Actually, this lack of participation by the base is obvious, and the year 1959, the most critical and important year for the Bolognese PCI so far, affords some good examples. In Party documents we read:

> . . . the cells lack the necessary political vitality and will to adjust to the actual situation. According to a recent examination by the Federal Control Commission, in some sections of town it is evident that the latter do not even perform the duty—democratic and in the statute—of showing the statute and program to newcomers.[35]

> In these years there has been a decline in the absolute number of cells in the province, a reduction of the number of factory cells in town as well as a reduction of feminine cells. . . . This illustrates an even more serious and worrying fact, namely, the weak political life of the cells. Compared to a limited number of cells that meet every two weeks there are many cells that never meet or that only meet a few times a year. Furthermore, in the latest Congresses, the absence of over 50 per cent of the members of the cell-assemblies was noted.[36]

[35] Federazione Bolognese PCI, "Relazione di attività della commissione federale di controllo," Documento interno (Bologna: PCI, 1959, 6 mimeographed).

[36] Federazione Bolognese PCI, "Giudizi del comitato federale," Documento interno (Bologna: PCI, 1959) 29-X-59, p. 29, mimeographed.

The fact is that no more than 35 per cent of the members of the Party participate regularly in the cell activities. Remedies have been proposed, but they have met with little success. A de-emphasis of politics is the most important remedy suggested, as already illustrated by the Festival dell'Unità. Since the 1950's, the Party has attempted to make the cells into social meeting points (in contrast to their original political purpose), while sections have become recreative circles. Thus the Bergonzini section in Bologna is fully equipped with a bar, card tables, billiards and ping-pong tables, a dance hall ("The Red Moon"), a grocery store, and two conference rooms which are more often used for movies than for political discussions. In this way the Party can satisfy the desires of both the old and the young. In the case of the latter the Party has spared no efforts, particularly in the transformation and exploitation of front organizations like ARCI (Associazione Ricreativa Culturale Italiana) and UISP (Unione Italiana Sport Popolare), which reveal less political orientation than other groups.

In conclusion, while the Communist Party has many shortcomings, especially its inability to expand and to win over the younger generations (a weakness common to all other parties in Bologna), it remains the strongest group on the local scene, well served by its formidable organization and its capacity to enter into every aspect of human life.[37] However, confronted by these shortcomings, the PCI has attempted to modify its strategy and tactics, and this attempt may indicate that dynamism is still a key factor for the local PCI.

In all its activities in Italy, the Communist Party is aided by the country's lack of a democratic tradition. Then, too, Italy's political institutions are characterized by a general absence of continuity, and in the postwar years normal political life has been hampered not only by the extremist positions of its parties but by an inability to understand the meaning of a democratic political process.

In the early years the Party's success was due largely to the deplorable economic conditions which plagued the now-rich town of Bologna. If we look at the changing strategy of the local Communist Party, we can distinguish not only permanent propaganda themes

[37] "The means employed to gain victory will be different according to the profession or the political opinion of each voter; universal problems will be exemplified by application to specific cases; and the concrete wants of that particular family or that particular voter will be considered." G. Parmeggiani, "Per una grande vittoria elettorale," La Lotta, April 5, 1961, an. XIII, n. 14.

but also a period of violence (1945–56) and a new, peaceful line since 1956. After World War II, violence was the Party's principal ally in its attempt to win power in Bologna, which became one of the angles of the so-called death triangle controlled by partisan forces. With the exclusion of the communists from the government in 1947 and the subsequent lack of reaction on the part of Togliatti—who maintained that the Party was a government party—it was clear that the possibility of a violent take-over had passed. To satisfy the Party's ordinary member, the posture of violence was maintained; even in 1950 the seventh local Congress of the federation examined "The capitalistic society [which] has had its day, is in a state of putrefaction, and is awaiting to be swept away."[38] By 1956 belief in the revolution had died, and the Khrushchev report at the twentieth Congress of the CPSU and the elaboration of an Italian path to socialism saved the Bolognese Party from the unhappy task of preaching violence in which no one believed and of the end of a capitalistic society which very few wanted. During this period the Bolognese Party had emphasized certain themes which, inasmuch as they form the base for all the political propaganda and *battage* performed by the Party, can be considered traditional. First among these is insistence on the role played by the communists during the Resistance[39] which culminated in April 1945 with the town's liberation. The effective role of the Communist Party has already been pointed out, but what is surprising is that the Party has been able to monopolize the popularity engendered by the Resistance. The Party appears to have achieved this by seizing active control of the ANPI (*Associazione Nazionale Partigiani Italiani*) and, more passively, by the inertia of the Christian democrats, who not until 1965 started propagandizing their own Resistance role. This, however, is an argument that is convincing to the older generations who lived with fascism. But today, while the PCI strikes the same chord, it does not elicit the same response: 47 per cent of its own electorate still sees the Party as the

[38] VII Congresso Federazione Bolognese del PCI, *Tesi* (Bologna: PCI, n.d. [1950] 29.
[39] Examples abound. One can quote: G. Dozza, "Discorso del X Anniversario della Resistenza," *La Lotta*, April 28, 1955; L. Arbizzani, "Del 1921 una lunga e gloriosa battaglia per la liberta di tutti," *La Lotta*, April 22, 1955; "Il Contributo dei comunisti alla testa del popolo bolognese," *La Lotta*, November 23, 1956; "Storia dell'antifascismo bolognese," *La Lotta*, April 5, 1962.

main Resistance fighter, but 46 per cent does not commit itself at all. The communists' second constant theme is to stress the contrast between the efficiency and morality of the Communist Party, on the one hand, and the bungling and corruption of the Christian democrats on the other. In particular, the communists point to the way in which important towns like Rome or Florence[40] are administered, not to mention the villages around Bologna; good targets, too, are Christian democratic scandals, Church intervention in politics, the activities of the prefect, and the centralization of all decisions in Rome. With respect to centralization, for example, the communists can point to the fact that it took the local administration nine years to wangle a government permit to open a municipal pharmacy and only eight weeks to get it into operation, or that thirty-eight months were required to get the plans for a school approved and only eighteen to have it built.

It is against this background that a man like Dozza must be understood.[41] The record of Dozza's local adminstration is prestigious: financial orthodoxy crowned by a balanced budget, a more equitable distribution of taxes, a sound policy of investments, low-priced housing for workers, and the least crowded schools in all of Italy. The importance of the name Dozza on the communist list of the Two Towers (a symbol from which the hammer and sickle are excluded) is reflected in the preferential votes he receives:[42]

	1946	1951	1956	1960	1964
Dozza (%)	48	53	56	53	51
PCI (%)	38	40	45	45	44
Votes	18,000	30,000	31,000	24,000	22,000

In Dozza many discern a guarantee of moderation, especially against "Young Turks" like Guido Fanti and Umbro Lorenzini, and the achievement of a kind of delicate balance with the upper middle class in Bologna. However, since 1958, when his health began to decline, Dozza has become more or less of a rubber stamp for Loren-

[40] Guido Manzoni, "Due Amministrazioni a Confronto: quella di Dozza e quella di La Pira," La Lotta, February 16, 1956.

[41] See Italy, Time Magazine, November 20, 1964, pp. 38–39.

[42] Compiled from Comune di Bologna, Ufficio Elettorale, "Elezioni politiche e amministrative," Bologna, 1965, mimeographed, n.p.

zini, the assessor for local finances, and Fanti, secretary of the local federation and the mayor since April 1966.

The Party's final theme, endlessly repeated and constantly used, is its inter-class composition. It is true that the Party devotes attention to all classes through its various associations: women (*Unione delle Donne Italiane*), intellectuals (*Circolo Gramsci*), partisans (ANPI), sports (UISP), associations of communist doctors and lawyers, associations of small craftsmen, tenants, anglers, bowlers, refugees, and others. But it is equally true that socially the Party has always been dominated by the proletariat and the lower middle class.[43]

Between 1956 and 1959 the Bolognese Party began to evolve a new line, the result of the more Italian approach to socialism developed by Rome and the coming to power of the modernizers (*rinnovatori*) in Bologna. Despite a setback suffered in 1963, these modernizers have attempted to continue this new and broader policy. It's prime sign is the search for broad alliances; in this aspect it can be seen as the reaction to socialist attempts at unification (with the PCI excluded) which began in 1956, culminated in the proposals of a center-left government in 1959, and became even more concrete with the union congress of November 1966. However, in the case of Bologna, the year 1956 was also the Party's most dangerous electoral campaign, and it was obliged to seek alliances among all social classes even when this line was not completely orthodox. Theoretical justification for this policy was found in Togliatti's 1946 writings on "The Middle Class and Red Emilia,"[44] which maintained that communism and the middle class were compatible so long as the middle class was defined as "the gamut of social groups included between the capitalist and the salaried worker."[45] Beginning in 1956, the Communist Party in the Bolognese municipal committee devoted considerable attention to the problems of small shopkeepers who were finding it difficult to compete with large supermarkets and Party-controlled consumers' cooperatives. One concrete result that won many shopkeepers

---

[43] See PCI Federazione Bolognese, IX Congresso, "Documenti per delegati" (Bologna: PCI, 1960), which gives the following: workers 46.2 per cent, housewives 25.7, employees 3.7, craftsmen 5.5, shopkeepers 3.4, liberal professions, 0.2, pensioners 9.5.

[44] Palmiro Togliatti: "Ceto medio ed Emilia rossa," *Discorsi sull'Emilia* (Bologna: Arte Stampa, 1964) 7–36.

[45] *Ibid.* 9.

to the PCI was the Party's attempts to prevent the opening of new supermarkets, though little was done to curb communist-controlled cooperatives.

In 1958–1959 the modernizers developed Togliatti's theory of alliances even further, to the point that alliances contracted with artisans or small industrialists dependent on a monopoly could be approved—though what was meant by small industrialists was never defined. This was in perfect harmony with the situation in Bologna where over the preceding ten years the economy had changed from one based on the pre-eminence of agriculture to one depending more on small industry. In fact, in the town of Bologna in 1962 there were 10,503 craftsmen and 972 small industries employing 37,713 persons.[46] To win the favor of this politically reserved and rather conservative social class, the Communist Party held numerous discussions in the municipal committee that were calling for a symposium on the problems of Bologna's economic and industrial development and of "recognizing the social function of the 60,000 small enterprises in Emilia."[47] The most logical move was to help these trades concentrate their efforts and thereby eliminate wasteful competition, and this the Party did. Moreover, the PCI did not try to dominate the newly constituted associations. In 1963 there had sprung up associations of carpenters for bulk purchase of wood, of furniture dealers to facilitate credit sales, and of transportation enterprises. All of these have been aided by a credit cooperative operated by the Party.

Within this general framework of new alliances, opportunities were seen for luring the Christian democrats—and particularly the Christian workers of the ACLI—to share in a new majority in the town hall.[48] However, these efforts were useless, and Lorenzini's proclamation that "the times of war have come to an end, the time of dialogue has started"[49] fell flat. Nevertheless, these new and broader policies were seen by many as playing in favor of the Party, which had been able by this means to interest many citizens in the Quarter

---

[46] Comune di Bologna, Annuario statistico 1963, appendix one.

[47] Federazione Bolognese PCI, "Comitato cittadino," March 8, 1958, mimeographed.

[48] Mario Soldati, "I problemi di Bologna e la svolta a sinistra," La Lotta, May 5, 1962.

[49] Umbro Lorenzini, "E finito il tempo dell'assedio . . .," La Lotta, June 28, 1962.

Councils and in the possibility of creating noncommunist adjuncts to the mayor.

Another revealing aspect of the Party's new line is its immigration policy. The arrival of immigrants solicited by the town hall plainly fulfilled the needs of an expanding industrial town and provided the means for taking advantage of possibilities offered by the economic boom. However, the town hall followed a careful policy in resettling the new immigrants, the greater part of whom came from the red countryside. Most of them were directed to parts of town where the Party was most strongly entrenched; there, not only was work found for them when necessary, but they could be controlled by a closed system of communications as well.[50] For the Party this meant an increase in votes and also a stabilization (perhaps even a slight increase) in the total Party membership and in the proportion of Party members to the whole population.

Finally, since 1959 the efforts of the Communist Party to dispel its reputation for hostility to Catholics have been very evident. Although nonhostility had been the traditional line of the Italian Communist Party, it had been out of favor since 1948–1949. Now, with the center-left alliance of socialists and Catholics, the new papacy, and the opening of a dialogue with the Churches of Eastern Europe, it was restored. After recalling the importance of religious tolerance, Togliatti declared, "You have the full right to practice the religion and the cult of your conviction."[51] This attempt to win over Catholics and, even more, to attract Bologna's numerous indifferentists— who spurned open collaboration out of fear of eternal damnation —was recognized by the Church for what it was. Taking clear-cut positions both in the pulpit and in the little synods of 1961 and 1962, the Church launched a counterattack, the success of which is not clear.

Looking at the strategy followed by the local Communist Party, one may well ask what part ideology has played. Above all, it must be borne in mind that the Bolognese people are essentially practical

[50] "In this way [the Party] controls the picture of reality to which the working class and other elements are exposed and manipulates the picture in such a manner as to deepen their sense of alienation and destroy all hopes for constructive change within the framework of the existing political and social systems." See G. Almond, *The Appeals* 369.

[51] Palmiro Togliatti, *IX Congresso Regionale PCI, 1959* (Bologna: PCI, 1959) 56.

(the town reached its highest development when governed by the merchants' corporation) and are more concerned with economic well-being and food than with words. In fact, like most

> ... peoples of Western Europe [they] have been played false too often by ideologies—by liberalism, by nationalism, by socialism and by Fascism—until now there has developed on a substantial scale a kind of integral disbelief in all ideologies.[52]

The communists have understood this perfectly and have made the necessary compromises, thus becoming "a purposeful community devoted to combatting the many grievances of [a] difficult life"[53] and content with paying lip-service[54] to the Party's ideology. A good example of this compromising spirit can be found in the daily Unità, which tends more and more to be an information paper increasingly neglectful of the ideological aspects of the class struggle.

As a matter of fact, while communists in Bologna have been successful in identifying themselves with the people, they have been almost total failures in giving these people an ideological formation. Furthermore, this identification has exceeded all ordinary limits in that the Party has identified itself as much (if not more) with the bourgeoisie as with the workers. While preaching the necessity of change, the Communist Party has attained a state of equilibrium, a kind of gentlemen's agreement with the capitalist class based on the theory that good business will win as much for the workers as agitation; and this agreement has been put into practice and maintained by a conservative administration to the satisfaction of entrepreneurs and workers alike.[55]

In Bologna, the Party benefits from this agreement which, while avoiding capitalist hostility, at the same time bestows enormous prestige on the Party nationally. Thus, we understand why Bolognese communists have no desire for a change: they have become bourgeois and antirevolutionary; they have reached a state of development which in their own terminology can only be called "immobilism." For the bourgeois, more appropriately, it can be qualified as coexistence.

---

[52] Almond, The Appeals 397.

[53] Ibid. 376.

[54] Umbro Lorenzini, in an interview, repeatedly came back to the point that Marx was not applicable to Italy in toto, that the concept of profit had to be maintained.

[55] See appendix six, pp. 211–212.

6: THE BOLOGNESE COMMUNIST PARTY: STRENGTHS AND WEAKNESSES

So far, we have been concerned essentially with outlining the Party organization in Bologna. It is now time to consider the strengths and weaknesses of the local PCI.

Most important of all the Party's sources of strength is its centralized structure, a factor which has helped it become a monolithic bloc capable of coping with all kinds of crises, whether general or local. Examples of this strength in action are numerous, and one may cite the destruction of the Stalinist myth and the reaction to the Hungarian uprising among others. More specifically related to Bologna, there are examples such as the elimination of the modernizers or the ousters of important Party members like Cucchi and Soldati for heresy and of Soave for improper moral conduct. As will be seen later, these cases tend to emphasize both the isolation of the base from the summit and, simultaneously, the base's passive obedience to orders. This centrality of power not only enables the Party to finance itself in Bologna but also, through contributions to national headquarters, to bear a major share of the Party's financial burden in other areas of the country. Thus, the Bolognese Party can wield a strong influence in Rome. To the Party's structure can also be attributed its ability to mobilize large crowds. Even if this ability were the sole point to be considered, it would, of itself, stamp the Communist Party as the one true mass party in Bologna. While many members are only partially sold on the communist cause, the over-all membership is so large that no other party can rival it, and the energy that is available from this huge membership is sufficient to solve most problems.

Finally, along with the Party's organizational and numerical advantages, the total subordination of socialists to communists since 1947 has been a factor of strength. The center-left coalition has not been strong enough to splinter this alliance on the local level, and as a result the leftist parties have been able to administer the town ever since the end of World War II. This point will be considered in greater detail in the following chapter, since much of the popularity and much of the potential for recruitment which the Party has enjoyed have stemmed from its competence in local administration.

The communist press deserves special mention; national in scope, it has local editions, and these insure that the whole paper is read. In keeping with Party aims to win over all strata of the population, the Party press at first sought to produce a large diversity of journals and newspapers. Some were aimed at the general reader, others at the intellectual, the Resistance partisan, women, children, sportsmen, workers, lawyers, doctors, etc. However, it soon became clear that this approach was unsuccessful, and from 1959 to 1962 specialized publications gradually gave way to more general and better-conceived newspapers, intended to sell and to make money. Headquartered in Milan and Rome, the national communist daily newspaper *Unità* has editorial offices in Bologna and prepares a special Bolognese insert of two pages devoted to local problems. As with other Italian newspapers, it is not easy to obtain reliable circulation figures, and even those given to delegates at Party congresses appear suspect. Furthermore, a distinction must be made between the daily *Unità*, for which no special sales effort is made, and the Sunday issue, which is promoted heavily. The average figures available for the province of Bologna follow:[1]

(in thousands)	1949	50	51	52	53	54	55	56	57	58	59
Unità (Sunday)	49	52	57	59	61	61	58	60	58	60	60
Unità (Thursday)	17	19	23	27	28	25	23	23	20	21	20
Unità (Other days)	15	17	19	21	23	19	17	17	15	15	14

It can be safely estimated that some 50 per cent of this circulation is distributed and sold in the town of Bologna. In any case, figures for 1962–1963[2] show that the communist press has not increased its sales; moreover, a trend in this direction appears unlikely with Party membership remaining constant.

[1] PCI Federazione di Bologna, IX Conferenza Regionale, "Documenti per delegati" (Bologna: PCI, 1959) n.p.
[2] PCI Federazione di Bologna, X Congresso Provinciale, "Documenti per delegati" (Bologna: PCI, 1962) 12, mimeographed.

	1962	1963
Unità (Sunday)	26,135	28,500
Unità (Daily)	7,420	8,500

Nevertheless, when these figures are compared with the 5,000 circulation claimed for the Catholic *Avvenire d'Italia*, the weakness of the latter newspaper becomes evident. Again, the 45,000–60,000 circulation of the noncommunist *Resto del Carlino*, which a great many communists buy regularly, attests to the value of emphasizing local news.

The *Unità* is actually one of the best Italian newspapers of its kind. While the news is not presented objectively by any means and while no stone is left unturned to feature communist propaganda, on the one hand, and attack capitalism and American imperialism on the other, it is still a fact that readers of this paper are quite well informed (though with a definite bias) about current events. Furthermore, since 1958 less and less space has been devoted to news of the USSR, Eastern Europe, and China, and discussion of ideological questions (except in editorials) has practically disappeared. Simultaneously with the demise of the many specialized journals, the *Unità* introduced special columns, for women on Sundays and for children on Thursdays (supplement, *The Pioneer*). However, the secret of *Unità*'s strength is not its intrinsic quality but its distribution system, each cell being responsible for selling a certain number of copies, particularly of the Sunday edition. Door-to-door distribution is the rule, and the paper is often forced on its recipients in red neighborhoods. Since distribution is often accompanied by a five or ten minutes' conversation, the very task itself has proved helpful in exerting control over political beliefs. Use of the bulletin board system has enabled the newspaper to reach people who may not be on the subscription list at all. In strategic points throughout the town (bus stops, crossings, etc.) a copy of each day's issue is displayed in this way, so that all can at least glimpse the headlines. To say that there are one hundred of these boards scattered throughout Bologna is probably a gross understatement.

In Bologna the national communist newspaper was formerly supplemented by a local federation weekly, *La Lotta* (the fight), which was published uninterruptedly from 1944 to 1964 and reserved to the *avant garde*. Briefly, this newspaper may be described as closely

tied to the federation's point of view which up to 1956 was purely
Stalinist, with emphasis on "miraculous" Soviet accomplishments,
and from 1956 until its death in 1964 was favorable toward local
autonomy. In both phases, La Lotta devoted a large proportion of
its columns to ideological questions, to congress debates, and the like.
Officially, the paper halted publication because it was losing money.
From another viewpoint it simply never won public favor. In 1962–
1963 its sales were as follows:[3]

	1962	1963
Circulation	2,900	3,000
Subscription	552	740
	3,452	3,740

Apparently, it never exceeded a circulation figure of 6,000, which is
remarkably low if we consider the forced-distribution arrangement
that was available through the communist cells. Undoubtedly, financial reasons were the final cause of the paper's demise. But it is only
fair to point out, too, that 1964 saw a notable decrease in the influence of the modernizers in the local federation: for some eight years
previously the Lotta had closely followed their line. It could also indicate that ideological questions no longer interest the proletariat.

Finally, it is interesting to note that the Lotta plays the role of
the Party's campaign organ. Given the name of Due Torri (The Two
Towers), the symbol of the city, the newspaper completely forsook
ideological questions during election campaigns and pointed out,
instead, the accomplishments of the local administration. During the
campaign it printed 20,000–40,000 copies and distributed them free
of charge to the entire populace.

The Party's specialized "quality" journals are aimed at cadres and
intellectuals, except the Noi Donne (We Women), a bi-monthly selling approximately 2,000 copies in town. Rinascita, a journal for intellectuals which since 1959 has been issued weekly, sells 500 copies in
Bologna, while Critica Marxista (monthly) probably does not reach
more than 200 subscribers. Another communist publication is Il
Commune Democratico (the democratic commune), a monthly published irregularly for local administrators; in Bologna its circulation

[3] Ibid.

has decreased from 240 copies in 1950 to 120 in 1964, most of them purchased by the town hall. Since 1960 this publication has been supplemented by an annual, Agenda Amminstratore Democratico, and a bi-monthly, Notiziario.[4]

To sum up, while the strength the Party derives from its press is by no means negligible, it appears definitely limited to the daily Unità. And this organ's circulation would be far less than it actually is, were it not for the structure of the Party. But if we realize that the local Carlino is not considered a party newspaper (though it is liberal) but as the traditional Bolognese paper, we must conclude that, insofar as the strictly political press is concerned, Unità is the only publication that truly blankets the city.

A third source of Party strength may be found in the front organizations it controls, especially the cooperatives and the trade unions. Since the first days of the socialist movement in Emilia, cooperatives represented a tradition which even fascism had to acknowledge. The fascists did this by renaming the organizations, but even so they were unable to suppress them.[5] Moreover, since they were founded by a political movement, it was only natural that they themselves should become political. It was no surprise, then, that the end of the War found the left holding the reins of leadership in the cooperatives.

In Bologna in 1945 the Ente Comunale di Consumo (founded 1917) controlled 23 retail stores (18 of them in town), plus materiel and capital worth 80 million lire.[6] In the province it was associated with 7 other consumer cooperatives, 35 production and building cooperatives (in particular, the Cement Coop), 8 agricultural groups, and the Cooperative for Reconstruction and Maintenance of Low-cost Housing, the latter owning 1,300 apartments and 32 stores in town. The administrative councils of these organizations were largely controlled by old-line socialist militants, some with anarchist leanings, who felt that each cooperative was free to take a political stand as it wished, regardless of the attitudes of the parties. However, in Bolo-

---

[4] [G. Galli], "Il PCI e la DC nelle amministrazione locali," Bologna, 1965 (manuscript) n.p.

[5] A. Basevi, Sintesi storica del movimento cooperativo italiano (Roma: Rivista della Cooperazione, 1953) 16–19.

[6] CSAS, Organizzazioni cooperativistiche social-comuniste e l'azione del PCI con particolare riguardo all'Emilia Romagna (Bologna: CSAS, 1948) 20–21, mimeographed.

gna, the consumer cooperative was to a great extent dependent on the town hall administered by socialists and communists. Since the communists played the dominant role in this coalition, they found it relatively easy to infiltrate the administration of the cooperative and, by 1947, to seize the key positions for themselves.

However, this was not the same as controlling the National League, which dominated all the cooperatives of the left. The League was still led by prewar socialist militants. The great debate revolved around the question "Should cooperatives be apolitical?" Obviously, the League's administrators answered affirmatively. The communist position was set forth by the Hon. Luigi Longo in October 1946 at the Congress of Roman Communist Cooperators:

> If apolitical means apartitical we agree, but it is an error to believe that cooperation should be apolitical.
>
> It is evident that cooperation has economic motives or objectives, and they can only be attained through political action.[7]

When it came time to vote in 1947, the communists were still part of the national government and had completed their infiltration of the Emilian cooperative movement. It was a foregone conclusion that, backed as they were by the Nenni socialists, they would take over League control. At the twenty-third Congress in Reggio Emilia, the socialist-communist motion won some 85 per cent of the votes, and article 1 of the Statute (apolitical) was amended to apartitical, thus proclaiming the political engagement of all cooperatives in the fight for democracy, peace, and the emancipation of workers. As the Bolognese were to state later, "Cooperatives are an auxiliary instrument in the class struggle for the emancipation of workers."[8] Having won control of the organization, the Communist Party began reorganizing. A single type of statute strengthening the central and provincial organs of the League was promulgated for all cooperatives; the League became, in effect, an instrument of the Communist Party, and its fortunes rose or fell with that institution.[9]

For political and, even more, for financial reasons, the Communist

---

[7] Direzione PCI, "Attività dei gruppi Parlamentari, riservato ai delegati del VII Congresso," *ibid.* 31.

[8] Federazione Provinciale delle Cooperative, *Atti e documenti della cooperazione bolognese 1955–1958* (Bologna: STEB, 1958) 61.

[9] [G. Galli], "I Fiancheggiattori del PCI," Bologna, 1965 (manuscript) p. 202.

Party's control of the League of cooperatives is a key factor in its strength. In 1962 in Emilia (where Bologna and its province represent some 50 per cent of the population) the League had under its wing cooperatives doing a total annual business of 75 billion lire (125 million dollars). Moreover, these are strategic groups, controlling 5 per cent of the nation's agriculture and food sales and 7 per cent of the building industry. These figures are merely prudent estimates.[10]
The distribution in the province of Bologna is as follows:[11]

	Cooperatives		Consumption Coops		Production Coops		Agriculture Coops	
	No.	Membership	No.	Membership	No.	Membership	No.	Membership
1947	394	106,457	83	66,612	260	16,963	51	22,882
1950	385	117,654	71	73,068	168	12,753	49	25,878
1955	384				117	15,200		
1956	297	95,380	64	59,318	101	7,430	33	19,514
1963	256		63		108			

The cooperatives located in Bologna include nearly all trades, from building enterprises to undertakers, from porters to bakers and butchers, from electricity to milk, from fruit to marble, and others. The most important of all is probably the *Cooperative di Consumo del Popolo*, a specialist in the distribution of grocery products, with 46 stores in town, 7 in the immediate environs, and a controlling interest in some 80 other stores. In 1955[12] its annual volume of business was 3.2 billion lire (5 million dollars); in 1962, 8.2 billion lire (13 million dollars).[13] Like a normal capitalist entrepreneur, it sets prices

[10] *Ibid.* 212. The author points out that this is the first time nationwide figures have been published.
[11] Sources:
    1947–1950 "Forza e attività delle organizzazione di massa. Dati statistici," confidential, VII Congresso PCI, Roma, 1950, pp. 37–39.
    1955 Atti e documenti della cooperazione bolognese 1955–1958 18–29.
    1956 CSAS, *Organizzazioni* 25.
    1963 Federazione Provinciale delle Cooperative e Mutue, *Lineamenti di una programmazione pluriennale* pp. 37–49.
[12] CSAS, *Organizzazioni* 30.
[13] Federazione Provinciale delle Cooperative e Mutue, *Lineamenti* 44.

that are the same as elsewhere, and it never hesitates to dispose of
stores that are uneconomic. However, it has certain advantages for
the consumer, not the least of which is the ready extension of credit
to members in good standing. Collecting the balance is relatively
easy in the case of a Party member. Next in importance is the *Cooperativa Italiana Fornaciai*, the province's top cement producer, which,
besides owning several sand, marble, and granite pits, is the largest
manufacturer of prefabricated panels and beams. The CAMST (*Cooperative Albergo, Mensa, Spettacolo e Turismo*) owns two movie
houses, one of which is in the center of town; a travel agency; three
bars; four restaurants (including one in the Central Station); one
hotel; and a pasta factory. Its earnings undoubtedly run well over 1
billion lire (1.5 million dollars). Here again the criterion is business
as usual. The restaurants are among the most attractive in town and
maintain prices that are competitive with the cheapest *trattorie.*
Despite the culinary tradition of the Bolognese, CAMST did not
hesitate to introduce self-service. And in accord with the class division of railway accommodations, one restaurant with two separate
sections (first and second class) is operated at the station to cater
to travelers. The only difference from other restaurants is that the
waiters are less friendly and less obsequious than elsewhere. Apart
from regular income, the advantages for the PCI are many. CAMST
caters to all town hall receptions—and general public funds pay for
party-benefit events. Moreover, it is reported that the after-meeting
snacks enjoyed by local administrators belonging to the majority
party include the finest imported wines. A far cry, indeed, from ordinary proletarian habits! As to the tourist trade, while many trips to
Eastern Europe are promoted, CAMST knows no prejudices. One
of their posters proclaims: "For Easter to Lourdes, with CAMST."[14]

The centralized Party structure is also found at the cooperative
level. Besides the provincial federation, created in 1945 and controlled by the PCI since 1947, Provincial Consortiums were initiated
in 1946 (in 1950 for the rest of Italy). These Consortiums were
assigned the task of purchasing goods in large quantities, a policy
which, theoretically, causes lower prices. In fact, however, the Consortiums were overstaffed, and while benefits were dispersed more
widely, prices either remained the same or increased. Following the

[14] *La Lotta,* March 15, 1962.

Congress of Reggio Emilia this trend toward concentration grew even stronger, and large holdings were established on a national scale: Italian Alliance of Consumption Cooperatives (AICC), of Agricultural Cooperatives (AICA), of production (Laborcoop), of Import-Export (Italcoop), of agricultural machinery (ICMA), of cloth (Tessilcoop). "A commercial organization of exploitation, with a quasi-monopolistic character, for the wholesale buying of products to be sold to the provincial consortiums"[15] now existed. The result of mingling these two factors of specialization and centralization was not as successful as had been predicted, and ended with the creation

> . . . of new obstacles, preventing an effective participation of the base, with which . . . in the majority of cases, the formal exercise of power has become merely a power that consists in the ratification of decisions taken elsewhere.[16]

Since the Party reached the peak of its strength in 1950, a constant, steady decrease in the membership of cooperatives can be noted. Thus, in 1952 the Municipal Committee for Coordination of Cooperative activities was established, and this was supplemented in 1955 by area associations designed to study the problems of each group of cooperatives.[17] The aim of these two groups was to terminate the downward trend in membership, and the cooperatives did experience renewed popularity between 1957 and 1961. However, the economic miracle is more convincing as an explanation for this. Actually, the only cooperatives that have hiked their membership substantially have been those connected with the building industry (37 to 49 per cent), and this increase stems largely from nonactive capitalist members who buy apartments on speculation. Meanwhile, in the second most important sector, consumption, a 3 per cent decrease in cooperative membership in town has occurred[18] at the very moment when the town's population is registering a sharp increase. In view of this downward trend, the cooperatives are beginning to appear as not much more than front organizations controlled by the Party: while not increasing membership, they do provide the PCI with a regular source of income. The fact of the matter is that members are

---

[15] CSAS, Organizzazioni 5.
[16] Federcoop, Bologna, Il Socio delle cooperative. Conclusione 9.
[17] Lineamenti 47–48.
[18] Ibid.

not interested in participating in a movement or a debate where there is little left for them to decide, where until 1959 "any comments on any question had to include at least twenty minutes of talk about the problem of the fight for peace."[19] The red cooperatives still do business today, but they are unable to broaden their social base (by age or by social class) beyond the membership of the Communist and Socialist parties. To the majority of their members, the cooperatives are seen less as economic enterprises offering services than as simply the offshoots of a political party.

In 1958 the Party had 200 political functionaries and 1,500 technicians in the local cooperatives,[20] and to remain a member of the cooperative required a Party card. Prior to that date, the political purpose of the cooperatives was even more evident: in 1949 the Bolognese cooperatives voted 90 million lire (145,000 dollars) to support workers on strike. In 1950, the second symposium of cooperatives agreed to mobilize the whole movement against the government's sabotage actions. In 1954, 100,000 people were helped by the Party cooperatives.[21] After 1958, when the modernizers came to power in Bologna and the general emphasis was on efficiency, the cooperatives returned to the concept of business without active politics, and an increase in benefits to the cooperatives was rationalized as an increase in benefits to the Party.

As a result of controlling the cooperative organization in Bologna, the Communist Party has become the largest entrepreneur in the province, to the point that one can speak of "red capitalism." The base is the municipal administration, which lets all the contracts it can to the cooperatives it controls. This is done openly when bids are not necessary (on contracts involving less than 3 million lire), while larger contracts are divided for the same purpose. In other cases, it is a matter of favoring the communist cooperatives at the time of bidding, often by informing them ahead of time of certain contract clauses that the administration will not require to be fulfilled. In defense of the cooperatives, it must be acknowledged that, because of their financial power, they are usually better equipped than private entrepreneurs and can win the bid anyway. While it might mean

[19] Federcoop Bologna, Il Socio 18.
[20] CSAS, Organizzazioni 36.
[21] Ibid. 19.

working at cost or at a loss, even this may not be disastrous. The PCI needs ways to keep Party members occupied. Furthermore

> . . . a large share of the benefits is reinvested, no longer in the cooperatives but in limited liability companies or in private companies entrusted to reliable members of the Party.

> In such a way . . . a real and proper capitalistic structure has been created, which is in a state of continuous expansion. . . . This phenomenon is peculiar to Bologna.[22]

The financial advantages to the Party are clear and have already been mentioned. To cite an example, after a pasta factory was destroyed by arson in 1954, the 600,000 dollars in insurance money that was collected was not used to rebuild, but in all probability went into the Party coffers.[23] Moreover, indirect financing of the Party by the cooperatives it controls must be listed among these advantages. A great many communist cadres receive their formation in the cooperative movement, and in many cases they frankly admit turning back to the Party part of their salaries in sheer gratitude for having been provided with a job. The cooperatives finance most of the Party's cultural projects, like the Circolo on the main thoroughfare via Rizzoli (characterized by the luxury of the decor and the emptiness of the rooms), as well as some that are not so cultural, such as the Festival dell'Unità. Finally, the cooperatives' policy of assistance to old people and children (holiday camps and Christmas presents) is interpreted in most cases as a Party gift program. The financial benefits, however, are not the only advantages. Of the 6,000–7,000 people in the province who depend on the cooperatives, the great majority are members of the Party on which their livelihood depends, to the extent that the Party card has been called the bread-card.

The second front organization which accrues positive benefits to the Communist Party is the trade union CGIL (Confederazione Generale Italiana del Lavoro). Originally a conglomerate association controlled by the left (June 1947: PCI, 52 per cent; PSI, 30; DC, 12),[24] it was formally dissolved in July 1948 when the Christian democrats walked out. Already in the hands of the Communist Party

---

[22] CSAS, Organizzazioni 35.
[23] Ibid. 30.
[24] [G. Galli] "Movimento sindacale e ruolo dei partiti politici," Bologna, 1965 (manuscript).

and the Nenni socialists, the union died for other reasons than simply that the cold war was beginning. In fact, the PCI and PSI were accusing the capitalists, especially the agrarian capitalists who formed the core of the DC party, of being the leaders of fascism. The DC had no answer to this and, realizing it was being hamstrung in the union as then constituted, decided to establish its own group. An idea of the predominance of communist influence in the Bolognese CGIL can be obtained by noting that while the breakup cost the CGIL 800,000 members in all of Italy, it lost none in Bologna.[25] In the province of Bologna the membership figures are as follows:

	Province[26]	Town[27]
1949	237,250	
1950	227,700	
1956	215,433	161,820
1965	246,000[28]	

Actually, the CGIL organizes some 75 per cent of all organizable workers; however, it must be noted that in Bologna only 32 per cent of the members participate in the union, and only 3 per cent are really active.[29] Thus, in 1958, elections for the internal commissions (enterprise committees) were held in only 229 of some 500 companies,[30] and the CGIL was able to garner 70.7 per cent of the votes as compared to the 22 per cent of its Catholic opponent, the CISL. While these figures reveal that the PCI does not enjoy a monopoly over potential union members, they also disclose that at least two key sector associations do follow Party instructions down the line, even to the point of appearing more violent than the Party itself. These are the building-industry workers controlled by the cooperatives and the public transportation union which the town hall dominates.

The importance of the union to the Party is plain: the size of its membership (twice that of the Party) and the economic and finan-

---

25 Ibid.

26 [A. Ardigò], "Studi sull' organizzazione del PCI in Emilia-Romagna" (Bologna: CSAS, 1958) 22, mimeographed.

27 "La Situazione sindacale a Bologna," Il Mulino 8, no. 87 (March 1959) 146.

28 Vinicio Araldi, Emilia rossa (Roma: Vito Bianco, 1964) 64.

29 [Galli], "Movimento."

30 "La Situazione sindacale," p. 148. Only 31,975 people voted.

cial advantages it brings in its wake are the most noteworthy. More-over, the unions existed before the Party, and in a certain sense their association with the Party enhances its prestige. Furthermore, the union still retains revolutionary ideals which apparently have been abandoned by the Party: the association between a dynamic union and a rigid Party benefits the latter more than the former.[31]

This truth becomes all the more obvious if the extent of the Communist Party's influence over the union is considered. As a matter of fact, the union expands when the Party expands and decreases when the Party decreases.[32] In Bologna the Party controls 75 per cent of the key positions, 90 per cent if left-wing socialists are included; and this has made it possible for the Party to substitute its own personnel for the union's whenever it is deemed necessary that the CGIL follow a particular line. Consequently, the Party can maintain a constant political discourse with the base, acting sometimes as the union, sometimes as the Party.

Besides these profitable front organizations, the Communist Party maintains a number of other groups, largely for reasons of prestige. In theory these are nonpolitical, but in reality they always comprise leftist leaders, with members of the Communist Party invariably holding the key positions. Their principal purpose is to broaden the social base of the Party, but they are also conceived of eventually, as a reservoir of votes, cadres, and finances. In all cases it is the Party which controls these four functions and thus superimposes itself upon the organizations so that they are left with practically no freedom to maneuver within their own spheres of interests.

In the town of Bologna there are three of these groups worth mentioning: the UDI (women), the ANPI (partisans), and the ARCI (recreation). In the case of the UDI (founded in September 1944), Bologna seems to be one of the most efficient provinces. Figures at hand list 33,000 members in 1958 and 20,000 in 1963,[33] with 250 "reference points" (the great number of these contact points seemingly indicating the groups' lack of organization). The majority of the members also belong to a cell, thus demanding a kind of dual citizenship, while the Party supports an association that can only

[31] See Jean Meynaud and Claude Rise, "Il Movimento sindacale in Francia e in Italia," Nord e Sud 9, no. 35, (September 1962) 24.
[32] [Galli], "Movimento."
[33] Ibid.

develop in those social strata that the PCI already controls.

The ANPI[34] was created in May 1945 to further a truly democratic regime and to give moral and material aid to its members and to the families of deceased partisans. In 1947 the Christian democrats left the association, and two years later it was entirely controlled by communists and socialists. The majority of its cadres were absorbed by the local federation, and it was left with one leader and a few functionaries whose duty it was to maintain the ideals of the Resistance and interpret modern Italian history according to the communist outlook. Its membership in Bologna,

1950	18,000
1959	11,600
1963	6,532

is exclusively communist and left-wing socialist, and its decrease is attributable not only to deaths but also to disinterest, as the memories of the War fade away. A brief examination of its newspaper, *Patria Indipendente*, is enough to prove that ANPI's positions invariably coincide with those of the Communist Party, especially in such matters as imperialism and American aggression.

More interesting, inasmuch as it illustrates a method of penetration, is the ARCI (Italian Association for Recreation and Culture) which is an instrument

> . . . to give workers, in an always increasing proportion, a chance to devote their free time to largely democratic and politically educational circles which should be modern and equipped for relaxation, recreation, culture, and sport.[35]

The Association was created in May 1957 and by September of that same year 19 circles had been established in Bologna; in 1961 it controlled 201 circles in the province, 60 of which were in the city.[36] Its influence is greatest in the area of movie distribution, and this is surely worth consideration. Two periods in its history, from 1957 to

---

[34] Interview with cadre Willy Beckers.

[35] E. Lalli, "Per una politica democratica del tempo libero," *Quaderno dell' Attivista* 12 (July 1957) 9.

[36] E. Biondi, "Relazione del presidente provinciale dell' ARCI al congresso Provinciale culturale di Bologna," *Le Ore Libere* 5, nos. 10–11 (April-May 1961) 49.

1962 and from 1962 to the present, should be noted.[37] The first period was devoted to organization, with increasing membership the main object. As a consequence, the Association's activity hinged on the following considerations: the absence of a theater in a village or a part of town, the greater animation of the circle and higher consumption of drinks when a movie was shown, the necessity of giving women some recreational opportunities, and finally cultural needs— only 30 per cent of the films then shown were of high quality.

Starting in 1962, as new university-trained cadres began to arrive on the scene, the emphasis was put on quality (the Association distributing 154 films divided into 35 series), and on careful selection (according to the tastes of the audience to which the films were to be shown). Thus, between September 1962 and March 1963, 548 films were shown, 146 of which were regrouped into 42 series. The most popular of these series are: Russian, 10 out of 42; Czech, 10; Italian neorealism, 4; Flaherty, 3; and American, 3. Of these 42 series, 14 were shown in 2 circles and 28 in 12 others. The conclusions of the authors of the study from which these statistics were extracted, in summing up the impressions of the critic, the manager, and the four Association representatives who led the debates following the showings, are most interesting. First of all, they remark on the difficulty in employing a cultural activity as a means of reaching the diverse membership of the communist-controlled circles, the leaders and patrons of which are more apt to be sensitive to purely recreational or purely political propagandistic activities. Second—and this follows from the previous point—only very limited results may be expected, and even these must be carefully planned for. Since this is the case, it must be admitted that for the Communist Party this activity is one of prestige only.

In general, and especially as far as those associations which have a more openly political aim are concerned, it may safely be said that the Party does not create them or take them over in order to permeate them with a given ideology but rather to control them politically. However, from the moment the PCI takes over an association, that association loses its usefulness as a pressure group, since, with its

---

[37] Luciano Pinelli and Guido Ronconi, "Problemi del cinema contemporaneo," Le Ore Libere 8, nos. 18, 19 (November-December 1963) 106–115 (see also for what follows).

autonomy gone, it must necessarily rely upon Party cadres and often Party finances. In reality, the influence of such groups is restricted to individuals already committed to communist ideals. Thus, such organizations as UDI, ANPI, and to a lesser extent ARCI are no more than organs of prestige, for they neither increase communist voting strength, nor guarantee fruitful contacts with specific sectors of public opinion, nor, finally, enlarge the social base from which the Party draws its cadres and leaders. The fact is that in Bologna the PCI is wealthy enough to maintain them as "luxuries."

The basic weaknesses of the Bolognese Communist Party seem to derive from internal dissensions among the local leaders, and from disagreements between the Bolognese communists and their Roman bosses. These points deserve particular attention, not only because of the weakness they reveal (actually, all major crises have thus far been resolved) but especially because they demonstrate how the principles of democratic centralism and of Rome's final authority over the Bolognese are employed. Simultaneously, the frank expositions of dissident members emphasize weak spots in the Party's organization and policy.

To begin with, all conflict between Party leaders and individual members on questions of morality must be excluded. As a matter of fact, on these grounds the Party is a severe judge, as the municipal assessor Giuseppe Soave had the opportunity to learn.[38] A communist assessor is not supposed to spend his time chasing municipally-employed secretaries or janitors. Invariably, the ostracism employed when a member is expelled on moral grounds is helpful to the Party, which can then point with pride to its lofty moral rectitude.

Most dangerous to the Party are those attacks by individuals or groups which either assail the centrality of the communist organization, and thus question the necessity of a monolithic Party, or which denounce immobilism and thereby destroy the myth of a progressive Party by focusing attention on the accord reached by the Party and the capitalistic groups it is supposed to combat. Illustrations of both modes of assault can be found in the Bolognese federation. In January 1951, following the Provincial Congress of Reggio Emilia, the Cucchi-Magnani case exploded. Aldo Cucchi was a professor of legal

[38] "Epurazione silenziosa nel PCI bolognese," *Documenti sul Comunismo* 2, no. 28 (July 10, 1962) 5.

medicine at the University of Bologna and a militant in the ranks of the Communist Party since 1936. A former commander of the Seventh GAP and the Sixty-second Bolero Brigade and holder of the highest partisan decorations, Cucchi had served as municipal counselor of Bologna and had been elected to Parliament with 7,000 preferential votes.[39] Suddenly, following the line of Magnani, the secretary of the federation of Reggio Emilia, Cucchi resigned from the Party. For over two weeks this pair was to have the honor of the front page in all Italian newspapers except the Unità. The reason for their resignation was announced in a proclamation to "Comrades, partisans, and workers" on January 29, 1951. In effect, the two deputies opposed the concept of total submission to Moscow and rejected the authority of the Cominform, both of which positions had been adopted at the Provincial Congress.
They stated,

> . . . we believe that communists must unconditionally and without subterfuges declare themselves ready to defend the national territory from all future aggressions, from wherever they come.[40]

Clearly, this meant even against the USSR. And their stand was all the more relevant with the Korean War in progress and General Eisenhower's recently completed visit to Rome. In February, the two expanded their thoughts in a pamphlet and declared it impossible to hold real discussions within the Party where "the line is mechanically accepted, where nobody dares to raise objections."[41]

The repercussions for the Party were immense. On the international scene, the Titoists (Pobeda, February 6, 1951) rejoiced, and the Figaro (February 5, 1951) devoted an editorial to the question. In Italy both deputies enjoyed a considerable following, particularly in Reggio and Bologna, and they received many letters of support calling for a truly national Communist Party following an autonomous line.[42] The Party had been taken completely by surprise, having had no reason to question the attachment and devotion of the two men.

---

[39] "I Deputati Magnani e Cucchi abbandonano il PCI" Giornale dell'Emilia, January 28, 1951.
[40] In ibid., January 31, 1951.
[41] V. Magnani and A. Cucchi, Dichiarazioni e documenti (Bologna: Luigi Parma, 1951). Reproduced in Il Giornale dell'Emilia, February 16, 1951.
[42] Giornale dell'Emilia, February 2, 9, 13, 1951.

Dozza, on January 28, mentioned a "moral breakdown";[43] and just before that, between January 25 and 28, efforts were made to force the two deputies to retract their resignations. On February 2, in the words of the Bolognese federation, Aldo Cucchi became . . . "the despicable figure of the traitor, of a man with no principles and no character, a weasel, an agent provocateur of the enemy."[44] That same day he was dismissed from the communist parliamentary group for "indignity" (no resignations are acceptable to the Party), and two days later the ANPI announced the ouster of this most famous partisan of the Bologna area. The following months witnessed a few more defections, but the Party, which had constantly minimized the affair in its press, kept control of the situation. A greater vigilance was imposed, and Cucchi was soon forgotten by the mass of the people.

The case of the Bolognese modernizers is even more interesting because this time the criticism came from the summit of the federation, and a split between Rome and Bologna seemed possible. The growth of this movement took place over a long period of time and can be connected with the problems inherent in local administration. From 1950 to 1953 Emilia had been switching from an economy based solely on agriculture to one that combined industry and agriculture. The local Communist Party had not adequately grasped the situation, and when Dossetti in his 1956 campaign pointed to this as an example of Party immobilism, both the Party's ordinary members and its younger administrators were inclined to agree with him. The latter had grown increasingly restive under the sharp rein of the Stalinist-generation leaders, and they yearned for power.

The second element in the situation was twofold: admission of the possibility of different national ways to socialism; and the Russian intervention in Hungary. Until 1956 the only valid model had been the USSR; the crushing of the Budapest uprising destroyed any belief in Russian humanism that communist intellectuals might have held. Thus, on the one hand there was a climate of unrest and a desire for rejection of the rigid Stalinist methods upon which the Italian Party was based, and on the other hand there loomed an opportunity to bury the past (particularly, the Party's failure to inspire an autonomous revolutionary spirit) without being declared heretics.

---

[43] "Accusati di tradimento . . .," *ibid.*, January 29, 1951.
[44] *Ibid.*, February 2, 1951.

The situation was ripe for action, and as protagonists, the "new wave" of Bolognese communists were men who could make their influence felt by virtue of the positions they held in the local administration and the Party. The most noteworthy of the leaders were Assessors Zangheri (the theoretician of the modernizers), Panieri, Bondi, Soldati (member of the Central Committee of the PCI), and Lorenzini; the Federal Vice-Secretary Fanti; the president of the Federal Control Commission, Vigna; the municipal counsellor, Murotti; and the administrators Caselli and Bettini. However, at this moment there was no question of revolt; this new generation, which had risen to power through the Resistance and been indoctrinated in Party schools, had no intention of attacking the Party's masters. What it wanted was to demonstrate its dynamism and its ability to administer a city according to modern criteria (and this was an indirect criticism of Dozza) by progressing along a purely Italian road to socialism.[45] The basis for this nationalist viewpoint was found in the Hon. Giorgio Amendola's theory which had emerged victorious over the centrality opinion advocated by the Hon. Ingrao at the Seventh National Congress.

Addressing the municipal assembly in Bologna, Amendola would later declare,

> . . . the Emilian communists, the 47,000 Bolognese communists, must fulfill their duty as an *avant-garde*. . . .

> The problem of power cannot be resolved in one town, in one province or region . . . [it cannot be expressed] in local or municipal terms.

> A more intensely democratic life must be developed in the Party.[46]

The authors of the thesis to be discussed in the Ninth Regional Conference were quick to expand on these directives when they declared that the Party had been hampered by "attitudes of petty reformism . . . conservatism and sectarianism,"[47] that its concept of local administration was characterized by rigidity as "an end in itself,"[48]

---

[45] Alberto Mario Rossi, "Il Partito comunista in Emilia," *Il Mulino* 12, no. 123 (January 1963) 30.

[46] Giorgio Amendola, *Discorso all'assemblea cittadina dei comitati di sezione* (Bologna: PCI, 1958) 4, 5, 27.

[47] IX Conferenza Regionale del PCI, *Tesi di discussione Documento interno* (Bologna: PCI, 1959).

[48] *Ibid.*

and that even communist cooperatives were not immune to "capitalistic tendencies."[49]

The subtitle given the Ninth Regional Conference indicated the
line of attack the Bolognese intended to pursue: "For a democratic
and socialist renewal of Emilia Romagna and Italy."[50] The delegates
were quick to point out what was wrong within the Party, and they
spoke with a liberty of expression never heard before. Guido Fanti
pointed to the federation's lack of organic policy,[51] and the delegate
Cicchetti quickly added that because of this,

> The appeal of the Party's ideals has progressively diminished, to the
> point that for years in our work we have been unable to win over a
> worker or an employee.[52]

In his angry criticism of the federation's conduct, Fanti went on to
denounce the "particularism and sectarianism which exist, the anti-
quated conception of relations between Party . . . and mass organization,"[53] and the Party's lack of democracy. He concluded by affirm-
ing how essential it was to "put the leadership in contact with the
base . . . to stimulate collegial work . . . [to avoid] a sectarian tendency
to restrict the use of Party strength to a small circle of comrades."[54]
More concretely, one delegate declared that "the policy concerning
cadres had been one that reduced their roles to merely the practical
work and discipline of comrades who always say yes and are not
supposed to create problems."[55]

While the attack upon the Party's rigidity was undoubtedly violent, the real point at issue was the concept of local administration
held by the Party. As the first speaker said, "to our administrative
competence there has been no corresponding, adequate political
direction."[56] And Fanti called for the abandoning of limited horizons
and "petty reformism"[57] in favor of a "new course"[58] which would be
more beneficial to the Party.

[49] Ibid.
[50] IX Conferenza Regionale "Documenti per delegati" (Bologna: PCI, 1959).
[51] Ibid. 30.
[52] Ibid. 135.
[53] Ibid 38–39.
[54] Ibid. 42–44.
[55] Ibid. 86.
[56] Ibid. 2.
[57] Ibid. 12 and 28.
[58] Ibid. 13.

The period from the conclusion of the Conference until February 1962 can be truly called the high point of the Bolognese modernizers. Criticism of the Party continued; the federation was judged "insufficiently collegial"[59] and Secretary Ghini "not in command of the situation."[60] Dozza had to condemn his own system of administration, and declared that "this conservatism leads to ordinary administrative activity which does not correspond to the complex vision of the general policy of the Party. . . ."[61] As a result, a new policy of local administration was developed, the theory for which was published in the review *Rinnovamento*. It was based upon the creation of new alliances with all antimonopolistic forces—thus to benefit the entire regional society and not only the working class.[62] Its aim was to democratize public life and local administration, to evaluate problems with more precision,[63] and if necessary to destroy the myth of a balanced budget which had been represented as the greatest accomplishment of the communist administration.[64] In fact, a new plan for expansion of the town was drawn up; the first steps for decentralizing the local administration were taken; and the mayor selected representatives from among the opposition parties. Most of the old Stalinists were also removed. At the Tenth Congress of the Italian Communist Party, Guido Fanti was bold enough to urge the delegates to follow the "Bolognese way to socialism."[65]

Thus far, the Bolognese remained orthodox communists: they had criticized the failings of their own federation, had done little to alter it, and had developed a plan that fitted into the framework of the Italian way to socialism. The Twentieth Congress of the Communist Party of the USSR and the destruction of the Stalinist myth were the issues that would create confusion among rank and file members

[59] Federazione di Bologna, "Giudizi del comitato federale sull'attività della Federazione Bolognese del PCI dall'VIII Congresso," October 1959 (Bologna: PCI), mimeographed.

[60] Federazione di Bologna, "Riunione del comitato federale sulla relazione di attività dell'VIII Congresso ad oggi," confidential (Bologna: PCI), n.d. [1959] n.p., mimeographed.

[61] *Ibid.*

[62] Introduction to *Rinnovamento* 1 (January 1960) 5.

[63] Umbro Lorenzini, "Comune e vita democratica," *ibid.* 49–54.

[64] Paolo Fortunati, "Lineamenti politico-economici della finanza locale," *Rinnovamento* 1 (February 1960) 28–37.

[65] Quoted in Gianluigi Degli Esposti, "La Fine dei rinnovatori bolognesi," *Il Mulino* 13, no. 140 (June 1964) 682.

of the Bolognese group and put them on the road to heresy. At a
meeting with all the other federal committees at the end of 1961,
Bologna, represented by Guido Fanti, raised the possibility of creating a minority and majority within the Party. Meanwhile, Cicchetti
was questioning the whole concept of democratic centralism when
he declared, "We have no proof whatsoever to support the view that
democratic centralism has guaranteed a democratic life in the Communist parties."[66] Togliatti, who was present as an observer, responded
by inviting the comrades "to study and research";[67] as a matter of
fact, the Bolognese were pushing their idea of regional action too far
and were no longer in accord with the Party's over-all policy; simultaneously, their views on democratic centralism were undermining
the very foundations of the Italian Communist Party.

The life of the modernizers was not easy; the views they had expressed would soon bring their movement to an end. By April 1960
the review *Rinnovamento*, torpedoed by the local Stalinists, had
ceased publication. And before its demise, its editorials betrayed
either a fatal lack of confidence on the part of the modernizers[68] or
at least a desire to protect themselves. At the end of 1961 the Tenth
Congress of the Communist Party confirmed the victory of Ingrao's
theory over Amendola's, and Togliatti began a gradual reorganization
of the Bolognese Party. He sent a repesentative of the "tough" line,
Iginio Cocchi, to the *Camera del Lavoro* and a Stalinist, Enrico
Bonazzi, to the small Peasant Association, providing the latter with
plenty of free time to handle other matters, in particular the task of
probing the strength of the "heretics" in the base. The Tenth Provincial Congress in 1963 was the turning point. Many Party members
were ready to abolish democratic centralism and thus adopted a position which was equivalent to destroying the monolithism of the
PCI. Fanti, who had sensed the way the wind was blowing—and
possibly thinking of succeeding Dozza—knew this was going too far,
and he returned to an orthodox position.

> We have been too tolerant in allowing individual comrades and organi-
> zations to adopt attitudes which in practice not only differ from but are
> even opposed to the orientations and decisions taken collegially.[69]

[66] Quoted by A. M. Rossi, in *Il Mulino* 36.
[67] *Ibid.*
[68] "Considerazioni sul nostro lavoro," *Rinnovamento* 1 (April 1960) 3–6.
[69] Rossi, in *Il Mulino* 39; Fanti's views are developed in "Il PCI in Emilia,"
Critica Marxista 1, nos. 5–6 (September-December 1963) 246–263.

For those who sincerely believed in the Bolognese modernizers' line, this marked the end. This conviction was particularly strong with Mario Soldati, who convened a secret meeting of the "faithful" following the Tenth Provincial Congress.[70] The strategy agreed upon called for Lorenzini to replace Dozza in the 1964 campaign, so that the new line could be maintained in the local administration. It was believed that Lorenzini was ambitious enough to try to outdo Fanti and, furthermore, that it would be more difficult for the national Party to oust a mayor than an ordinary member of the federation. Unfortunately, the substance of this meeting was repeated to Fanti by Panieri, and the control commission suspended Soldati, Caselli, and Castellucci, while Vigna resigned.[71] The accusation made against these men involved their participation in a "serious episode of political uncouthness," a "union set up outside party lines"—in reality, fractionalism. Since Lorenzini had not been present at the Soldati meeting, he promptly changed sides and returned to the orthodox Togliatti line. Soldati, who had been one of the most famous Bolognese partisans and one of the most popular members of the local Party, returned to private life. He made neither an attempt to defend his position nor any effort to embarrass the Party; he knew his ideas were irretrievably condemned.[72] To all appearances, the new policy was upheld by Lorenzini, finance assessor and acting mayor of Bologna, whom the Party maintained in power in the belief that his ambition to succeed Dozza would make him reliable. As a result, any reaction by the ordinary members who had really believed in the new democratic line developed by Amendola and the Bolognese revisionists was well nigh impossible. The only concrete sign of their disappointment was a slight decrease in Party membership in 1963–1964.

In trying to compare the strengths and weaknesses of the Bolognese Communist Party, one conclusion is certain: the strengths are predominant. In fact, any weakness arising out of internal opposition is negligible when compared to the strength deriving from the organization of the Party. This organization is such that the Party is able to

---

[70] See Degli Esposti, in *Il Mulino* 682–689 for what follows.

[71] "Lotta per il potere tra dirigenti PC," *Il Resto del Carlino*, January 28, 1964.

[72] Killed in an automobile accident on October 23, 1965, Soldati received an official party funeral. The only mention of his heretical views was a reference to his "anticonformistic and complex personality." The funeral oration was given by L. Bergonzini, a second-class member of the federation.

check all opposition at the point of origin and to crush it whenever necessary.

The sole hope of a revisionist resurgence depends on a wavering of the federal secretary. This is highly doubtful, however, since backing by a majority of the PCI would be required, and federal secretaries are not men of such national eminence that they could win such support. Controlled by men in his own federation, supervised from above in Rome, a secretary must submit if he does not want to fall into oblivion.

7: THE COMMUNIST PARTY AND
LOCAL ADMINISTRATION

For twenty years the PCI has ruled Bologna and has been deriving considerable benefit from its privileged position, growing stronger as it fends off each assault launched against it. Today, the Party is the prime beneficiary of the impression of continuity it has created, of the fact that its own conservative attitudes coincide with those of a large proportion of the population, and especially of the system of alliances it has established wherein its socialist partners are completely dwarfed.

Until 1956, when the socialists and communists were formally allied, the predominant position of the left was practically uncontested. Since that time, the communist majority continues to be strong enough to forestall any other combination.[1] As a matter of fact, while an alliance between the DC and the MSI is wholly inconceivable (though some would have liked it in 1951), even a combination of the center-left type, including the liberals, would have garnered only 30 seats, at the most, in 1960 and 29 in 1964. This kind of coalition could govern only if it received the backing of the extreme right.

[1]

	1946	1951	1956	1960	1964
PCI	24	33	29	28	28
PSI	16	6	4	5	4
PSIUP					1
DC	19	10	17	17	14
PRI	1	1			
US		6			
PSDI			5	5	5
PLI		2	2	3	6
MSI		1	3	2	2
Gigante		1			
	60	60	60	60	60

149

The situation appears no different today, and the refusal of two PSI municipal counselors to go along with the new unified Socialist party thus assures the PCI of a majority until the next elections. Consequently, the communists' argument that under the circumstances they constitute the only party that can actually govern the town appears valid. It carries all the more weight if it is pointed out (as the PCI *does* point out, with pleasure) that the probabilities of a center-left coalition obtaining a majority are minimal. In other words, the Bolognese can choose between the present administration, which has proved quite satisfactory, and the appointment of a prefectoral commissar, which is an unknown quantity but which would probably spell the end of the democratic process of local government and lead to the domination of Bologna by a clericalized state. This kind of reasoning can still be effective in a town where the State has never been considered an ally but always an enemy, and consequently the PCI may not be in as precarious a condition as some of its adversaries claim.

Communist concepts of local administration have varied not only according to the local situation but even more so in relation to the Party's general situation. Since the mid-fifties the Party has been in danger of being cut off from the main trends of Italian political life. Bearing this in mind, we can better understand two different positions it has adopted. During the period from 1945 to 1956, when a revolutionary take-over of the country appeared possible (the possibility was genuine, at least until 1947, and was then artificially sustained for the benefit of the masses) and when the rigid Stalinist approach was mandatory, local administration was seen simply as a means of seizing power and of retaining control of the unions. Spurred by the 1956 DC attacks on the Party's alleged immobilism, and particularly since the Italian road to socialism was mapped out in 1958, control of the local administration has been considered a means of coming to power legally rather than a way of seizing power extralegally. It is also seen as a way of proving that the Party has the right to share in the national decision-making processes and thus to avoid being isolated.

These two attitudes are reflected in positions taken by the mayor of Bologna, who in 1947 proposed in Parliament a measure "for a democratic life of the local administrations." Such a law would grant a larger degree of autonomy and would demand "the abolition, pure and simple, of judgment according to merit" by the prefect. Briefly, it proposed

> . . . to give the communes the financial means for an autonomous life which would avoid the humiliating and antidemocratic conditions in which they found themselves during the fascist period when they had to suffer the excesses of the central government.[2]

This line calling for more autonomy was proposed again in a press conference in 1951.

> We do not want to see the autonomy of local government, the strongest guarantee of democratic life in a country, suffocated.
>
> [We] call for a strong and massive intervention from the grass roots as the *sine qua non* for an orderly public life.[3]

On the one hand, greater autonomy would allow the PCI a freer hand if it intended to seize power by illegal means, and, on the other, demands to abolish prefectoral controls would be bound to enlist the sympathies of a majority of democrats.

In keeping with the Italian road to socialism, the positions taken by the Communist Party change radically: the accent is now no longer on autonomy but upon participation in the decisions of the State.

> The municipalities are not outside the State, but are its primary constituent nucleus, the necessary foundation, the thread of the cloth. . . .[4]
> The elected local organs are neither in opposition to the State nor instruments for local demands against the central government. They are an organic expression of the State . . . [from which they derive] powers and competence that are of the same nature as the powers of decision which the State exercises, differing only in a quantitative measure.[5]

The switch from defending local autonomy to demanding a share in the State's responsibilities regarding local administration can be

---

[2] Giuseppe Dozza, *Per una vita democratica delle amminstrazioni locali*, (Roma: Camera dei Deputati, n.d. [March 17–24, 1947], n.p. This proposal of law was in harmony with the seldom applied article 5 of the Constitution.

[3] Giuseppe Dozza, "Il Reato di essere sindaco," *Rinascita* 8, no. 4 (April 1951) 7.

[4] Giuseppe Dozza, *Relazione della Giunta*, March 16, 1960 (Bologna: Comune di Bologna, 1960) 3, mimeographed.

[5] Giuseppe Dozza, *L'Amministrazione bolognese all'inizio del nuovo mandato* (Bologna: Comune di Bologna, 1965) 8–9.

viewed as a tactical move to avoid isolation. But on a more general level, the PCI's changing policies can be attributed to the fact that the Party does control key municipalities and, thus, can see at first hand the deplorable state of the Italian system of local administration: in 1965, Italy's municipalities still operated according to criteria established in 1865 and modified by the fascist regime in 1932. Not only is financial autonomy denied de facto[6] but also any local decision can be vetoed de jure for political reasons.

Looking at the benefits the Communist Party derives from local administration, one can see that in Bologna the Party not only has excellent grounds to complain about the general system but also that it has an adequate concept of what local administration should be. A Bolognese administration notable for its honesty and competence lends irrefutable strength to the PCI argument.

The prime criticism lodged against the communist administration is its alleged inability to plan for the future. This was the main theme of the 1956 campaign and will be examined later when the matter of financial policy is studied. More to the point are attacks on the municipality's unsound budget policy, which became evident when payments were refused the city's suppliers in both 1964 and 1965. As a matter of fact, the administration was able to pay its own employees in those two years only by means of short-term, 8 per cent borrowings. In part, the city's plight was the result of granting salary increases before the local budget was approved by the Central Financial Commission in Rome. But the argument of the municipality also appears convincing: had the financial commission approved the 1964 budget in 1964 and not on January 7, 1965—a delay that made it impossible for the city to contract a loan for 1964—the municipality could have obtained aid and thus been able to meet its expenses.[7] The real problem is that the PCI has all too little influence in Rome, and its efforts to push through an ambitious policy are doomed to failure. Until 1956 the PCI could be attacked because of shoe-string budgets that balanced; today it is assailed because it is too bold.

---

[6] Tito Scipone, "Situation of Municipal Finance in Italy," Review of Economic Conditions in Italy 13 (March 1959) 164–179.
[7] Gli Argomenti del Consiglio Comunale contro le riduzioni al bilancio per il 1964 (Bologna: Comune di Bologna, 1965) 69–72.

The phenomenon called *sotto governo*, to which the preceding remark is not irrelevant, appears to be relatively limited in Bologna. Undoubtedly, considerable padding takes place in the town hall, and all proposals of the *Giunta Municipale* have a political flavor reflecting the views of the Communist Party,[8] but what else should one expect? Even Dossetti acknowledged that the *Giunta* is a political organ, and thus it is scarcely surprising that it takes positions on the atomic bomb or the Vietnamese problem which are identical with those of the Communist Party. Finally, exploitation of the tendency to identify the town hall and the Communist Party is normal. An amazing example, although perhaps in reverse, was the juxtaposition of an exhibit featuring the model of a new garbage disposal system and a gigantic, colored poster calling for more recruits to the Communist Party (January 1965). All in all, whatever communist opponents may say, this kind of action cannot be considered dishonest. Moreover, financial honesty is guaranteed by the rigidity of prefectoral controls. Proof of this is the fact that only one fairly serious attempt was made to attack the PCI on these grounds.[9]

Not only is the communist administration honest but, by Italian standards, efficient and satisfactory as well. This becomes evident in any comparison of Italian cities, even though Bologna itself is far from perfection. The same man, Giuseppe Dozza, was in power from 1945 to 1965, and his governing policies varied according to whether economic considerations or political circumstances prevailed. The period from 1945 to 1956 was characterized by reconstruction and modernization, an entirely normal emphasis if we take into account the destruction caused by war, the old structures that should have been razed long before, and the failure to initiate new construction during the fascist period. Since 1959, new programs—which may be best described as a kind of *aggiornamento*—were undertaken to answer Dossetti's criticism that the communists did not understand the changes that had occurred in the province's economic structure. Not merely a negative response, these undertakings also corresponded to the Party's new line that administration *per se* was not enough.

[8] Giuseppe Dozza, *I Problemi fondamentali dello sviluppo di Bologna* (Bologna: Comune di Bologna, 1965) gives a good example of the unification of socialist forces, pp. 11–12.
[9] Ettore Toffoletto, *Nella Bologna del compagno Dozza* (Bologna: ABES, 1954).

Unfortunately for the town, this new phase has come too late. In this connection, before assessing the accomplishments of the local administration, it must be remembered that when the Italian economic miracle was in its ascendant phase, i.e., between 1956 and 1961–1962, immobilism[10] prevailed in Bologna. By the same token, the bold initiatives later undertaken by local administrators coincided with a descending economic spiral. Thus, it is almost certain that these new programs face rougher going than if they had been started in 1956 or 1958.

The principal objectives of the local administration, insofar as they developed during the 1952–1959 period, can be classified under the headings of current administration, municipalization, and financial policy. So far as financial policy is concerned, the Bolognese communists have always been orthodox in the sense that revenues must cover expenditures. This is evident from a survey of the budgets of the period,[11] and this enviable record in local finance enabled the Communist Party throughout Italy to point to Bologna as a model of local administration even though the reality differed somewhat from the impersonal statistics. The truth is that an appreciable share of the budget was covered by extraordinary taxes, and investments could only be maintained by increasing the municipality's indebtedness. In 1958, for example, the budget actually showed a deficit of 849.6 million lire. A 35 to 50 per cent hike in the tax on consumer goods was necessary to cover this deficit.[12] However, the fact is that

[10] Franco Nasi, "Bologna rossa mia," *Il Giorno*, May 12, 1965.

[11]

	Revenue	Expenditures
	(in millions of lire)	
1951	6,899	6,830
1952	7,688	7,445
1953	10,409	10,254
1954	10,663	10,356
1955	15,715	15,583
1956	14,072	14,070
1957	15,284	15,172
1958	17,611	17,338
1959	18,161	17,878

Comune di Bologna, *Valutazioni e orientamenti per un programma di sviluppo della città di Bologna e del comprensorio* (Bologna: Zanichelli, 1964) 353.

[12] Fernando Felicori, "Bologna non è il Comune modello," *Via Emilia*, February 1, 1958, pp. 10–11.

the Bolognese were, in general, quite content with this situation and were proud of the fact that they had a balanced budget; moreover, in this accomplishment the PCI found its strongest ammunition for increasing its following in local elections as opposed to general elections.

Regarding investment policy, it is clear that in all Italian cities—and not just Bologna—deficit financing and bond issues represent the only way a program of investment can be undertaken,[13] financing by ordinary revenue being impossible. In executing this policy, Bologna, because of its budgetary stability, has always found it relatively easy to obtain the funds necessary to finance the projects approved by the town hall and the Giunta Provinciale Amministrativa (prefect). To sum up, even as we ponder the expenditure and investment policy of the town, Bologna must be recognized as one of the few Italian cities that can easily cover the interest it must pay for financing its investments.

The greatest part of the town's revenues comes from the family tax and the sales tax, both of which have been stepped up sharply as investments have increased.[14] What must be considered is the reasoning behind the method of the tax levy. The town hall has made it a point to "progressively reduce the proportion of taxes which are paid by the working class and the less favored groups of the popula-

[13] Quello che abbiamo fatto (Bologna: PCI, 1964) 14. These figures are estimates and should be decreased by approximately one third, the amount of loans not granted.

(in millions of lire)	Covered by Loans	Covered by Revenue	Total
1951	89	218	307
1952	3671	271	3942
1953	1600	314	1914
1954	1085	485	1570
1955	4969	442	5411
1956	2548	1240	3788
1957	5513	1317	6830
1958	3563	914	4477
1959	4031	1244	5275

[14] Comune di Bologna, Valutazioni 358–359.

	Family Tax	Consumption Tax
1953	100	162
1956	132	227
1959	197	264

tion."[15] Thus the sales tax yields less than 40 per cent of the total revenue; it is distributed as follows:

	Essential Goods	Luxury Goods
1954[16]	45.7	54.3
1960[17]	43.6	56.4

So far as family tax is concerned, 56 per cent of the population is exempt; 30 per cent pay some 14 per cent, 14 pay 50, and 0.3 pay 37.[18]

In the matter of tax policy the local administration has attempted to distribute the levies in proportion to the incomes of the different groups of the population. Generally speaking, it seems that the PCI has adhered quite closely to these lines, though many grounds for compromising the tax bill apparently arise, particularly for the more fortunate social categories.

A second major point of local administration policy is municipalized enterprise. All public utilities are controlled by the town hall, especially those which are normally passive, such as the transportation system. In this respect, town hall policy has been marked by constant but maddeningly slow efforts at modernization,[19] but even these efforts have put Bologna in the forefront of Italian towns. Examples that might be cited include the total mechanization of garbage collection and disposal and the progressive transformation of the transport system from tramways to trolley and standard buses, which was completed in 1962. The caution displayed has been the breeding ground for many of the attacks leveled against the PCI administration, and it has already been admitted that their policy was too conservative. But in defense of the PCI, it must also be said that those who accused it of not being bold enough would also have been the first to brand it as nothing but a spendthrift.

Municipalized pharmacies are probably peculiar to Bologna and constitute an example of progressivism. Their underlying purpose is to provide the town hall with a cheaper way to supply people of

[15] *Quello che abbiamo fatto* (PCI) 18.
[16] Renato Nicolai, *Il Sindaco e la città* 12.
[17] *Quello che abbiamo fatto* (PCI) 19.
[18] *Ibid.*
[19] See "Azienda municipalizzata gas," *L'Azienda municipalizzata gas e acqua dalla liberazione al 1960* (Bologna: Maregrani, 1960).

limited means with needed medicines. Previously, these were purchased in private stores, which were then reimbursed by the town hall. Under the municipalized pharmacy system, the town hall buys the medicines at a wholesale price and thus saves a considerable amount. From the one pharmacy which opened in 1959 in the town hall, there are now eight blanketing the entire town,[20] despite the strong protests of the pharmacists' lobby.

Finally, normal administrative policy must be considered. So far as public works, street and building maintenance, lighting, and expansion of services are concerned, it appears that the policy has corresponded to the necessities of the town. The same can be said for housing policy, whereby the town hall has directly or indirectly financed some 15 per cent of all construction between 1952 and 1960.[21]

Thus, if the entire period from 1952 to 1959 is considered—a period the local administrators boast of as a "modernization" period —it is at once obvious that the essential works have been accomplished but that a conservative policy, reflected in the budget, has been followed. Though a goodly portion of the ordinary maintenance is inevitably done shortly before election time—1956 is a good example—by and large what had to be done has been done, but nothing more. This lack of foresight is the most serious criticism that can be leveled at the local administrators, who have been content to expedite the city's current affairs while paying little heed to its future needs; they have refused to consider the city in the broader context of the regional and national economies.

The years 1959–1960, when the height of the economic expansion was reached and when the communists adopted a new concept of local administration, were also notable as a period for undertaking new projects. To discover the origin of these initiatives, the best place to look is the 1956 platform of the Christian democrats. The new line emphasizes the modernization of services (mechanographical center, computers), the adoption of sociological methods to survey the town's necessities, and the creation of a modern and efficient center for statistical studies. The over-all goal may be summed up in the word "planning," *programmazione*, and is consonant with a general

---

[20] Comune di Bologna, *Notiziario settimanale*, January 25, 1965.
[21] Comune di Bologna, *Valutazioni* 213.

trend throughout Italy that was made specific in 1960 at the Venice
Conference on Local Administration and Planning. Two possibilities loomed on the horizon at that time: regulation of present programs or imposition of a new policy. As might be expected where
strong local administration is concerned, Bologna chose the second
solution.

The Bolognese plan deals with

> . . . the choices, the instruments, and the objectives upon which the
> plan must be founded; the role of the government in a modern planning
> policy: the role that is to be played by the local administration in elab-
> orating and putting into practice a democratic policy of economic and
> social expansion.[22]

Briefly, the plan is designed to establish an organic pattern for the
necessities and priorities of Bologna (seen in the larger complex of
its immediate surroundings) for the years 1963–1970. The possibility
of increasing current expenditures to the point where by 1970 they
will more than double those of 1963[23] has been foreseen, as well as
a quadruple increase in investments during the same period. The
plan itself, which comprises an impressive volume of some five hundred double-column pages, is divided into four parts: a study of the
characteristics and trends of development of Emilia and its economy;
an analysis of the general political and politico-economic problems of
the Bolognese economy, plus the steps required (either centrally or
locally) to find the solution to these problems; an organic exposition
of the problems of the town, by sectors, according to their economic
and social incidence; and, finally, the financing of the plan in the
town's budget. The projects undertaken in the politico-administrative
field and in the administrative field alone, together with their financial consequences, form integral parts of the plan.

As a pioneer among Italian towns in working out its plan, Bologna
has completed the division of the city into fourteen quarters,[24]
according to the provincial law. It has established a council for each
quarter, presided over by a delegate of the mayor, and these councils
became operative in June 1964. The purpose of the division is twofold: on the one hand, the quarters serve as administrative and civic

---

[22] Comune di Bologna, Valutazioni xxi.
[23] Ibid. 333. From 17 to 37 billion lire.
[24] Il Decentramento democratico," Valutazioni 124–133.

centers (distribution of certificates, information, social assistance, etc.), and on the other, through their council they form a link of communication between the population and the town hall. The mayor's delegate is the personally appointed representative of that official, and according to an agreement among all parties except for the right, the number of representatives to which each party is entitled is determined by the percentage of votes registered in municipal elections. The council, in turn, is composed of twenty members, chosen by the municipal council according to the distribution of seats in the town hall. Though the project is expensive (1.65 billion lire over the period 1963–1970), it appears particularly well suited to a town like Bologna which has been undergoing a period of rapid expansion and where it is imperative that the central organs of local government be informed of the requirements of each part of town. Furthermore, the establishment of such positions as those of mayor's delegates and the councils—which eventually will be elected by each quarter—is a step toward democracy. Undoubtedly, it can be viewed as a communist move to politicize all aspects of public and administrative life; however, in an effort to produce constructive opposition the democratic parties have supported the project. Consequently, each quarter now has the means to make its influence felt in a more decisive manner.

Other administrative measures[25] during the period 1960–1964 have been in response to economic necessities, especially in the matter of housing. In fact, since the price of land largely determines the cost of an apartment, the town hall has purchased some 290,000 square meters for the construction of low-cost housing, reselling the property at the low price of 3,000 lire per square meter. This move has not only stimulated the building industry but has also helped end speculation in possible building sites on the outskirts of town.

The local school construction policy has put Bologna in the forefront of Italian towns so far as new projects are concerned. The plan that was adopted sought both to increase the number of buildings and to decentralize as well, at a cost of 8.5 billion lire. While in 1960 only three of the town's quarters—all in or near the center—had secondary schools with space available for 12,048, by 1964 there was a project in the works calling for a school in each of the quarters of

[25] *Quello che abbiamo fatto* 21–37.

town with seats available for 13,800 over-all. This despite the fact that the center of town would lose some 4,000 seats. Simultaneously, the University has received some 500 million lire for scientific research; 700 million was pledged for the newly created faculty of political science, and 50 million has been distributed in scholarship aid. Finally, during the period 1960–1964, 3 billion lire has been allotted to build a highway (autostrada) around the town, while 200 million was appropriated for the local airport.

This ambitious policy has been complicated both by an economic depression and by the length of its term (1970). The inevitable consequence has been a serious financial upset—so grave an upset that Bologna is now on the same level as other Italian towns which have been forced into deficit financing.[26] When the Bolognese budget was balanced, the Central Finance Commission had little to say about a reasonable amount of borrowing. But when the city began to operate on deficit budgets, with borrowing almost quadrupled, it became a different matter. As a result, when the 1963 deficit was set at 3.2 billion, the Central Financial Commission rightly felt that circumstances demanded an austerity policy. This group promptly decreed that the deficit for 1964 should be sliced from 3.2 to 1.9 billion lire,[27] with the State covering 12.5 per cent (against 15.3 in 1963) of the town's ordinary budget. Unable to find credits in Italy to cover the extraordinary expenses of investment, Bologna's city fathers managed

[26] Valutazioni 353. Quello che abbiamo fatto 14. Thus the evolution of the budget:

	Revenues	Expenditures
1960	20,485	20,262
1961	23,012	22,515
1962	21,700	21,700
1963	17,391	20,621 — 3,230
1964	20,225	27,075 — 6,850

	Financed by Loans	Extraordinary Revenue
1960	5,705	950
1961	4,936	1,145
1962	5,788	1,109
1963	19,748	6,231
1964	22,419	5,581

[27] L'opposizione del Comune alla decurtazioni imposte dalla CCFL (Bologna: Comune di Bologna, 1965) 64.

to negotiate a loan of 11 billion lire[28] on the West German financial market. The loan was subject to approval by Italian authorities, who refused to grant permission because of the town's poor economic situation. On the one hand, the incident illustrates the confidence outsiders have in the administrative ability of the Bolognese communists; but, by the same token, it indicates that the plan the Bolognese are pursuing, adequate and necessary as it may be, requires improved economic conditions and less rigidity on the part of the Central Finance Commission. Even should an economic upswing be foreseen, there is no reason to believe that the Commission will be any more lenient with the Bolognese administrators than it has been thus far.

In conclusion, it can be said that the local administration has performed its task adequately and that it has undertaken desirable projects (though later than they should have been undertaken), especially so far as an organic development plan is concerned. But, above all, it is interesting to observe that the Party has been able to convince voters that the new projects are its own, and not what they really are—the entire 1956 Christian democrats' platform. What is even more remarkable is that the local administrators have even been able to persuade their electorate that when their plans meet with failure, the responsibility is not theirs but that of the central DC government. They point, of course, to the central government's refusal to approve credits that could have been obtained abroad, if not in Italy.

Finally, if the communist administrators had initiated their organic plan sooner, during the economic boom days, the chances for success would have been far greater. Today it is obvious that either the plan's financial commitments must be revised or else extended well beyond the original date of 1970. If the latter alternative is chosen, the plan will necessarily be far less effective.

So far as one can judge, this ambitious scheme has shared the fate of many other such ambitious undertakings which have remained on paper only. Shelving of the development plan is not being admitted, though its partial postponement has been attributed to the uncooperative attitude of the central government. Other reasons can be found, such as the struggle in the PCI for Dozza's succession, which

---

[28] *Quello che abbiamo fatto* 16. Thomas Storling, "Lenin Pure Among the Capitalists," *Weekend Telegraph*, November 19, 1965, pp. 9–12.

has led the Party to devote less time to local affairs. With the modernizer Lorenzini (and "liberal" might be a better word) having been shunted aside in favor of Fanti, the latter still must establish his position. More rigid than many of the "new wave" he once headed, Fanti needs a period of calm and quiet: shelving the plan and ignoring its partisans, while at the same time employing the pretext of government opposition, could be a convenient way of obtaining the necessary tranquility.

The question remains: Would the opposition have done any better had it been in power? The communists have actually attempted to put into effect most of the points that were in the local Christian democrats' program of 1956. But when this program was first proposed, Roman Christian democrats were not very sympathetic. The difficulties encountered by the communist administrators today are probably no different from those that would have confronted the Christian democrats had they won the 1956 election. The only difference is that the latter would have started their plan five years before the communists.

Furthermore, if the budgets of towns administered by communists and by Christian democrats are compared,[29] there is no apparent difference. Each does the best job it can with the insufficient means at its disposal. In fact, "the comparison proves that there is no pattern in budget-making that can be attributed to the political coloration of the *giunta*."[30] DC and PCI criticisms of each other on the grounds that administration of certain towns proves the total ineptitude of the party in power are contradicted by facts: both parties administer their budgets in the same way, and in Bologna it is highly improbable that the DC would act very differently from the way the PCI does now. The same answer would apply to the question, "Should local administration be only administration or also politics?" In Bologna Christian democrats call for a purely administrative concept of local government; elsewhere, where they are in power, they appear to view local administration as a completely political matter. In Italy the problems of democratic government are accentuated by the imbalance of the economy and the crying discrepancies of social situations.

---

[29] [G. Galli], "DC e PCI nelle amministrazioni locali," Bologna, 1965 (manuscript).
[30] *Ibid.* 227.

Until some kind of satisfactory arrangement can be found, the PCI will have excellent grounds for voicing its criticisms.

Considering the accomplishments of the local administration in Bologna, especially when compared to the opposition's achievements in those towns where it holds sway, the fact that the communist policy has proved quite satisfactory must be admitted even though its conservatism, paradoxically, has discouraged the development of new industries more than its leftist political orientation. It is only normal that a party benefits when it does a good job of administration. This, plus the factors of strength outlined in previous chapters, explains why some 45 per cent of the Bolognese vote PCI. In any case, benefits now accruing to the Communist Party for its efficient local administration would similarly accrue to any other group that administered the town efficiently.

Some of the benefits derived are uniquely connected with the Communist Party. Economic benefits are practically impossible to prove; that area of administration described as "sottogoverno" is held in tight check by rigid prefectorial controls, though its existence cannot be denied. For example, the administration has always favored the communist-controlled cooperatives for public works, and the latter give kickbacks to the Party. However, the administration demands fairness in the advertising of bids and in their fulfillment. But the red cooperatives are, in fact, far better equipped—and sometimes more efficient—than many of the private enterprises. Thus they can quote equal or lower prices quite readily.[31]

Nevertheless, the benefits really worth considering are the political ones, and paramount among these is the association of the Communist Party with the socialists in the town hall. This association stems from pre-1950 national alliances which today are maintained only on a local level. The alliance is not presently one between equals as it was in 1946; but if the Socialist party wants to remain in power, it must accept a situation wherein it has lost the initiative. Yet, for-

---

[31] It is true, however, that in some cases conditions imposed by the town hall can only be accepted by the cooperatives; the building of an underground passage, wherein a clause required that traffic not be interrupted and invoked a one-million-lire penalty for every day of interruption, might be cited. This was an impossible clause in view of the nature of the work, and only the red cooperatives could accept it since they knew that application of the "no-interruption" clause would be waived.

mally, it remains independent, and this fact is of considerable value to the Communist Party, since it gives voters the illusion of a choice between two different parties. This explains why the Communist Party, so long as it can control the socialists, has not felt it necessary to obtain an absolute majority. In other words, the possibility of unfavorable repercussions among the electorate that could result from such a move is being given due weight.

The second political benefit stems from the continuity of the local administration as personified by Dozza. Twenty years of continuous and prosperous administration constitute a record in any country, and the attractiveness of the local programs helps to explain the influence of the Party on the lower middle class and on circles craving for a protective policy the Party was actually anxious to establish. Even the University has not been immune to this influence, though in this case it is largely a question of personalities; among the past rectors of the Bolognese institution is a communist (Forni), and some of its most distinguished professors have agreed to be "independent" candidates on the Two Towers list in local elections (Olivo, Flora, Favilli).

Furthermore, control of the town hall and the municipal enterprises has enabled the Party to place its members throughout the entire administration, and these people depend on the Party for their daily bread. Today the town hall has over 6,200 people on its payroll (excluding teachers), and merely to meet this payroll requires 46.5 per cent of the city's normal revenue.[32] Town hall personnel have increased by more than 80 per cent since 1959; as is usual in Italy, the number of ushers is far greater than their usefulness.

Finally, the financing of investment programs admits the administration to circles which under normal circumstances it would be unable to penetrate. Local banks like the Cassa di Risparmio are examples. This particular bank loans money for town hall programs and thus has a prime interest in seeing administration promises fulfilled. Moreover, such institutions may very well prefer to grant new loans rather than see confidence in the administration decrease. On the other hand, groups with as widely disparate backgrounds as the Municipal Theater (Teatro Stabile) and the Institute for Nuclear Physics also furnish examples of administration penetration. The

[32] [G. Galli], "DC e PCI" 217.

former depends almost exclusively on grants from the town hall and tends to produce slanted plays. The survival of the latter hinges on Euratom contracts and a yearly subsidy from the town hall; should either contracts or subsidies cease, a desperate financial situation would ensue, and thus the Institute's employees look with favor on the local administration.

In sum, while operating within very narrow limits, the Communist Party in the town hall has still been able to provide a satisfactory, though conservative, administration. By apparently changing its policy in the early sixties, it has cut the ground from under its opposition. Two questions remain to be answered: "What do the people think of their administrators" and "Has voting communist become a habit that no longer depends upon accomplishments?"

8: THE BOLOGNESE AND THE PCI

From a dynamic movement in 1945–1947, the PCI in Bologna, with the exception of the 1959 experimental period, has become progressively more static and monolithic. In spite of this, no signs of decline are visible in the electoral returns, while the proportion of Party votes remains constant in local elections and increases in general ones. The question to be answered is why the Bolognese vote for the PCI; and in this context we must also ask if the Party really has won the allegiance of as large a segment of the population as it contends it has. In attempting to answer these questions, two guidelines should be borne in mind. First, the PCI should be successful at the polls to the degree that it successfully projects its own image as the only proper political movement to represent the burgeoning lower-income brackets of the town's expanding population. Second, this in no way means that the voters will perceive what the Party truly is, believes, and stands for, though some may perceive these things and decide it is easier to live with them than to fight. The alienated state of Italian political culture and the apathy of the Italians with regard to political participation tend to support this contention.[1]

If we grant that the aim of the Communist Party is not only to convince others of the rightness of its immediate program but also of the validity of its ultimate aims and if the guidelines mentioned are supported by our findings, we might conclude that the PCI has failed in Bologna or, at least, that it has only partially succeeded. This conclusion could hold good even though the attractiveness of certain immediate aims, plus the apparatus' intrinsic strength, and the fact that the Bolognese have grown accustomed to living with extremist movements and history enable the PCI to maintain its strength for the present. Proceeding along this line, we now turn our attention

[1] See Gabriel Almond and Sidney Verba, *The Civic Culture* (Princeton: Princeton University Press, 1964) 154–155 and 402–403.

167

to the attitudes of the population vis-à-vis the PCI in general, that is, with respect to the role it performs as a local administrator.

Since we are concerned essentially with the communist electorate,[2] it is interesting to survey the degree of information it possesses and the sources from which this derives. There is little doubt that the apparatus automatically provides Party members (who represent one third of the communist electorate) with select sources of information, such as cells, sections, and unions, to say nothing of the total domination the extreme left exercises over certain quarters of the town. This, however, is helpful only to orthodox Party members in good standing, and such exclusive sources of information do not aid the PCI electorate at large. Moreover, it is our belief—and this will be touched upon later—that exclusive sources of information are not the same as effective sources. Consequently, we will first examine the ordinary sources of information, paramount among which is the press.

The 59 per cent of the Bolognese population who read newspapers regularly (more than three times a week) appears to be above average (Table XIII), with men represented more strongly than women; and the division by parties indicates a correlation between undecided voters and little or no reading.

Table XIII

FREQUENCY OF READING
(in per cent)

	Total	Male	Female	A*	B*	C*
Every day	47	58	36	41	61	17
More than 4 times a week	4	5	3	2	6	2
3–4 times a week	8	6	10	9	6	10
1–2 times a week	10	12	8	14	10	5
Less than 1 time a week	2	1	3	2	2	3
Never, or hardly ever	29	18	40	32	15	63
	100	100	100	100	100	100

* Communist, noncommunist, and undecided voter, respectively.

This cannot be attributed exclusively to an inability to read, since 21 per cent of the undecided voters as compared to 14 per cent of the

[2] Represented by A in tables; B and C indicate respectively the noncommunist and the undecided voter.

PCI electorate have received at least a secondary education; this inde-
cision could just as well be traced back to disinterest and disgust. On
the other hand, the noncommunist group, 52 per cent of which has
had secondary education, would appear better informed. It may be
that the 34 per cent of PCI voters who never, or hardly ever, read
rely instead on the exclusive sources of information at the Party's disposal. It can be assumed that many of these are Party members and
among the less educated.

It is interesting to consider which newspapers the PCI electorate
reads more often.

Table XIV

MORE-OFTEN-READ NEWSPAPER[3]
(in per cent*)

More often read	Total	Male	Female	A	B	C
Il Resto Del Carlino	51	63	40	33	73	27
L'Unità	15	17	12	39	2	—
Stadio	5	9	1	3	4	10
L'Avvenire D'Italia	4	4	3	1	7	—
Carlino-Sera	3	3	2	1	4	3
Avanti!	1	2	1	1	1	2
Il Corriere Della Sera	1	2	1	—	2	—
Il Giorno	1	1	1	1	2	—
La Stampa	1	2	—	1	1	—
Adults that read less than once a week	(31)	(19)	(43)	(34)	(17)	(66)
	113	122	104	114	113	108

* Percentages exceed 100 per cent because of multiple responses.

The supremacy of the local *Carlino*, which can surely be described
as eminently conservative, is striking. Even the communist electorate
relies heavily upon it, while the B group relies exclusively on the
orthodox papers or on its own press (*Avvenire*) and the C group
reads the *Carlino* or the sports paper *Stadio*, but not the *Unità*.
To tell the truth, the communist electorate in general and even some
party members use an opposition paper from which to gather their
information. In the majority of cases this would tend to classify them

[3] Totals are over 100 per cent since some people have indicated more than
one newspaper "more often read."

among those not particularly interested in the political content of the paper and probably more attracted by the local news and the sports columns. The undecided do not read the *Unità*, though some will vote for the PCI; these voters rely upon the leftist sports-oriented *Stadio* and on the *Carlino*, which also devotes a sizable amount of space to the same sports subjects. Some conclusions can be drawn with respect to those who regularly read more than one newspaper and with whom the *Unità* ranks as the most popular second newspaper for the PCI electorate without, however, outdistancing the *Carlino*.

Table XV

MOST-OFTEN-READ SECOND NEWSPAPER[4]
(in per cent*)

	Total	Male	Female	A	B	C
Il Resto Del Carlino	52	64	41	35	74	27
L'Unità	17	19	14	45	2	—
Stadio	7	13	2	5	7	14
L'Avvenire D'Italia	4	4	3	1	7	—
Carlino–Sera	3	4	3	1	4	3
Avanti	2	2	1	2	1	2
Il Corriere Della Sera	1	2	1	—	2	—
Il Giorno	1	1	1	1	2	—
La Stampa	1	2	—	1	1	—
Adults that read less than once a week	(31)	(19)	(43)	(34)	(17)	(66)
	119	130	109	125	117	112

* Multiple responses.

It therefore appears that a higher than ordinary percentage of the population has a regular source of information through the press; this proportion of informed people is much greater if to the press is added those traditional Party channels wherein efforts are expended on the less educated groups of the population. In spite of this, answers to questions about matters heavily stressed by the parties (and in particular, by the PCI) indicate a considerable disinterest in, or ignorance of, all political matters, whether local or national. Before considering this at length, it can be concluded that a high percentage

[4] *Ibid.*

of the communist and undecided electorate is less concerned with a newspaper's political content than with its local columns (shows, necrology, classified advertisements) and sports. All of the latter are found in the *Resto del Carlino*, and significantly this paper reigns supreme as the traditional Bolognese newspaper.

Considering the faith that the PCI electorate displays in its Party and the unorthodox views these electors defend, it could well be inferred that the PCI nonetheless fails to interest, convince, and inform those who vote for it. Many of the votes it receives could then be viewed as "protest-votes," if not mere "habit-votes," rather than as votes arising from clear conviction. One question in the sample was devised to test how effective were the most commonly used communist slogans on the general population and the PCI electorate. The results are summarized in Table XVI.

Table XVI

WHAT WOULD HAPPEN IF THE PCI WERE IN POWER
(in per cent)

	Yes	No	Do not know	Total
1. One would live *better* than now	21	35	44	100
2. There would be *less* liberty	32	23	45	100
3. There *would be* complete religious freedom	23	30	47	100
4. The worker's standard of living *would not* increase	21	27	52	100

There seems to be a general consensus that if the PCI were in power things would be no better. If the negative and "Do not know" answers are considered, it is clear the PCI does not convince the people. Furthermore, if the same questions and answers are studied according to sex,[5] the negative approach is taken more often by men than by women while the latter have more doubts, which hints at the importance of the feminine vote for the PCI in Bologna. Considering the answers of the communist electorate, the voters' basic lack of information on matters constantly raised by their Party is striking.

[5] See appendix five, pp. 203–204.

Table XVII
WHAT WOULD HAPPEN IF THE PARTY WERE IN POWER, COMMUNIST ELECTORATE
(in per cent)

	Yes	No	Do not know	Total
1. One would live *better* than now	53	7	40	100
2. There would be *less* liberty	12	45	43	100
3. There *would be* complete religious freedom	23	30	47	100
4. The worker's standard of living *would not* increase	21	27	52	100

Undoubtedly there is faith in the Party, but in the answers to the first and last and second and third questions a discrepancy can be noted. Taking into account the large percentage of "Do not know" answers on matters essential for the Party image and the sizable number of answers contrary to Party teachings, it must be concluded that many communist voters are uninformed about their own Party, that they accept the PCI as a whole and vote for it even while ignorant of what it pretends to defend. This is confirmed by answers to questions on the center-left and on the most democratic party.

Ever since the beginning of the center-left experiment, with the threat of isolation it poses to the PCI, it has been subjected to the Party's most violent attacks, both in the press and in Parliament. Yet, the communist electorate itself does not hold such radical views, some 20 per cent viewing it favorably and 35 per cent holding no clear opinion on the question.

Table XVIII
THE CENTER-LEFT GOVERNMENT
(in per cent)

	A	B	C
Very satisfied	1	3	—
Rather satisfied	10	18	3
Neither satisfied nor unsatisfied	9	26	7
Unsatisfied	33	23	3
Very unsatisfied	12	3	—
Do not know	35	27	87
	100	100	100

THE BOLOGNESE AND THE PCI

As to which parties are democratic and which are not, views on the PCI are rather divided, though females are prone to see it more democratic than not. It is true that females also hold less clear opinions on this matter (lack of information, education, interest), but all in all the PCI is not considered undemocratic (Table XIX) by the general population.

Table XIX
THE PCI A DEMOCRATIC PARTY
(in per cent)

	Yes	No	Do not know	Total
Males	· 32	37	31	100
Females	29	25	46	100

Simultaneously, 72 per cent of the PCI electors consider the Party democratic, 1 per cent antidemocratic, while 27 per cent are undecided. This demonstrates clearly that the PCI has succeeded in disguising the role played by the apparatus, thus making it a party acceptable to democrats. Contrariwise, the high percentage of undecided among the PCI electorate might be considered as an indication that those who have been exposed to the Party hierarchy are not convinced of its democracy. In responses to the question, "Which is the most democratic party?" (Table XX), it is interesting to observe that while 40 per cent of the communist electorate sees the Party as the most democratic, equally as many have no illusions about the Party's democracy.

Table XX
THE MOST DEMOCRATIC PARTY
(in per cent)

	Total	Males	Females	A
PCI	14	15	13	40
DC	12	11	14	1
PSDIC	8	12	—	—
PSI	6	7	5	2
PLI	5	5	4	—
MSI	1	(.)	1	1
None of these parties is democratic or the most democratic	12	11	13	16
Do not know, no answer	42	39	46	40
	100	100	100	100

Moreover, only 14 per cent of the total population sees it as the most democratic party, even though it polls 45 per cent of the total vote.

In summarizing the various elements submitted, it can be affirmed that the PCI has *not* succeeded in proving to its electorate what it really intends to be and that a large share of this electorate entertains very few illusions about the Party. The high percentage of women who consider the PCI democratic—plus the fact that there are more females who will *not* pronounce it antidemocratic than there are those who are categorical in this matter—illustrates the strength the PCI can wield among the feminine electorate. It might well be in this area that the Party has the greatest opportunity for progress. If the PCI is unable to convince the electorate of its more basic characteristics, it is inevitable that many specific aspects of its program concerned with local affairs will be totally ignored.

Almond and Verba have pointed out quite clearly that civic obligations are felt less in Italy than elsewhere.[6] Thus, in Bologna any great interest or participation in local affairs is not to be expected, and consequently considerable ignorance of matters concerning the local administration must follow. To whatever extent the attitudes of the Bolognese are similar to those of their fellow countrymen, they can nevertheless shed some light both on the basic character of the people and on the degree to which the PCI has failed to penetrate an electorate constituting nearly half the population.

To discover an answer to this, two series of questions were elaborated, one concerning the Bolognese and their local administrators and, the other, the Bolognese and the problems of the local administration. In the first part, the intention was to discover how informed and interested the population is in its administrators. Most striking of all is the universal acceptance of Dozza (Table XXI), an acceptance made plain by the preferential votes he receives, and this indicates, in turn, the Party's success in promoting his image and building his "myth," particularly among males. However, among the communist electorate only 3 per cent vote for the Party solely because of the man nominated, and this explains quite well why no major difficulties were encountered when Dozza was shoved aside in April 1966.

[6] Almond and Verba, *The Civic Culture* 169.

Table XXI

WHO IS THE MAYOR AND TO WHICH PARTY DOES HE BELONG?
(in per cent)

	Total	Male	Female
Know the name	92	96	88
Do not know	8	4	12
	100	100	100
Know the party (PCI)	91	96	85
Do not know	9	4	15
	100	100	100

From this point on, one is confronted by ignorance. The fight over Dozza's succession had been going on since 1959, and accounts had been carried by all the opposition newspapers, particularly the *Carlino*, which is read daily by many communist voters. Yet, just three months before the power was transferred, 89 per cent of the population did not anticipate it: the proportions were 81 per cent for the PCI electorate, 92 for its opponents, and 98 for the undecided. To the question about which party would triumph if a new mayor were to be chosen, of the 19 per cent who expressed an opinion, 75 per cent predicted the PCI. Thus, it can be seen that the PCI has created an image of strength among an uninformed population where the degree of information possessed by the PCI electorate is slightly greater than that of the opponents. This impression of ignorance is confirmed when the electorate is asked about the "modernizers" who rocked the PCI between 1959 and 1961, the views of whom filled the pages of the press in that period. Furthermore, since Soldati had passed away just two months earlier and had been given a Party funeral, it was felt his name at least should be remembered.

This may very well confirm our belief that a majority of the population is not interested in the PCI's internal affairs, perhaps because they realize that the PCI is the strongest party in any case. It can also be regarded as the admirable capacity the Party has for digesting all its internal crises; or as a fact of life that disputes at the summit are not felt at the essentially passive base; or even, possibly, that Communist Party members refuse to commit themselves on such ques-

Table XXII

THE MODERNIZERS
(in per cent)

	Total	Males	Females	A	B	C
Never heard of them	94	91	97	92	94	100
Yes, but remember no name	5	7	3	8	4	–
Yes, and remember the name of						
Soldati	1	2	–	–	2	–
Lorenzini	(.)	(.)	–	–	(.)	–
	100	100	100	100	100	100

tions. Furthermore, the ignorance the Party electorate displays concerning its leaders supports this view. Guido Fanti, the federal secretary and new mayor, and Umbro Lorenzini, the *de facto* mayor until April 1966, are practically unknown by the electorate. To the question, "Have you heard of . . . ?" one obtains the following response.

Table XXIII

BOLOGNESE POLITICIANS
(in per cent)

	GENERAL SAMPLE				COMMUNIST VOTERS			
	Ardigo (DC)	Fanti (PCI)	Felicori (DC)	Lorenzini (PCI)	Ardigo (DC)	Fanti (PCI)	Felicori (DC)	Lorenzini (PCI)
Yes	17	20	18	12	9	22	12	17
No	83	80	82	88	91	78	88	83
	100	100	100	100	100	100	100	100

This result implies that most communist voters who ignore the real Party program are likewise not concerned about the man for whom they vote. Like most Italians, they vote for a party, regardless of its opinions or figureheads, because of the distorted image of the party they have created for themselves. Moreover, if one considers that at least one third of the communist electorate holds membership in the PCI, it can be concluded either that Party statistics are artificially inflated (which is not very likely), that the base is not concerned with the summit and joins the Party for other reasons, or that there is practically no communication (but only anonymous controls) between the summit and the base. Both of these latter arguments are detrimental to a party which considers itself democratic.

The most important problem Bologna and its communist administrators face revolves around the budget, one that is devised to bring about a greater expansion of the town and is passive. This question is raised regularly in all spectrums of press opinion, the *Unità* being the most violent in denouncing the cuts decreed by the Central Commission for Local Finances. The Bolognese themselves, however, are not of this opinion, perhaps because they agree with the old saying that in any case the State will pay. They are concerned, above all, with practical problems such as schooling, housing, unemployment, etc. (Table XXIV) which affect their daily life and toward the solution of which the PCI has devoted so many major efforts. Only 1 per cent, actually, consider the budget an important matter.

Table XXIV
THE MOST URGENT PROBLEMS FOR BOLOGNA
(in per cent*)

	Total	Male	Female	A
Schools, public instruction, aid to children	25	25	25	26
Streets, traffic, parking, policemen, lighting	24	30	18	17
Hospitals, public health	17	14	19	14
Popular housing and town planning	15	18	14	18
Pensions, help to old people	8	6	10	8
Unemployment	7	5	8	10
Public gardens	6	8	5	4
Sport facilities	3	2	3	4
Public services	2	2	2	2
The budget, public finances	1	(.)	2	1
All problems will be solved	3	3	3	9
Other answers	2	2	1	1
I do not know, no answer	34	33	35	29
	147	144	145	143

* Multiple responses.

To the extent that the PCI can solve the practical problems that confront them, many Bolognese are ready to support it, a readiness reflected in the special following the PCI attracts in local elections. That the budget is of no real concern to the population does not mean that the financial situation of the town is ignored (Table XXV).

Table XXV

KNOWLEDGE OF THE FINANCIAL SITUATION
(in per cent)

	Total	Male	Female	A	B	C
Active	(.)	–	(.)	–	1	–
Passive	68	76	62	63	84	84
Balanced	2	2	2	4	1	–
I do not know, no answer	30	22	36	33	14	16
	100	100	100	100	100	100

On the contrary. But the fact is that there is no consensus on what to do about it. Consequently, the average man apparently feels the best policy is to overlook the problem upon which, in any case, he can have no influence. However, the degree of information the population has on this question, in contrast to its ignorance of other questions and its low ranking given to financial problems, is an indication of how important the budget was (and is) for the PCI. Until 1962 the balanced budget could be accurately described as a "myth," but even today the PCI insists it will re-establish this equilibrium, "myth" or not, by the turn of the decade.

If, on the whole, the general population can be considered adequately informed on the state of finances—even though not aware of the full implications of the situation—the same cannot be said with respect to the promises made by the PCI and not fulfilled. Once again this proves that people can often vote for a party and then remain unconcerned about its accomplishments. While some 23 per cent of the general electorate and 49 per cent of the communist electorate think that all the promises made in 1960 were fulfilled by 1965—61 and 44, respectively—express no opinion.[7] One per cent of the A group criticizes the public housing policy, 2 per cent the unemployment situation, and 1 per cent the pension schemes. In other

[7] See appendix five, p. 207.

words, they are vocal on questions which, in all probability, affect them directly. Yet in 1964 the percentage of PCI votes in local elections remained practically constant. The same is true with respect to opinions of the current administration, though less optimism is apparent in this case because of the financial situation. The answers to the questions "Do you believe the local administration can keep the promises it made before the last (1964) local elections?" and "Which promises will not be maintained?" are an illustration of this.

Table XXVI

PROMISES THAT WILL OR WILL NOT BE MAINTAINED
(in per cent*)

	Total	Male	Female	A
All promises will be maintained	15	13	17	34
Many promises will not be maintained because of lack of funds	5	8	3	7
No promises will be maintained	3	4	3	1
Schools	1	–	2	1
Roads, traffic	1	1	–	–
Public housing	1	–	2	1
Public transport	1	1	–	–
Other	1	1	(.)	1
I do not know, no answer	73	72	74	56
	101	100	101	101

* Multiple responses.

The rather large percentage of people who are not concerned whether promises are respected or not but who will give their votes to the PCI anyway is illustrated by remarks about the local administration's accomplishments. Most striking is the fact that this lack of concern for local affairs is common to all groups.

Table XXVII

ACCOMPLISHMENTS OF LOCAL ADMINISTRATION[8]
(in per cent)

	Positive	Negative	Do not know	Total
General sample	14.7	16.7	68.6	100
Communist	28.3	7.9	63.8	100
Anticommunist	8.7	27.7	63.6	100

[8] For a more detailed examination, see appendix five, pp. 204–206.

In concluding this survey about what the Bolognese think of their local administration, a few pertinent remarks should be made. The majority of the population is apathetic on all questions of local administration except for the two points (budget and mayor) upon which the PCI has built its reputation. Those few people who seem genuinely interested (Party members or not) are the ones who are directly affected by local policies on housing, schooling, and public transportation. People who vote for the PCI are not really interested in what it accomplishes. They vote PCI because they perceive that some of its goals are suitable for them. This explains the importance the Party attaches to the myths it has built up around its administrators and their actions; in other words, the Party image is of crucial importance, especially since the PCI has used and still uses Bologna as a point of comparison for other towns.

As a result, to determine why 45 per cent of the inhabitants of Bologna vote for the PCI is deemed an important question. To discover the answer, the most commonly heard slogans and ideas about Bologna were integrated into questions. The results for the general sample are summarized in Table XXVIII.[9]

Table XXVIII

OPINIONS OF THE PCI IN BOLOGNA (GENERAL SAMPLE)
(in per cent)

	True	False	Do not know	Total
The PCI is the only well-organized party in Bologna	40	22	38	100
In Bologna, the communists are too strong; the other parties should reorganize	34	11	55	100
In this part of the country the Resistance was fought almost exclusively by communists	22	29	49	100
Only the PCI has men really capable of administering Bologna	18	37	45	100
The PCI is declining in Bologna	11	29	60	100
The clergy of Bologna participates too much in politics	35	19	46	100

[9] See appendix five for detailed breakdown, pp. 208–209.

A general deep-seated belief persists in the strength of the PCI: the quality of its organization, in particular, is praised to the point that some 30 per cent of the opposition admits that only the communists are sufficiently prepared to wage a political battle. This PCI strength is also acknowledged by the communists themselves, and 10 per cent of their own electorate feels other parties should improve their organization and so make the political competition more worthwhile; this sentiment could be a hint that they would vote for parties like the PSI if there were a chance of success. However, it is also a fact that 38 per cent of the electoral body (respectively, 27 per cent of the PCI voters; 31 per cent men; and 45 per cent women) is either apathetic or else has no idea of that which is very evident: the overwhelming strength of the PCI. The 27 per cent of communist voters who do not grasp the strength of the Party is in all probability comprised of people who cast their vote for the Party while perceiving only the very limited objectives that can ameliorate their personal economic situations. Nevertheless, the feeling does exist, especially among communist opponents and, even more especially, by women than men, that the Party is losing the strength it once held. An objective examination of the PCI can warrant this conclusion, although in extenuation it must be said that the Party has not recently been so concerned with asserting its strength as it once was.

Over the last two decades the PCI has attempted to monopolize Resistance glory, and insofar as one can judge from written publications, it would seem to have succeeded. However, the sampling of opinion proves the contrary; in fact, the role played during the Resistance is of paramount importance only to PCI members, and even among the PCI 46 per cent (the younger members?) has no opinion to express. In studying communist efforts, one is tempted to say that propagandizing the Party membership about the PCI's role in the Resistance affects only those who fought in it. Heroic battles helped the Party get into the town hall, but today the strength of the Resistance myth is practically nonexistent.

Another myth cultivated by the PCI is also nearing its end. Until 1960 it was commonly heard that only the communists had men—led by the genial Dozza—who were capable of administering the town hall. After 1960, the personality of Dozza was played down by the young Turks in order to facilitate his replacement. In this respect the Party seems to have succeeded, though a large share (46 per cent) of the Party electorate is still convinced that only the PCI has the men who can cope with the situation in Bologna.

It has been said many times that a fundamental characteristic of the Bolognese is their anticlericalism. This is confirmed by our study where 35 per cent of the electoral body, communists and noncommunists, men and women alike, agrees that the clergy is overly concerned with politics.

To sum up, the factors of strength pointed out previously still seem valid, especially so far as the fundamental anticlericalism of the population is concerned. Anticlerical Bolognese simply cannot conceive of giving their votes to the DC. Then, too, the image of strength the Party has been able to project through an organization that has functioned for twenty years remains an important factor. Contrary to what was expected, the myths the Party has attempted to create around its Resistance role and the ability of its administration do not appear to have sunk deeply into the minds of the Bolognese, though they cannot be ignored. It is now possible to consider why people vote for the PCI.[10] The results of the sampling pertaining to the general population, men and women, and communist voters are summarized in Table XXIX.

Above all, the fact that 41 per cent either do not know or do not say why people vote communist is rather disquieting. If this response is due in part to disinterest in or ignorance of politics, a goodly percentage is also explainable by a desire to conceal genuine opinions. A similar reluctance was encountered when the interviewee was asked to indicate the Party he had either never voted for or would never vote for.[11] Several remarks can be made about the answers given. Twenty-one per cent of the populace gave answers generally favorable to the Party but went no further: in other words, they perceived only some very fragmentary aims. Reasons of accommodation or interest, successful administration, and possible personal benefits were considered to be good reasons for voting PCI by 14 per cent of the population, and this proportion coincides with the positive judgments that were made regarding the local administration. Explanations of PCI support arising out of Party ideology (17 per cent) are rather low and possibly reflect the practicality of the Bolognese. The answers

---

[10] For the DC see appendix five, p. 207.
[11] Appendix five, p. 203.

Table XXIX

WHY PEOPLE VOTE FOR THE PCI
(in per cent)

	Total	Male	Female	A
They hope to improve, to progress, etc., generical answers favorable to the PCI	21	21	21	20
It is the best party, the party of the working class; I have faith and believe in the PCI	9	9	9	24
Because I hope in a bettering of the conditions of the working class	8	7	8	10
By interest, convenience. It is better to be a communist in Bologna	7	9	6	1
Because of ignorance, illusions, belief in propaganda, etc., negative answers for the PCI	7	11	4	—
Because satisfied with the local administration	5	5	4	8
Because of Dozza	2	3	1	3
Other answers	(.)	(.)	1	1
Do not know, no answer	41	35	46	33
	100	100	100	100

given by the two sexes correspond so far as the over-all perception of Party aims and ideology is concerned. The similarity ceases there, however, and subsequent answers tend to confirm our opinion that women are not as negatively oriented to communism as men and that they are more interested in the global view of communism than in questions relevant to the local administration.

Most pertinent to our subject is the reason why communist votes are cast in the first place. The importance of ideological reasons cannot be ignored, since they are cited in 34 per cent of the answers. It is thought that a rather large proportion of these was given by members or strong sympathizers of the Party who are directly exposed to its influence. This would also tend to be confirmed by the electoral returns where one Party member is accountable for three votes. If ideology is important, there is also the 12 per cent motivated by egoistic reasons (interest, local administration, efficiency, Dozza), a percentage which corresponds rather closely to the general feeling. It is true that the general population assigns 7 per cent to motives of convenience while PCI voters attribute only 1 per cent to such motives; this does not appear to be too significant, however, since communist beneficiaries can hardly be expected to incriminate themselves. What finally becomes evident is that the local administration's success accounts for 8 per cent of the communist vote, a proportion that might grow if undecided voters were also considered. Twenty per cent of the communist electorate appraises the Party positively but in rather vague terms, a percentage which corresponds to the general sentiment. In other words, one fifth of the PCI electors understand the more general aims of the Party and are satisfied that it represents them best, but they are unable to offer a clean-cut explanation for their vote. A reasonable proportion of these can be considered card-holders whom the Party has been unable to indoctrinate with its most fundamental principles. To sum up, it seems that most active Party members vote as they do because of ideological motives, while one third of the communist vote comes from people who either see such a vote as in their interest or else have high regard for the Party's accomplishments in the town hall. The remaining third is probably made up of protest-voters, possibly in the lower income bracket, who seek to improve their lot and consider the PCI as the "party of the poor."

The extremism and anticlericalism of the population, plus the communist role in the Resistance, may well explain how the PCI came to power; and its organization may very well be the factor that maintains it there. But this strength may possibly be limited in time and more apparent than real. To whatever degree the PCI might decide to take radical stands—which so far it has carefully avoided—many Bolognese communist voters could readily switch their preference if radical measures were not in harmony with their interests. In the same sense, were communists to obtain an absolute one-party majority, a much stronger opposition might arise, as happened in 1948 when many believed the leftist front would triumph in Bologna. Communist strength, which today polls between 40 and 45 per cent of the popular vote, is bound to diminish as the economic situation improves. In Bologna and elsewhere, specialized workers cast their votes differently from the ordinary laborer: they favor the PSI and, more and more, the PSDI. Economic development is not conducive to progress for the Party, and this explains why it was in the Party interest to follow the cautious and conservative financial policies approved by the entrepreneurial class and why the development plan had to be shelved. While these policies slowed the development of the town, they brought the Party votes from all social classes. If the PCI were pushed to more radical stands by a unified socialist Party, it could prove to be the Party's downfall.

It can also be hypothesized that a key factor in the PCI's strength in Bologna, one which is not noted elsewhere, can be found in the feminine vote, which is roughly equivalent to the masculine vote. To attribute this factor of strength to the ignorance of Bolognese women is not a sufficient explanation; and the argument that women are both more emotional and less well-informed than men and that they, therefore, tend to vote for extremist parties is unsatisfactory and rests on no substantial evidence. It is our opinion that women constitute a secure reserve of communist votes in Bologna because they are as politicized, as anticlerical, and as dechristianized as the men.

What strikes the observer of the Bolognese scene (but conflicts sharply with the opinion of themselves held by the Bolognese) is the populace's general disinterest in participating in politics and its lack of information on political matters. This apathy has served the PCI well in its creation of a mythical image of efficiency and competence and has enabled it to win many an extra ballot. Bologna is a town of many apathetic people, plus a few parochial partisans who are essentially practical and among whom the myths cultivated by the PCI have played a dominant role. Thus the Party has been able to thrive and develop its organization. To the extent that these myths disappear—as they are doing today—and to the degree that the economic situation betters and Party cadres grow older, the PCI should tend to stabilize in Bologna, as has been happening during the last three years.

It is because of this apathy that we believe the PCI has failed in Bologna. In spite of all its efforts to politicize all questions and to win over the population—presenting itself to the poor as a revolutionary and to the rich as a conservative group—it has proved itself unable to interest a majority of the population, even if we include many supporters who vote for it as a reaction to their personal economic destitution. Furthermore, in accepting the conservative policies of businessmen, who considered these policies as a kind of economic protectionism, the PCI has played into the hands of the very class it sought to control. In the late 1950's, this occurred again when a younger and more dynamic entrepreneurial and political class appeared on the local scene, demanding more economic expansion even at the cost of stronger political competition. In brief, the PCI in Bologna is controlled by, as much as it controls, the milieu it has tried to change. In view of Bologna's past and also of its future, it is possible that what the city needs is a more dynamic left than the PCI is capable of providing. The new, unified Socialist party might be the answer.

Appendices

APPENDIX ONE

THE RESISTANCE

The Leftist Press of the Bolognese Resistance

1. *Rinascita*: regional organ of the Union for Peace and Liberty (PC-PSI-PdA). Two issues, August 18 and 28, 1943. Printed. 25,000 copies for Emilia Romagna.

2. *LaVoce dell'Operaio*: organ of the Bolognese working class. Two issues. Mimeographed and printed. 4,500 copies. Published by Agitation Committee for Factories.

3. *Avanti*: Socialist party. Twenty-one (two-page) issues. Printed. Unknown circulation.

4. *La Lotta*: organ of the Communist Federation of Bologna. Six issues, January 1944–March 1945. Printed. 4,500 copies.

5. *Orizzonti di Libertà*: PdA. One issue, March 1944 (four pages). Printed. Unknown circulation.

6. *La Voce dei Campi*: organ of Laborers. One issue, June 1944. Unknown circulation.

7. *Unità*: central organ of the Communist Party. Emilian edition. Twenty-five issues, July 1944–April 1945. Printed. 4,000–5,000 copies.

8. *Il Lavoratore Agricole*: organ of laborers. Two issues, July–September 1944. Printed. Continuation of *Voce dei Campi*.

9. *Tempi Nuovi*: intellectual group. A. Labriola. Two issues, July 1944 (16 pages); March 1945 (44 pages). Printed. Unknown circulation.

10. *La Rinascita*: organ of the Provincial Committee of the Youth Front. Four issues after July 1944. Mimeographed. (The group had up to 7,000 members.) Unknown circulation.

11. *Il Combattente*: organ of CUMER. Three issues, from August 1, 1944. Printed. Unknown circulation.

12. *Rivoluzione Socialista*: youth groups of PSUP. Three issues, from December 15, 1944. Typewritten.

13. *La Voce della Donna*: organ of Women's Defense Groups. Five issues, from December 1944. Mimeographed and printed. Unknown circulation.

14. *Compagna:* feminine groups of PSUP. Two issues, late 1944. Printed. Unknown circulation.

15. *Avanti-Unità and Unità-Avanti!:* published by PSI and PCI. One issue, December 1944. Printed. Unknown circulation.

16. *L'Ardimento:* organ of the Seventh Brigade GAP. One issue, January 1945. Printed. Unknown circulation.

17. *L'Attacco:* organ of Bolognese Brigade SAP. Two issues, January 1945. Mimeographed. 3,000 copies.

18. *La Squilla:* organ of PSIUP. One issue, April 1945. Printed. Unknown circulation.

Source: L. Arbizzani, "Periodici della Resistenza stampati a Bologna," *Garibaldini e partigiani* (Bologna: Galileo, 1960) 142–180.

Bolognese Partisan Brigades

Partisan Division Bologna (Mountain) "Wolf"

Brigade Red Star	(Independent, but Communist Commander)
36th Brigade Garibaldi	(PC)
Matteotti Brigade (Mountain)	(PSI)
Brigade Justice and Liberty	(PdA)
62nd Brigade Garibaldi	(PC)
66th Brigade Garibaldi	(PC)

Partisan Division Bologna (Plain) "Mario"

7th Brigade GAP, Arditi Gianni		(PC)
1st "	Irma Bandiera	(PC)
2nd "	Paolo	(PC)
63rd "	Bolero ——	(PC)
4th "	Venturoli	(PC)
5th "	Bonvicini	(PC)
6th "	Giacomo	(PC)
8th "	Masia	(PdA)
9th "	S. Justa	(DC) *
Brigade Matteotti Citta		(PSI) **

Operating Outside the Province

Divisione Nannetti (Belluno)	(PC)
Divisione Modena (Modena)	(PC)

Source: Antonio Meluschi, ed., *Epopea partigiana* (Bologna: ed. SPER, n.d.) [1947?] 1. (Categories supplied by present writer.)
* Formed in January 1945.
** Formed end of 1944.

APPENDIX TWO

Population Increase

1. Absolute figures

1921	205,452
1931	243,474
1941	321,957
1951	340,427
1961	448,679
1963	475,664
1964	482,438

2. Natural increase of population

	Births	Deaths		
1950	3,195 (9.4 ‰)	3,353 (9.9 ‰)	—	158
1955	3,768 (10.2 ‰)	3,498 (9.5 ‰)	+	270
1960	4,941 (11.4 ‰)	4,168 (9.6 ‰)	+	773
1961	6,399 (13.6 ‰)	4,437 (9.5 ‰)	+	1,962

3. Increase of population due to immigration

	Immigrated	Emigrated	
1950	10,800 (31.9 ‰)	4,303 (12.7 ‰)	+ 6,497
1955	15,317 (41.5 ‰)	5,666 (15.1 ‰)	+ 9,651
1960	20,899 (48.7 ‰)	7,333 (16.9 ‰)	+13,566
1963	21,957 (46.8 ‰)	10,932 (23.3 ‰)	+11,025

Source: Comune di Bologna, Ripartizione Statistica, Annuario statistico 1963 24, and Bollettino mensile di statistica (December 1964) 249.

Immigrants According to Origin

ORIGIN	1951	1952	1953	1954	1955	1956	1957	1958	1959	1960	1962‡	1963
Province of Bologna												
Mountain									1,118	1,623	1,492	1,366
Hills									2,756	3,233	2,367	2,231
Plain									3,872	4,717	3,445	3,263
Total Province	4,580	2,916	4,943	8,876	8,093	9,703	9,143	10,213	7,816	9,573	7,304	6,860
Other Provinces of Emilia									3,833	4,537	3,539	3,542
Total Emilia									11,649	14,110	10,843	10,402
Other Regions	4,375	4,230	5,529	7,074	6,902	8,782	8,704	10,239	5,742	6,417	7,038	7,784
Abroad†	143	75	81	117	312	218	224	344	276	372	562	644
General Total	9,098	7,221	10,553	16,067	15,317	18,713	18,091	20,796	17,667	20,899	18,443	18,830

Source: Compilation of Comune di Bologna, Annuario statistico (1951–1963).

† Abroad: mainly from former colonial possessions.

‡ Statistics for 1961 not available.

APPENDIX THREE

Vote Distribution in the Various Sections of Town 1956–1958

1. Variations of the electoral body 1956–1958

Zones	1956		1958		Variation	
	N°	%	N°	%	N°	%
Zone A	82,447	28.98	78,198	25.91	−4,249	−3.01
Zone B	24,276	8.51	27,118	8.98	+2,842	+0.47
Zone C	45,190	15.85	51,470	17.05	+6,280	+1.20
Zone D	62,716	22.00	65,616	21.74	+2,900	−0.26
Zone E	14,417	5.06	16,356	5.42	+1,939	+0.36
Zone F	56,057	19.66	63,074	20.90	+7,017	+1.24
Total	285,103	100.00	301,832	100.00	+16,729	——

2. Party variations, Zone A

Parties	1956		1958		Variation	
	Valid Vote	%	Valid Vote	%	Valid Vote	%
PCI	25,604	33.61	17,479	23.97	−8,125	−9.64
PSI	4,383	5.75	7,734	10.60	+3,351	+4.85
PSDI	7,056	9.26	7,502	10.29	+ 446	+1.03
PRI–Radical	1,237	1.62	1,629	2.23	+ 398	+0.61
DC	26,472	34.75	26,364	36.15	− 108	+1.40
PLI	5,849	7.68	6,959	9.54	+1,110	+1.86
Right	5,585	7.33	5,263	7.22	− 322	−0.11
Total	76,186	100.00	72,930	100.00	−3,256	——

3. Party variations, Zone B

Parties	1956		1958		Variation	
	Valid Vote	%	Valid Vote	%	Valid Vote	%
PCI	4,873	21.66	3,807	15.18	−1,066	−6.48
PSI	1,205	5.36	2,170	8.65	+ 965	+3.29
PSDI	2,136	9.50	2,602	10.37	+ 466	+0.87
PRI–Radical	601	2.67	788	3.14	+ 187	+0.47
DC	9,381	41.71	10,366	41.32	+ 985	−0.39
PLI	2,542	11.30	3,526	14.06	+ 984	+2.76
Right	1,755	7.80	1,825	7.28	+ 70	−0.52
Total	22,493	100.00	25,084	100.00	+2,591	——

4. Party variations, Zone C

Parties	1956		1958		Variation	
	Valid Vote	%	Valid Vote	%	Valid Vote	%
PCI	17,920	42.15	16,344	33.07	−1,576	−9.08
PSI	2,894	6.81	6,128	12.40	+3,234	+5.59
PSDI	4,217	9.92	5,411	10.95	+1,192	+1.03
PRI–Radical	604	1.42	839	1.70	+ 235	+0.28
DC	12,884	30.30	15,333	31.03	+2,449	+0.73
PLI	1,716	4.04	2,621	5.30	+ 905	+1.26
Right	2,278	5.36	2,742	5.55	+ 464	+0.19
Total	42,513	100.00	49,418	100.00	+6,905	——

5. Party variations, Zone D

Parties	1956		1958		Variation	
	Valid Vote	%	Valid Vote	%	Valid Vote	%
PCI	29,045	49.32	25,304	40.63	−3,741	−8.69
PSI	5,482	9.31	9,415	15.12	+3,933	+5.81
PSDI	5,594	9.50	6,623	10.63	+1,029	+1.13
PRI–Radical	653	1.11	814	1.31	+ 161	+0.20
DC	14,167	24.05	15,200	24.41	+1,033	+0.36
PLI	1,435	2.44	2,048	3.29	+ 613	+0.85
Right	2,516	4.27	2,874	4.61	+ 358	+0.34
Total	58,892	100.00	62,278	100.00	+3,386	——

6. Party variations, Zone E

Parties	1956 Valid Vote	%	1958 Valid Vote	%	Variation Valid Vote	%
PCI	8,921	65.32	9,195	57.93	+ 274	−7.39
PSI	1,100	8.05	2,135	13.45	+1,035	+5.40
PSDI	843	6.17	1,059	6.67	+ 216	+0.50
PRI–Radical	56	0.41	103	0.65	+ 47	−0.24
DC	2,332	17.08	2,702	17.02	+ 370	−0.06
PLI	135	0.99	281	1.77	+ 146	+0.78
Right	271	1.98	399	2.51	+ 128	+0.53
Total	13,658	100.00	15,874	100.00	+2,216	——

7. Party variations, Zone F

Parties	1956 Valid Vote	%	1958 Valid Vote	%	Variation Valid Vote	%
PCI	34,460	64.78	33,693	55.47	− 767	−9.31
PSI	4,829	9.08	9,179	15.1	+4,350	+6.03
PSDI	3,231	6.07	4,037	6.65	+ 806	+0.58
PRI–Radical	271	0.51	490	0.81	+ 219	+0.30
DC	8,582	16.13	10,578	17.42	+1,996	+1.29
PLI	722	1.36	1,118	1.84	+ 396	+0.48
Right	1,104	2.07	1,643	2.70	+ 539	+0.63
Total	53,199	100.00	60,738	100.00	+7,539	——

Source: A. Ardigò, "Il Volto elettorale di Bologna," in A. Spreafico and J. La Palombara, *Elezioni e comportamento politico in Italia* (Milano: Comunità, 1963) 820–831.

APPENDIX FOUR

The Questionnaire

I am an interviewer of the DOXA Institute. We are carrying out a public opinion survey among the Bolognese.

1. Let us consider daily newspapers (evening and morning newspapers and sports papers). Do you read any of these newspapers . . .?

   Everyday?   Once or twice a week?
   Over 4 times a week?   Less than once a week?
   Three to four times a week?   Never or almost never?

(If answer other than "less than once a week," ask):

2a. Which daily newspaper did you read most often in the last few weeks? Was it any of the dailies mentioned on this list?

2b. Have you recently read any *other* dailies *regularly*, that is, *at least once a week?* Which?

> Avanti!
> L'Avvenire d'Italia
> Carlino–Sera
> Il Corriere della Sera
> Il Giorno
> Il Resto del Carlino
> La Stampa
> L'Unità
> Stadio
> Other dailies:

3. In your opinion, are the people who a year ago were in favor of the center-left government satisfied or disappointed today with the government's activity during the past year?

4. In your opinion, is it possible to be a *good communist* (member of the PCI) and a good *Catholic* at the same time?

5. In your opinion, if the PCI held the majority in Parliament a few years later (please read every question) . . .
Would we *live better* than we live now?
Would there be *less freedom?*
Would *fewer opportunities* be offered to capable people?
Would there be *less unemployment* in Italy?
Would *wages and salaries* rise?
Would there be complete *religious freedom?*
Would there be *more injustice* in Italy?
Would the living standard of *workers not* improve?

6a. Which of these parties may be considered *sincerely democratic* and which may not be considered democratic?

6b. (For parties mentioned as democratic.): Which of these parties is the *most democratic?*

6c. (For parties mentioned as *nondemocratic*): In your opinion, may any of these parties be considered a *danger to democracy?* Which?

PCI
PSI
PSDI
DC
PLI
MSI
None

7. Do you know the name of the *Mayor of Bologna* and which party he belongs to?

8. If a *new* mayor of Bologna had to be elected in a short time, who has the *greatest chance* of being elected mayor of this town, in your opinion? Which party does he belong to?

9a. Have you heard about any members of the PCI in Bologna being called "modernizers" because of their political attitude? (If yes): Do you recall the names of any of these "renewers"? (If informant heard about "renewers"):

9b. What do you think about the ideas and attitudes of these communists who are defined as "renewers"?

10. Here is a list of persons who are more or less known in the political circles of Bologna. You should kindly tell me, for each person:
(a) *Have you ever heard of . . .?*

(b) (If yes): Have you heard good or bad opinions about . . .?

(c) In your mind if . . . (name of person) were appointed mayor of Bologna in the next few years, would he be able to fulfill his task well?

Ardigò	Fanti	Felicori	Lorenzini
(DC)	(PCI)	(DC)	(PCI)

11. If the majority of the Town Council of Bologna were made up of several parties, not just one party, which parties should it consist of?

12. In your opinion, which are the most pressing problems to be solved in this "commune"?

13a. Do you think that in the last few years the City Administration of Bologna maintained the engagements assumed (the promises made) at the end of 1960, before the (last-but-one) administrative elections?

13b. Which engagements has it not maintained?

14a. Do you think the City Administration of Bologna will be able to maintain, in the next 2–3 years, the engagements assumed (the promises made) at the end of 1964 before the (last) administrative elections?

14b. Which engagements will it not be able to maintain?

15a. Did the City Administration do anything right the last 2–3 years? (If yes): Which were its most useful, most advantageous decisions, initiatives, provisions in favor of Bologna and of families such as yours?

15b. In the last 2–3 years, did the City Administration do anything wrong? (If yes): Which and how many serious errors did they make? In other words, which were the decisions, initiatives, provisions most detrimental to Bologna and to families such as yours?

16. Now would you please express your opinion on what the administration of Bologna did in the last few years. In your mind, should a positive or negative opinion be given about . . .

Economic and industrial development of this "commune" (more industries, more jobs)?

Roads and means of transport?

Building of new schools in this "commune" and assistance to pupils and students?

Trade problems (opening of new shops, licenses, etc.)?
Ability to offer the same treatment to all citizens, independently of their political ideas?
Solution of problems regarding city quarters, administrative decentralization?
Ability to solve budget problems of this commune?
Ability to obtain loans and funds for local needs?
Fair distribution of taxes among all the categories of citizens?

17. Do you know whether the budget of the "commune" of Bologna for the past financial year showed a credit, a deficit, or a balance?

18a. At the present moment, is it better for the Bolognese that the City Administration make higher expenses for important public works, even if this implies a great deficit, or cut down expenditure to keep the budget in balance?

18b. (If answer other than "Do not know"): Why?

19. In the administrative elections in Bologna 20 to 25 per cent of voters vote for the Christian Democratic party. In your opinion, why do many people vote for the DC? In other words, what do they expect from the DC? What do they want the DC to do in Bologna?

20. In the administrative elections in Bologna, from 40 to 45 per cent of voters vote for the "Two Tower" list. In your opinion, why do many people vote for this list? In other words, what do they expect from the candidates of this list who, as is well known, are prevailing members of the Italian Communist Party?

21. One may hear various things said about the political situation in Bologna. (Please read every statement.) In your opinion, is it true or false that . . .

The PCI is the only well-organized party in Bologna?
Communists are too strong in Bologna; other parties should become stronger?
The Resistance movement was conducted in this area essentially by the communists?
Only the PCI has men who are well-prepared and capable of running the "commune" of Bologna?
The PCI is getting weaker in Bologna; it is no longer so strong and efficient as in past years?

In Bologna the clergy is too often concerned with political problems?

Other answer:

And now would you kindly answer some questions on your political preferences.

22a. In the interest of the "commune" of Bologna, which political party should get more votes during the next administrative elections? (If vague answer): Which party in particular?

(If "the socialists," "left-wing parties," and similar answers):

22b. Which party in particular: the PCI, PSIUP, PSI, or PSDI?

23a. Which of the lists mentioned on this facsimile of a voting paper *did you vote* for on the last administrative elections (November 1964)?

23b. Which of the parties represented by these symbols *did you never vote for*? Which do you feel you *will never vote for*?

Classification Data

24a. In your family are there any children or young people:
   under 6?
   between 6 and 11?
   between 12 and 17?

24b. How many persons does this family consist of (including adults, teenagers, and children)?

25. Is the informant the household head?

26. Occupation of informant and household head?

27. The informant (or household head) had:
   A dependent occupation (civil service, etc.)?
   An independent occupation (owner of a firm, professional, etc.)?
   Is unemployed?
   Other occupational condition, namely:

28. Does your family own . . .
   Radio set?
   TV set?
   Motor-vehicle?
   Car?

29. Last school attended by informant?
    Elementary school or no schooling?
    Lower secondary school, vocational school?
    Higher secondary school?
    University?

30. Informant's sex?

31. Informant's age?

For the Interviewer Only

32. Total monthly income of household (estimate):

    Up to 70,000 Lire   151,000–200,000 Lire
    71,000–90,000 Lire   201,000–300,000 Lire
    91,000–120,000 Lire   Over 300,000 Lire
    121,000–150,000 Lire

33. Economic and social standing of household:

    Upper   Lower middle
    Upper middle   Lower
    Middle

APPENDIX FIVE

Sample Returns

For Which Party Did You Vote in the Last Local Elections (1964)
(in per cent)

	Total	A
Due Torri (PCI)	17	47
PSIUP	–	–
PSI	2	–
PSDI	5	–
PRI	–	–
DC	6	–
PLI	5	–
PDIUM	(.)	–
MSI	(.)	–
Never voted	2	1
Refuse to answer	63	52
	100	100

What Would Happen If the PCI Were in Power
(in per cent)

	Males			
	Yes	No	Do not know	Total
One would live better than now	24	38	38	100
There would be less liberty	36	25	39	100
There would be complete religious freedom	26	33	41	100
The worker's standard of living would not increase	23	31	46	100

Females

	Yes	No	Do not know	Total
One would live better than now	17	33	50	100
There would be less liberty	29	21	50	100
There would be complete religious freedom	21	26	53	100
The worker's standard of living would not increase	19	24	57	100

Accomplishments of the Local Administration
(in per cent)

	General Sample						
	Compl. pos.	Mostly pos.	Neither pos. nor neg.	Mostly neg.	Compl. neg.	Do not know	Total
Economic and industrial development of the commune (new industries, new jobs)	3	9	3	8	7	70	100
Roads and means of transport	5	15	3	15	17	45	100
Building new schools and assistance to students	3	13	4	14	20	46	100
Trade problems: opening of new shops, licenses, etc.	3	5	3	5	10	74	100
Ability to offer the same treatment to all citizens independently of their political ideas	3	7	2	4	7	77	100
Solutions of problems regarding city quarters, administrative decentralization	6	14	3	4	4	69	100
Ability to solve budget problems of this commune	3	5	1	7	9	75	100
Ability to obtain loans and funds for local needs	3	7	1	3	4	82	100
Fair distribution of taxes among all categories of citizens	2	6	1	3	8	80	100

Communist Voters
(in per cent)

	Compl. pos.	Mostly pos.	Neither pos. nor neg.	Mostly neg.	Compl. neg.	Do not know	Total
Economic and industrial development of the commune (new industries, new jobs)	7	21	2	–	2	68	100
Roads and means of transport	9	29	2	13	13	34	100
Building new schools and assistance to students	8	24	4	9	16	39	100
Trade problems: opening of new shops, licenses, etc.	7	14	2	2	3	72	100
Ability to offer the same treatment to all citizens independently of their political ideas	7	15	3	2	1	72	100
Solution of problems regarding city quarters, administrative decentralization	11	22	1	2	–	64	100
Ability to obtain loans and funds for local needs	8	24	2	4	–	72	100
Ability to solve budget problems of this commune	7	12	2	2	–	77	100
Fair distribution of taxes among all categories of citizens	6	13	1	1	1	78	100

Noncommunist Voters
(in per cent)

	Compl. pos.	Mostly pos.	Neither pos. nor neg.	Mostly neg.	Compl. neg.	Do not know	Total
Economic and industrial development of the commune (new industries, new jobs)	2	4	5	16	12	61	100
Roads and means of transport	2	8	4	20	27	39	100
Building new schools and assistance to students	1	6	4	22	28	39	100
Trade problems: opening of new shops, licenses, etc.	1	1	3	9	18	68	100
Ability to offer the same treatment to all citizens independently of their political ideas	–	2	2	6	15	75	100
Solution of problems regarding city quarters, administrative decentralization	3	12	5	5	9	66	100
Ability to solve budget problems of this commune	1	1	1	10	18	69	100
Ability to obtain loans and funds for local needs	1	6	–	5	10	78	100
Fair distribution of taxes among all categories of citizens	–	3	1	5	15	76	100

Why People Vote for the DC
(in per cent*)

	Total	Male	Female	A
They have their ideas, believe in their ideology, are convinced, believe in the DC	10	10	10	10
Are afraid of communism, want to fight it	11	11	11	4
Are Christians, for religion, for the Church	8	7	9	10
Want well-being, liberty, a little democracy, and other positive answers for the DC	8	12	5	4
To defend their interests, by interest	6	8	4	12
They seek to create a majority to oppose to the present one because they want to change the communist administration	4	5	3	1
Because they do not know what they are doing, are ignorant, do not understand and other negative comments on the DC	4	5	3	8
Other answer	(.)	–	1	–
Do not know, no answer	50	43	56	52
	101	101	102	101

* Percentages exceed 100 per cent because of multiple responses.

Promises Maintained (and Not Maintained) by the Local Administration After the 1960 Local Elections
(in per cent*)

	Out of 100 interviewees			
	Total	Male	Female	A
All promises maintained	20	17	22	43
All that could be done was done	3	4	2	6
All of many promises were not maintained	7	11	3	2
Not maintained				
Road maintenance, traffic	5	5	5	–
Schools	3	4	3	1
Public building, housing, urbanistic plan	1	2	(.)	1
Hospitals	1	1	2	–
Unemployment	1	1	(.)	2
Pensions	1	–	2	1
Administrative decentralization	(.)	1	–	–
Sports development (stadium, etc.)	(.)	–	1	–
Other	1	1	1	2
Do not know, no answer	61	59	62	44
	104	106	103	101

* Multiple responses.

Opinions of the PCI in Bologna (Males)
(in per cent)

	True	False	Do not know	Total
The PCI is the only well-organized party in Bologna	46	23	31	100
In Bologna, the communists are too strong; the other parties should re-organize	38	12	50	100
In this part of the country the Resistance was fought almost exclusively by communists	25	33	42	100
Only the PCI has men really capable of administering Bologna	20	38	42	100
The PCI is declining in Bologna	8	33	59	100
The clergy of Bologna participates too much in politics	39	18	43	100

Opinions of the PCI in Bologna (Females)
(in per cent)

	True	False	Do not know	Total
The PCI is the only well-organized party in Bologna	34	21	45	100
In Bologna, the communists are too strong; the other parties should re-organize	31	10	59	100
In this part of the country the Resistance was fought almost exclusively by communists	18	26	56	100
Only the PCI has men really capable of administering Bologna	16	36	48	100
The PCI is declining in Bologna	12	26	62	100
The clergy of Bologna participates too much in politics	31	19	50	100

Opinions of the PCI in Bologna (PCI Voters)
(in per cent)

	True	False	Do not know	Total
The PCI is the only well-organized party in Bologna	69	4	27	100
In Bologna, the communists are too strong; the other parties should re-organize	10	20	70	100
In this part of the country the Resistance was fought almost exclusively by communists	47	7	46	100
Only the PCI has men really capable of administering Bologna	46	10	44	100
The PCI is declining in Bologna	2	55	43	100
The clergy of Bologna participates too much in politics	57	2	41	100

Opinions of the PCI in Bologna (Noncommunists)
(in per cent)

	True	False	Do not know	Total
The PCI is the only well-organized party in Bologna	29	42	29	100
In Bologna, the communists are too strong; the other parties should re-organize	62	8	30	100
In this part of the country the Resistance was fought almost exclusively by communists	10	55	35	100
Only the PCI has men really capable of administering Bologna	3	68	29	100
The PCI is declining in Bologna	20	20	60	100
The clergy of Bologna participates too much in politics	29	36	35	100

APPENDIX SIX

The Bolognese Business World and the Communist Party

During the months of November-December 1965, some fifteen interviews were granted to the author by Bolognese businessmen who agreed to discuss the political problems of the town frankly, provided their names would not be mentioned. The following is a summary of the opinions most frequently expressed.

The economic world of Bologna is based on small and medium-size units. Today, as in the past, it does not produce "big" businessmen or sizable industries (no budget is over 20 billion lire and there are no enterprises employing more than 1,500 employees and workers). In agriculture, the basic unit is generally small.

The Bolognese businessman, above all, takes into account the current situation, dominated as it is by the PCI, a domination that could only be increased if the regions were to be established. In consequence, though he sympathizes with center-right parties (PLI), he must consider the political climate of the zone in which he operates. A situation in which he would take clear-cut opposing positions would render profitable activity impossible or, at least, very difficult. Furthermore, he has been accustomed to such a situation since the days of fascism.

This being said, and considering the cumbersome Italian bureaucracy, business cannot ignore the presence of economic institutions (cooperatives) controlled by the PCI; nor, in the field of labor, the strong discipline imposed by the CGIL; nor in the field of bureaucracy, the dependence upon the town hall where taxation, licenses, building permits, etc., are concerned. Having the choice between agreement or bearing the consequences of disagreement, all Bolognese businessmen find it necessary to adopt the first solution, even if this means an ideological and sometimes a financial sacrifice. Agreement has been richly rewarded by the PCI, which has long known how to exercise its influence most meaningfully and thereby leaves a certain amount of flexibility to the entrepreneurs, especially the smaller ones.

Thus, relations of mutual interest have been created—and the initiative comes from the PCI, inasmuch as it is impossible to ignore the economic organs controlled directly or indirectly by the town hall and the Party. To perform his function of producer, the industrialist must enjoy normal, and even cordial, relations with the town hall, which is the biggest buyer on the local market. If an enterprise wants to build a plant in an area not yet classified as industrial, it is the town hall that must assent. When a company or a private citizen wants to build an apartment house, it is with the town hall that either of them must discuss the size of the building.

In the last several years, the town hall of Bologna has extended its authority over the adjacent communes where industries have tended ever more frequently to locate. For the industries, the aim is to make use of relatively cheap agricultural areas; for the communes concerned, this means an increase of revenue through taxation. What can be a favorable operation for both thus plays to the advantage of the PCI; the PCI controls the municipalities, and it is the Party, more than the municipalities, that consents to an agricultural zone being reclassified as industrial. And the consent is often accompanied by some form of compensation.

To sum up, the economic world of Bologna has been obliged to put ideology aside to operate successfully. It is true it has done this with ease and has become accustomed to the situation. However, a majority of businessmen feel this situation is an unhappy one. The domination of one party creates a rigid system that renders the entrepreneurs' activity timorous and uncertain. This rigidity certainly does not attract new initiatives from the outside, initiatives which otherwise would find fertile ground for cultivation in Bologna.

Selected Bibliography

A. BOOKS

Adams, John Clarke, and Barile, Paolo. *The Government of Republican Italy.* Boston: Houghton and Mifflin Company, 1961.

Almond, Gabriel. *The Appeals of Communism.* Princeton: Princeton University Press, 1958.

————, and Verba, Sidney. *The Civic Culture.* Princeton: Princeton University Press, 1963.

Amendola, Giorgio. *Discorso all'assemblea cittadina dei comitati di sezione.* Bologna: PCI, 1958.

Ammassari, Paolo. "Opinione politica e scelta elettorale." *Elezioni e comportamento politico in Italia.* Milano: Comunità, 1963.

Araldi, Vinicio. *Emilia rossa.* Roma: Vito Bianco, 1964.

Arbizzani, Luigi, ed. *Bologna è libera.* Bologna: ANPI, 1965.

————, ed. *Garibaldi combatte.* Bologna: La Lotta, 1965.

————. *Garibaldini e partigiani, almanacco bolognese 1960.* Bologna: Galileo, 1960.

————. *La Brigata di Pampurio.* Bologna: La Lotta, 1963.

————. *La Stampa clandestina nella Resistenza bolognese.* Bologna: La Lotta, 1962.

————. *Le Donne emiliane nella Resistenza.* Bologna: La Lotta, 1964.

————. "Lotte agrarie in Provincia di Bologna nel primo dopoguerra." *La Campagna emiliana nell'epoca moderna.* Milano: Feltrinelli, 1957.

————. *Sguardi sull'ultimo secolo. Bologna e la sua provincia.* Bologna: Galileo, 1960.

Archidiocesi di Bologna. *Annuario diocesano 1963.* Bologna: UTOA, 1964.

————. *Il Cardinale Lercaro.* Bologna: UTOA, 1964.

————. *Piccolo sinodo diocesano 1962.* Bologna: UTOA, 1963.

Ardigò, Achille. "Il Volto elettorale di Bologna." *Elezioni e comportamento politico in Italia.* Milano: Comunità 1963.

[Ardigò, Achille]. "Studi sull'organizzazione del PCI in Emilia-Romagna." Bologna: CSAS, 1958. Mimeographed.

Argomenti del consiglio comunale contro le riduzioni al bilancio per il 1964. Bologna: Comune di Bologna, 1965.

Atti Parlamentari. Legislatura XXV, Sessione 1919–1921. Camera dei Deputati, Documento XXI. Roma: Tipografia dello Stato, 1921.

Barbieri, Remigio. *Al di qua della Gengis Khan.* Bologna: Galileo, 1965.

Barzini, Luigi, Jr. *The Italians*. New York: Bantam, 1965.

Bassi, Enrico. *Avanti! dal 1943 al 1945. L'Edizione clandestina bolognese.* Bologna: CVL, 1965.

Battaglia, Roberto. *Storia della Resistenza*. Second edition. Torino: Einaudi, 1964.

Basevi, A. *Sintesi storica del movimento cooperativo italiano.* Roma: Edizione Rivista della Cooperazione, 1953.

Beckers, Willy. *Banden! Waffen Raus!* Bologna: Alfa, 1965.

Bedeschi, Lorenzo. *Malefatte della rossa Emilia.* Bologna: ABES, 1953.

Bergonzoni, Luciano. *Clero e Resistenza.* Bologna: Cantelli, 1965.

Chabod, Federico. *L'Italia contemporanea 1918–1948.* Torino: Einaudi, 1961.

Comune di Bologna. Ripartizione Statistica. *Annuario statistico 1963.* Serie II–3. Bologna: ARTIP, 1965.

————. Ripartizione Statistica. *Bollettino mensile di statistica.* December 1964. Bologna: ARTIP, 1965.

————. *Valutazioni e orientamenti per un programma di sviluppo della città di Bologna e del comprensorio.* Bologna: Zanichelli, 1964.

CUMER. *Due mesi di attività partigiana in Emilia-Romagna.* Bologna, 1944.

"Dati riassuntivi del censimento diocesano." *Il Cardinale Lercaro.* Bologna: UTOA, 1964.

Degli Esposti, Gianluigi. *Bologna PCI.* Bologna: Mulino, 1966.

Della Torre, Guiseppe. *Azione Cattolica e fascismo.* Roma: AVE, 1965.

Democrazia Cristiana. *Bologna a una svolta.* Bologna: Resto del Carlino, 1956.

————. *Libro bianco su Bologna.* Bologna: Resto del Carlino, 1956.

Dogan, Mattei. "Le Donne italiane tra Cattolicesimo e Marxismo." *Elezioni e comportamento politico in Italia.* Milano: Comunità, 1963.

————. "Stratificazione sociale ed elezioni." *Elezioni e comportamento politico in Italia.* Milano: Comunità, 1963.

Dozza, Giuseppe. *I Problemi fondamentali dello sviluppo di Bologna.* Bologna: Comune di Bologna, 1965.

————. *L'Amministrazione bolognese all'inizio del nuovo mandato.* Bologna: Comune di Bologna, 1965.

————. *Per una vita democratica delle amministrazioni locali.* Roma: Camera dei Deputati, 1947.

————. *Relazione della Giunta*, March 16, 1960. Bologna: Comune di Bologna, 1960.

Einaudi, Luigi. *Il Buon Governo.* Bari: Laterza, 1964.

————, and Repace, Alessandro. *Il Sistema tributario italiano.* Fifth edition. Torino: Einaudi, 1954.

Facchi, Pietro. *La Propaganda politica in Italia*. Bologna: Il Mulino, 1960.

Falconi, Carlo. *Le Organizzazioni cattoliche in Italia, 1945–1955*. Torino: Einaudi, 1956.

Federazione Provinciale delle Cooperative e Mutue. Bologna. *Atti e documenti della cooperazione bolognese 1955–1958. Quaderni di Battaglia Cooperativa*. Bologna: STEB, 1958.

Galli, Giorgio. *Storia del Partito Comunista Italiano*. Milano: Schwarz, 1958.

Guidicini, Paolo. "Aspetti della morfologia sociale di Bologna." *Elezioni e comportamento politico in Italia*. Milano: Comunità, 1963.

"Inchiesta sulla messa nel comune di Bologna." *Il Cardinale Lercaro*. Bologna: UTOA, 1964.

Jemolo, Arturo Carlo. *Chiesa e Stato in Italia negli ultimi cento anni*. Second edition. Torino: Einaudi, 1963.

Kogan, Norman. *The Government of Italy*. New York: Thomas Y. Crowell Co., 1962.

La Palombara, Joseph. "Orientamento dei giovani." *Elezioni e comportamento politico in Italia*. Milano: Comunità, 1963.

_____. *Interest Groups in Italian Politics*. Princeton: Princeton University Press, 1964.

_____, and Spreafico, Alberto. *Elezioni e comportamento politico in Italia*. Milano: Comunità, 1963.

Lercaro, Giacomo. *Sociologia religiosa e azione pastorale. Discorsi del Cardinale G. Lercaro*. Roma: Herder, 1964.

Longo, Luigi. *Un Popolo alla macchia*. Second edition. Roma: Editori Riuniti, 1965.

Meluschi, Antonio, ed. *Epopea partigiana*. Bologna: SPER, n.d. [1947].

Nenni, Pietro. *Storia di quattro anni, 1919–1922*. Second edition. Roma: Einaudi, 1946.

Nicolai, Renato. *Il Sindaco e la città*. Roma: Editori Riuniti, 1956.

Onofri, Nazario Sauro. *28 Giugno 1914, i socialisti a Palazzo d'Accursio*. Bologna: Quaderni della Squilla, 1964.

Organizzazioni cooperativistiche social-comuniste e l'azione del PCI con particolare riguardo all'Emilia-Romagna. Bologna: CSAS, 1948.

Pancaldi, Bertrando. *Verso la libertà*. Bologna: CVL, 1965.

Partito Comunista Italiano-Federazione Bolognese. *IX Conferenza Regionale. Tesi di discussione*. Bologna: PCI, 1959.

_____. *Federazione Bolognese. IX Conferenza Regionale. Testi*. Bologna: PCI, 1959.

_____. *Federazione Bolognese. VII Congresso Provinciale. Testi*. Bologna: PCI, n.d. [1950].

Pintor, Giaime. *Il Sangue d'Europa*. Torino: Einaudi, 1965.

Pryce, Roy. *The Italian Election of 1956.* London: Chatto and Windus, 1957.

Salvatorelli, Luigi. *La Politica della Chiesa in Italia* [R. Petrazzoni, ed.]. Bari: Laterza, 1957.

————, and Mira, Giovanni. *Storia d'Italia nel periodo fascista.* Second edition. Torino: Einaudi, 1964.

Salvemini, Gaetano. *Scritti sul fascismo.* Volume 1. Milano: Feltrinelli, 1961.

Secchia, Pietro, and Frassati, Filippo. *La Resistenza e gli alleati.* Milano: Feltrinelli, 1962.

Spreafico, Alberto. "Orientamento politico e identificazione partitica." *Elezioni e comportamento politico in Italia.* Milano: Comunità, 1963.

————, and La Palombara, Joseph. *Elezioni e comportamento politico in Italia.* Milano: Comunità, 1963.

Toffoletto, Ettore. *Nella Bologna del compagno Dozza.* Bologna: ABES, 1954.

Togliatti, Palmiro. *Discorsi sull'Emilia.* Bologna: Arte Stampa, 1964.

————. *Politica comunista.* Roma: PCI, 1945.

————. *La Via italiana al socialismo.* Roma: Editori Riuniti, 1965.

Toschi, Tommaso. *La Maschera e il volto.* Second edition. Bologna: ABES, 1953.

Valente, Concetto. *La Ribellione anti-socialista di Bologna.* Bologna: Cappelli, 1921.

Visentini, Luciano. "Osservazione sulla propaganda elettorale." *Elezioni e comportamento politico in Italia.* Milano: Comunità, 1963.

Webster, Richard A. *The Cross and the Fasces.* Stanford: Stanford University Press, 1960.

Zanobini, Guido. *Corso di diritto amministrativo.* Volume 4. Latest edition. Milano: Giuffrè, 1958–1959.

B. PERIODICALS

Arbizzani, Luigi. "Giacomo Lercaro, arcivescovo di Bologna." *Rinascita* 16, no. 11 (November 1959) 785–792.

————. "L'Avvento del fascismo nel bolognese 1920–1922." *Movimento Operaio e Socialista* 10, no. 2 (April-June 1964); 3–4 (July-December 1964).

Archidocesi di Bologna. *Bollettino Diocesano* (June 1953).

Ardigò, Achille. "Indagine sul comportamento elettorale a Bologna." *Il Mulino* 8 (April 1958) 207–216.

————. "Note sulle strutture delle città emiliano-romagnole." *Civitas* 9, no. 10–11 (October-November 1958) 41–78.

Biondi, Emilio. "Relazione del presidente provinciale dell'ARCI al congresso provinciale culturale di Bologne." *Le Ore Libere* 5, no. 10–11 (April-May 1961) 45–59.

Biral, Bruno. "Giugno 1956." *Il Ponte* 12, no. 6 (June 1956) 936–940.

Bollettino Doxa (November 15, 1964).

Bonazzi, C. "Aspetti della Resistenza bolognese." *Rinascita* 9, no. 4, 207–211.

Citti, Vittorio. "Voto e ceti sociali." *Il Mulino* 7, no. 78 (April 1958) 216–238.

"Considerazioni sul nostro lavoro." *Rinnovamento* 1, no. 4 (April 1960) 3–7.

Contessi, Pier Luigi. "Bologna sbattezzata." *Il Mulino* 5, no. 58 (July 1956) 411–415.

d'Amato, Luigi. "Il Voto di preferenza." *Rassegna Italiana di Sociologia* 3, no. 2 (April-June 1962) 205–238.

Degli Esposti, Gianluigi. "La Fine dei rinnovatori bolognesi." *Il Mulino* 13, no. 140 (June 1964) 682–688.

D. F. "Pratica religiosa e atteggiamento politico a Bologna." *Questitalia* 5 (November-December 1962) 650–663.

"Diritti e doveri del clero." *Bollettino DOXA* 17 (1958).

Dozza, Giuseppe. "Il Reato di essere sindaco." *Rinascita* 8, no. 4 (April 1951) 6–12.

Dozza, Giuseppe. "La Fine del fascismo a Bologna." *Rinascita* 12, no. 4 (April 1955) 285–288.

Edelman, Murray. "Causes of Fluctuations in Popular Support of the Italian Communist Party since 1946." *Journal of Politics* 20 (August 1958) 535–553.

"Emilia." *Rivista di Cultura* (April 1955). Special Issue.

"Epurazione silenziosa nel PCI bolognese." *Documenti sul Comunismo* 2, no. 28 (July 10, 1962) 5.

Fanti, Guido. "Il PCI in Emilia." *Critica Marxista* 1, no. 5–6 (September-December 1963) 246–263.

Fortunati, Paolo. "Lineamenti politico-economici della finanza locale." *Rinnovamento* 1, no. 2 (February 1960) 28–38.

"Il Clero e le elezioni." *Rinascita* 5, no. 3 (March 1948) 98–99.

"Italy." *Time Magazine*, November 20, 1964.

Jerkov, Antonio. "Cronaca." *Il Punto* (August 29, 1959) 4.

————. "La Chiesa cattolica e le elezioni italiane." *Problemi del Socialismo* 6 (April 1963) 477–479.

Lalli, E. "Per una politica democratica del tempo libero." *Quaderno dell' Attivista,* no. 12 (July 1957) 9.

"La Situazione sindacale a Bologna." *Il Mulino* 8, no. 87 (March 1959) 146–149.

Lorenzini, Umbro. "Comune e vita democratica." *Rinnovamento* 1, no. 1 (January 1960) 49–56.

"Lei è stato in chiesa." *Bollettino DOXA,* 3–4, February 26, 1962.

Magri, Lucio. "Le Amministrative a Bologna." *Dibattito Politico* 12 (April 9, 1956) 15–17, 22.

Matteucci, Nicola. "Dossetti a Bologna." *Il Mulino* 5, no. 57 (June 1956) 382–391.

Meynaud, Jean. "Chiesa cattolica in Italia e in Francia." *Nord e Sud* 9, no. 36 (October 1962) 22–41.

————, and Rise, Claude. "Il Movimento sindacale in Francia e in Italia." *Nord e Sud* 9, no. 35 (September 1962) 24–43.

Nicolai, Renato. "Realizzazione della amministrazione democratica della città di Bologna." *Rinascita* 13 (March 1956) 150–155.

Pedrazzi, Luigi. "Cattolici non democristiani." *Il Mulino* 10, no. 108 (September 1961) 636–644.

————. "Il Ritorno di Dossetti." *Il Mulino* 5, no. 54 (March 1956) 225–229.

Pinelli, Luciano, and Roncone, Guido. "Problemi del cinema contemporaneo." *Le Ore Libere* 8, no. 18–19 (November-December 1963) 106–115.

Prandi, Alfonso. "Il Pericolo del comunismo e la coscienza cristiana." *Il Mulino* 13, no. 143 (September 1964) 957–969.

————. "La Campagna elettorale nella provincia emiliana." *Il Mulino* 5, no. 57 (June 1956) 403–411.

————. "L'Opposizione cattolica e la religiosità italiana." *Il Mulino* 3, no. 36 (October 1954) 622–640.

————. "Nota sulla politica dei cattolici." *Il Mulino* 3, no. 32 (June 1954) 422–430.

"Religione e politica." *Bollettino DOXA* 4–5 (March 23, 1963).

Rossi, Alberto Mario. "Il Partito communista in Emilia." *Il Mulino* 12, no. 123 (January 1963) 28–42.

Scepis, Giovanni. "I Sistemi elettorali e loro classificazione." *Amministrazione Civile* 2 (March-April 1958) 59–68.

Scipone, Tito. "Situation of Municipal Finance in Italy." *Review of Economic Conditions in Italy* 13 (March 1959) 164–179.

Secchia, Pietro. "L'Organizzazione del partito e del suo lavoro tra le masse al centro della Resistenza contro il fascismo." *Quaderno di Rinascita* 2, n.d. [1962] 85–89.

Settembrini, A. "La Chiesa in Italia." *L'Astrolabio* 1 (June 25, 1963) 36–39.
Storling, Thomas. "Lenin Pure Among the Capitalists." *Weekend Telegraph*, November 19, 1965, pp. 9–12.
Vicariato di Roma, *Bollettino d'Informazione* (March-April 1956).
Wiskemann, Elisabeth. "Socialism and Communism in Italy." *Foreign Affairs* 24 (April 1946) 484–493.

C. UNPUBLISHED MATERIAL

[Ardigò, Achille]. "Dalle previsioni ai risultati delle elezioni amministrative del 1956 nel comune di Bologna. Indagine campionaria." Bologna: CSAS, n.d. [1957] n.p. [29]. Typewritten.
[————]. "Relazione sull'influenza territoriale dei centri religiosi (Parrocchie) sull'orientamento politico (eseguite sui dati ricavati dalle elezioni amministrative del 1956.)" Bologna: CSAS, n.d. [1958] n.p. [3]. Typewritten.
Citti, Vittorio. "Voto e ceti sociali nel 1958." Bologna CSAS, n.d. [1959]. Typewritten.
Comune di Bologna, Ufficio Meccanografico. "Elezioni amminstrative 1960, elezioni politiche 1963. Risultati ufficiali per sezioni elettorali," n.d. [1964].
"Elezioni politiche e amministrative. Risultati," n.d. [1965]. Mimeographed.
[Galli, Giorgio]. "I Fiancheggiatori del PCI." Bologna, 1965. Manuscript.
[————]. "Il PCI e la DC nelle amministrazioni locali." Bologna, 1965. Manuscript.
[————]. "Movimento sindacale e ruolo dei partiti politici." Bologna, 1965. Manuscript.
Partito Comunista Italiano. "Forza e attività delle organizzazioni di massa. Dati statistici." Riservato. VII Congresso Nazionale del PCI. Roma: PCI, 1950.
————. "Forza e attività del partito. Dati statistici." VII Congresso Nazionale. Roma: PCI, n.d. [1950].
————. Federazione Bolognese. "Campagna di tesseramento e proselitismo 1966." Bologna: PCI, 1965.
————. "Comitato cittadino. 8-3-58." Bologna: PCI, 1958. Mimeographed.
————. X Congresso Provinciale del PCI. "Documenti per delegati." Bologna: PCI, 1962. Mimeographed.
————. "Federazione Giovanile PCI." Bologna: PCI, n.d. [1960].

————. "Giudizi del comitato federale." Documento interno, 29-X-59. Bologna: PCI, 1959. Mimeographed.
Partito Comunista Italiano-Federazione Bolognese. IX Conferenza Regionale del PCI. "Tavole statistiche. Documenti per delegati." Bologna: PCI, 1959.
————. IX Congresso Federazione Bolognese PCI. "Tavole statistiche. Documenti per delegati." Bologna: PCI, 1960.
————. "Relazione di attività della commissione federale di controllo." Documento interno. Bologna: PCI, 1959. Mimeographed.
————. "Riunione del comitato federale sulla relazione di attività dall'VIII Congresso ad oggi." Riservato. Bologna: PCI, n.d. [1959]. Mimeographed.
————. VII Congresso Provinciale del PCI. "Documenti statistici." Bologna: PCI, 1950.

D. NEWSPAPERS

Dailies covering the period 1944/45–1965:
 Avvenire d'Italia (clerical, DC).
 Il Resto del Carlino, Giornale dell'Emilia (conservative, PLI).
 La Stampa (independent, PLI).
 Unità (PCI).
Weeklies:
 La Lotta (PCI).
 La Squilla (PSI).
 Notiziario Settimanale (Comune di Bologna).
 Via Emilia (DC).
  As well as
 Il Giorno, May 12, 1965.
 Il Risveglio, May 21, 1956.
 The Times, July 9, 1965.

INDEX